Henry J. Van Lennep

Travels in little-known Parts of Asia Minor

Volume II.

Henry J. Van Lennep

Travels in little-known Parts of Asia Minor
Volume II.

ISBN/EAN: 9783742825780

Manufactured in Europe, USA, Canada, Australia, Japa

Cover: Foto ©Thomas Meinert / pixelio.de

Manufactured and distributed by brebook publishing software
(www.brebook.com)

Henry J. Van Lennep

Travels in little-known Parts of Asia Minor

Ancient Temple at Baoul.

TRAVELS

IN

LITTLE-KNOWN PARTS

OF

ASIA MINOR;

WITH ILLUSTRATIONS OF BIBLICAL LITERATURE
AND RESEARCHES IN ARCHÆOLOGY.

By Rev. HENRY J. VAN LENNEP, D.D.,

THIRTY YEARS MISSIONARY IN TURKEY.

IN TWO VOLUMES.—Vol. II.

WITH MAPS AND ILLUSTRATIONS.

LONDON:
JOHN MURRAY, ALBEMARLE STREET.
1870.

CONTENTS OF VOL. II.

ILLUSTRATIONS TO VOL. II.

VOL. II.   b

MAPS FOR VOLUME I.

Abbreviations on the Maps.

K. is used for Keuy (village).   K.B. is used for Khsülbash.
T.   „   „   Turkish.   A. . „   „   Armenian.
          G. is used for Greek.

Map IV. Chap. XII.

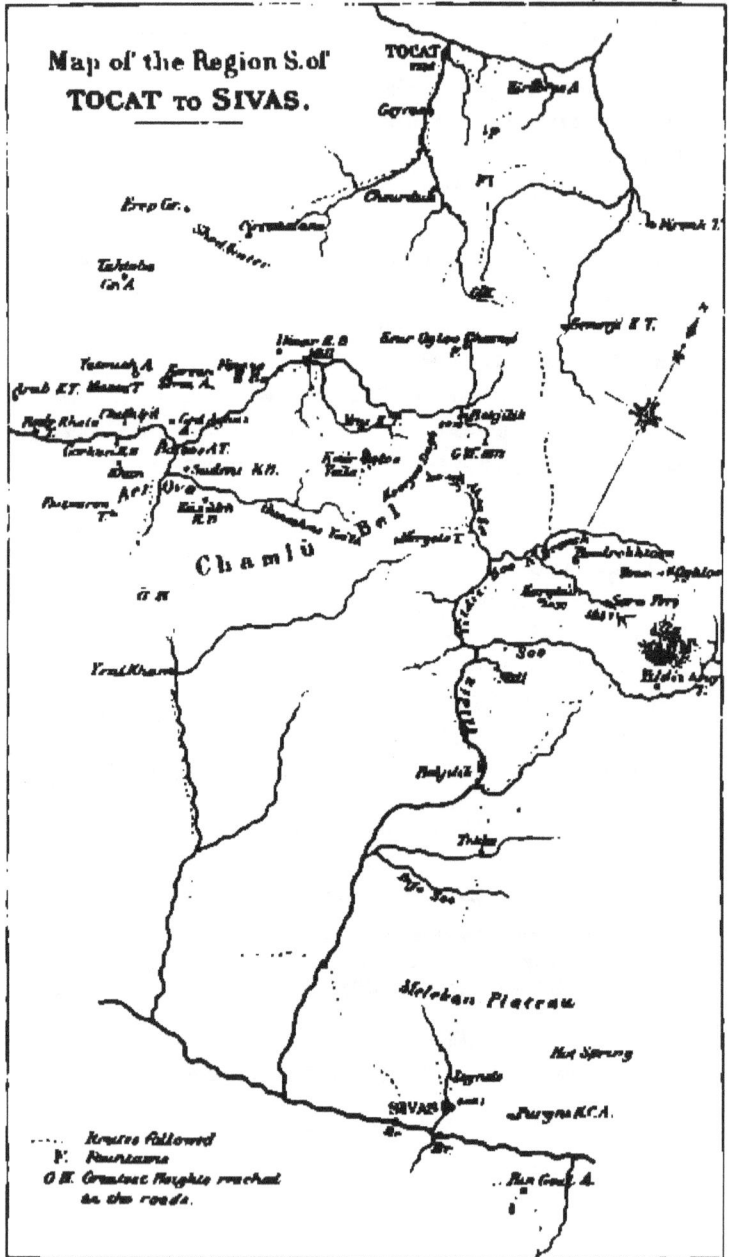

Map of the Region S. of
TOCAT to **SIVAS.**

TRAVELS IN ASIA MINOR.

CHAPTER XIII.

Resumption of narrative — Case of kidnapping — Religious persecution — Vice and immorality of Europeans — Expedition into the Chamlu Bel Mountains — Village of Keiras — Interesting ruin — Ali's "dam" — Rifle competition — The plain of Art Ova — Waylaying stags — Feat of horsemanship — Nature of soil — Monster ant-hill — Yaïla of Emir Oghloo — The Salep Plant — Fight with dogs — Return to Tocat.

WE now resume the narrative of our visit at Tocat, which has met with a long interruption for the purpose of initiating the reader not only into the history of missionary labours in this place, but also into the general character and condition of the people of Asia Minor. We left off the story of our travels upon our arrival at Tocat, from Constantinople and Samsoon, after a six days' overland journey by way of Amasia. Here are a few extracts from my Journal:—

May 20th.—Several of the chief Armenians of the town have applied to me to use my influence in a case of not unfrequent occurrence in this land. There is an Armenian girl of fifteen, whose widowed mother has a very doubtful reputation, and whose own conduct has not heretofore been above blame. This girl has

fallen in love with a young Turk, and she has expressed
her intention to turn Mohammedan for the purpose of
marrying him.   Thereupon she was kidnapped from her
mother's house, and with the consent of the latter, by
our old friend Haji Mardiros Agha, now the first *chorbajy* * of the Armenians, who keeps her in confinement;
but as she persists in her determination to renounce her
religion, he will be compelled to let her go.   The
Armenians, clergy and people, have employed every
means in their power in order to induce this girl not to
abjure the religion of her fathers.   They have worked
upon her conscience and her fears of hell and purgatory;
they have promised to marry her to a handsome young
Christian, with plenty of money for her dowry; but all
in vain.   She doubtless knows that they do not intend
to keep their word.   On the other hand, she does not
know, poor thing, that her " beau ideal " is quite likely
to divorce her in six months, or less.   But " love is
blind."   And now these people come to me, hoping
that I may be able to induce the Turkish authorities
not to allow this marriage to take place.   I told them
it was wholly out of my power.   I added that this
occurrence was the natural result of their mode of
bringing up their children, and of the example they
set them; and for my own part I should not much

---

* *Chorbajy* means, literally, a soup-maker; it is the only title
which Turks will consent to give to Christians in the room of Mr.,
keeping for their own exclusive use those of Agha, Effendi, &c. Though
the word *chorbajy* cannot properly be said to retain its original
meaning, it would yet be a mortal offence to apply it to a Turk.

regret to see all such people embrace a religion whose licentious tenets accord with their own immoral lives.

22nd.—The following case has lately come under my notice. It illustrates the kind of persecution now prevalent all over the empire toward those whose minds have become too much enlightened any longer to practise the superstitious observances of Eastern Christianity, as well as the manner in which the clergy succeed in enforcing obedience to the antiquated precepts of their Church. When we left this place in 1861 to visit America, there was here a young Greek, twenty years of age, who was a member of the Evangelical Church. Finding he could not make a living by labouring at his trade as a saddle-maker, he had just begun to learn the carpenter's business, which was much more promising; but finding no one in Tocat willing to teach him, he went to Sivas and bound himself as an apprentice to a skilful Protestant carpenter. Having served his apprenticeship he returned to Tocat, and remained five months absolutely without work, owing to his being a Protestant and to the prohibitions of the clergy. Compelled by starvation, he outwardly conformed to the Greek Church, and has found plenty of work ever since. He now openly declares that he has not changed his views in the least, and proclaims himself a Protestant; but he is obliged to go to the Greek church, and to keep away from the Evangelical preaching: moreover his relatives hope to secure his complete reformation by marrying him to a pretty young girl who has no leaven of truth in her heart.

23rd.—It seems strange to find that Europeans, brought up under more or less of Christian influence and amid an atmosphere of virtue and morality, so frequently become vicious and immoral as soon as they lose the restraints of home. We have had here, for several years past, a few persons who were considered very respectable in Europe and at Constantinople, but who have while here made the name of *Frank* a by-word for lewdness and immorality. The only way in which we can mitigate the reproach in such cases, is to point out the fact that these people are Roman Catholics, and their manners only correspond to those of the Armeno-Catholic priests here, who are their Father-confessors, and whose reputations are such that no respectable man of their own religion will allow his wife to confess to them unless he is present. It is, however, difficult to know what course to pursue toward these strangers : we owe them the rites of hospitality ; but in thus doing our duty the people deem us their friends, and think we approve of their lives.

30th.—The young men of our party have been begging for an expedition into the Chamlù Bel Mountains close by, in the hope of coming across some stag, or other beast of the forest. The season is altogether too far gone. The nomadic tribes are already far up on the mountain, with their herds, flocks, and tents, and they must have frightened away the poor game into the most inaccessible recesses. Yet, as this region has never been explored by a European, and the work upon the chapel and school can proceed for the present without my superintendence, I have decided upon an absence of nearly a week. Every preparation being joyfully made, and taking as guide our old friend Ali, the Turkish mountain sportsman of bear and stag celebrity, we started this morning at 5·45. Our direction was south, through the beautiful valley where lies the usual winter road to Sivas by the Art Ova and Yeni Khan. This charming valley, scarcely a mile in width, is extremely fertile, being filled with gardens, orchards, and cultivated fields of barley, Indian corn, and tobacco, with melon and cucumber patches; it is watered by a stream flowing through the centre, under a continuous bower of trees and climbing vines. The mountains on both sides rise to a height of full a thousand feet, and appear quite as fertile and productive, for the most part, as the valley itself. We reached the Turkish village of Keïras at 6·45. It is a collection of miserable stone huts with flat roofs, indicating wretchedness in man amid the rich productions of nature. It possesses a flour-mill; walnut-trees are abundant, and vegetation profuse. A portion of the water of this stream is turned off at the head of the valley into a canal which runs along the western slope, and supplies most of the city by means of pipes running down from the canal to the houses. The eastern portion of Tocat is similarly supplied with a canal, fed by a fine

spring issuing from un ler a great rock high up on
the hills which bound the valley eastward. The rest
of the water in the valley stream feeds several mills, and
is used in the copper foundry; but there is not enough
to keep the establishment at work during the summer
months. At 7 the valley became very narrow—a
mere gorge, with the stream at the bottom, and scarcely
room on its margin for the road. On the opposite
bank lies a natural cave, in tho perpendicular limestone, where the wild pigeons make their nests. Here
the strata of the rock offer the most extraordinary
contorsions, showing that the region has been subjected
to powerful volcanic influences; this is further proved
by the occurrence of trap rock. There are several flour-
mills here, at short distances from each other, owing to
the rapid inclination of the ground. The very last in
the gorge is occupied by a Protestant miller, whom I
had not yet seen, and who, spying us from far, joyfully
ran out to meet us. His demonstrations of gladness and
affection appeared somewhat unusual to my companions.
At this place a narrow path climbs the hills to the
right, leading to Greek villages in that direction. At
7·30 we reached the bridge at the head of the valley,
and crossing it, continued straight on. A road here
runs off to the left, taking a south-easterly course, and
leading into the mountains; some people go by it to
Sivas, and we returned this way from our present trip.
There is near this road, and barely fifteen minutes' ride
from the bridge, a very interesting ruin which I visited

several years ago, and which I will now stop a moment
to describe. It crowns an isolated limestone rock, some
500 yards long and 100 wide, and has an elevation of
about 200 feet in its highest part. The hillock has an
irregular rectangular form, with perpendicular and inap-
proachable faces on the south-west, north-west, and north-
east. On the latter is cut out a plain tomb, which it would
require a very long ladder to reach: it is open, and must
be empty. The summit of the hillock appears to have
been occupied as the area of a castle or small fortified
town, for one can yet easily trace the remains of a
strong wall along the only side which is rendered accessible by the sloping surface; but the ruins within are
so completely destroyed that no conjecture can now be
formed of the nature of the buildings once standing
there. There is, however, just such a tunnel as I
have described in speaking of the ancient fortifications
of Amasia and Tocat; it points down deep into the
rock, at an angle of 45°, and the steps are in a better
state of preservation than those of the others. This
fortification defended an important pass out of Pontus
into Cappadocia, at the time when that kingdom still
maintained its independence; just as the fortress of
Tocat seems originally to have merely been a fort to hold
the important pass it commands, for it is not probable
there was any town there as long as Comnena Pontica
flourished, distant two leagues only up the Iris.

At 9·15 we reached the "*dam*" of Ali, our guide.
There was once a village here, but it is in ruins. Ali

owns these fields, and keeps a "*dam*" or stable in
repair, in which he stays with his cattle at the time of
ploughing and harvest. These fields being at a considerable elevation on the mountain, and moreover
isolated, with the primeval forest close by, his crops
are very often devoured by the wild boars and stags,
and even bears not unfrequently come down in the night
to get a meal. Being a Muslem, he cannot eat the
former, and kills them in pure self-defence, though he
sometimes succeeds in selling one to some Christian, who
carries it off, if he can reach it before the sharp-scented
vultures have feasted upon it. I once came here in
search of game at the season when meat is scarce in town;
I well remember that we hauled a wild boar, we had
killed, up into a tree, out of the reach of the wolves and
foxes; but when my messenger arrived with a horse to
carry it away, he found that the vultures had already
eaten so much of it that the remainder was not worth
removing. Since then I have followed the practice of
dragging our game home upon the snow, which is easily
done, Tocat being situated upon a much lower level.
We stopped here by a fine stream of water to eat breakfast. While thus engaged, the men who had charge of
our horses began to brag of their shooting powers and
the quality of their guns; so they set up a mark on the
other side of the ravine, at a distance of 150 yards.
The boasters missed it, but Ali hit it at the first shot,
and we were all greatly amused to see a large hare start
up from a bush only a couple of yards from the mark

they had been trying to hit. Our would-be great shots had no end of jokes cracked upon them in consequence; it was said their bullets instinctively sought the hare, &c. I had one of Sharp's breech-loading rifles with me, and challenges were made to try it against the rifle of one of the men. I consented to do so, provided the mark were placed at least 300 yards off; and the result of my firing was such that the other party refused to take his turn. The top of the hill we soon afterwards reached was formerly occupied by a single guard-house, but the place has now been given up to a number of Circassian families. The air is good, but we saw very few signs of industry; only a few fields were cultivated by them. As they show no inclination to break up the fallow ground, their only resource, when the allowance now paid them by the Government comes to an end, will be to take forcible possession of the fields of their Christian neighbours, as they have begun to do elsewhere; or to levy black-mail, for which their position upon this main road is admirably adapted. Their fields are not fenced off with stone walls, like those of other people; they are protected by a slight fence, made mostly of wild cypress or fir sticks. There were several graves separated by the road from the village, and surrounded by similar fences, only more solidly constructed. The only monuments raised within these enclosures are stout sticks planted upright, one at the head and another at the foot of the graves. It is said that these Circassians do little as yet for their

support. They are mostly slaveholders, and their slaves
are expected to work for them; they have hitherto
been supported to some extent by the Government,
but more by the sale of their slaves' children, both boys
and girls, which are purchased by Muslems.

The rock about here is sandstone. After leaving
the village we went down to a fine stream and fountain,
shaded by a large tree. We reached Finezeh at 1·30 P.M.
This is a Kùzùlbash village of fifteen houses, in a very
dilapidated and ruinous condition. We pitched our
tent on the grassy lawn, and were soon stretched upon
our bearskins, sipping the never-failing and ever-
welcome cup of tea. The plain of Art Ova spreads out
southward, growing constantly wider, and covered with
unbroken fields of grain or pastures for cattle. The
villages, mostly Armenian, seem from this point to be
thickly scattered over it, and in several of them the
church is a prominent building, rendered visible from a
great distance by being whitewashed. I have repeatedly
crossed this plain in several directions, as well as
skirted it on its western edge. It is fertile everywhere,
but apt to be a little swampy in the centre;
though very productive now, its soil might easily be
turned to much better account. The usual road to
Sivas crosses it from north to south near the western
edge, and going right over the Chamlù Bel, passes
by Yeni Khan, a large village composed of two distinct portions, the one Turkish, and the other Christian, separated by a small stream and bridge. The

Christian village is, as usual, the more prosperous of the two.

· Looking round from our tent-door in front of Finezeh, in a direction opposite to that of the Art Ova, we could see Dinar, a Kůzůlbash village, lying near the edge of the plain to the north-east of us, and about two miles distant. On the east of us, and at about the same distance, are hills, which we visited, of hard red conglomerate, containing many pebbles of red and blue jasper. The plain contains gypsum near its edge under the soil, and it is dug out and carried to Tocat. In the evening Ali came to tell us that he intended to spend the night on the edge of a small salt-marsh or spring near by, for the purpose of watching for stags. Game has now retreated to the depths of the forests, both on account of the flocks which are leaving the plains and going up the mountains, and because the flies are beginning to trouble them. But there are isolated springs of brackish or salt water, called *Choorak*, which these animals seek with great avidity, and frequent, even in the immediate neighbourhood of villages, as in the present case; the native sportsmen kill more stags by waylaying them there than in any other way. The *Choorak* in this instance was hardly two miles from the village. The young men were extremely anxious to go, but I would not consent on account of the cold nights at this elevation. Ali went about midnight. He hid in some bushes on the edge of the spring, and towards dawn, having fallen asleep, he was suddenly awakened by a sort of grunt a few steps from him, followed by the sound of retreating footsteps. We examined the ground in the morning, and found that a good-sized buck had come within a few yards of him, and then beat a hasty retreat across the field, where his tracks were deeply impressed in the soft soil. Ali would not have been caught napping but for the fatigues of the preceding day.

Tuesday, 31st.—Struck tent and started at 6·15. Wasted some time in trying to get possession of a fine specimen of the black stork, which was enjoying a *gourmand*'s breakfast of frogs in the stream. Crossed over a hillock into a charming little valley filled with orchards of fruit-trees and fields of maize, and watered by a gushing stream which descends from the mountain to the E.N.E. Flowers were blooming in profusion on every side, and we could readily have yielded to the temptation to stop here awhile. Went up the valley along a well-shaded path until we reached, at 7·15, a flour-mill built up the stream; we found that we were proceeding in a wrong direction, and, crossing the river, we turned up the opposite hill and took a steep and rocky road, leading right up the mountain, through forests of pine, wild cypress, and fir, with a precipitous ravine upon our right, at the bottom of which we heard, and occasionally caught a glimpse of a mountain-torrent tumbling over the rocks. The scenery was thoroughly Alpine and truly enchanting. The tongues of all were loosened; one after another of the party sang his favourite ditty, or his " song of home," and finally came a grand chorus. One of the party had fully made up his mind that he could never learn to ride on horse-back, and to prove his assertion he was wont to relate various narrow escapes and actual tumbles, some of which were sufficiently ludicrous. Not content with this, he had exhibited his prowess the day before on the Kùzùl Enish; for he rode a steed whose full, luxuriant tail trailed upon the ground, while the mane, reaching almost as low, nearly hid the head and face of the animal. Our knight, anxious to secure the greatest amount of comfort, had arranged himself upon the top of soft cushions, scientifically strapped, with a complete arrangement of saddle-bags, cloaks, changes of garments, gun in its case, and pistols, and was, more-over, fully rigged after the most approved style of high-topped boots, silver spurs, and broad wooden stirrups, " à l'Américaine." We were all progressing with due order and solemnity, gazing with admiration at the ingenuity and ready resources of our knight, when, as luck would have it, a fly of the " worser " sort broke upon the quiet of the scene by stinging the otherwise gentle steed to the quick. In an instant the whole scene was changed; our knight disappeared in a cloud of dust and horse-hair, with here and there a protrud-ing limb at various angles of elevation, while from the chaotic mass issued half-smothered cries of " Whoa, whoa — stop him — whoa!" Several jumped off their horses and rushed to the rescue; quiet soon returned;

our knight emerged safe and sound, but half over on
one side, desperately holding on to the front and back
of the saddle. The adventure now became the theme
of comment and song; a parody of a popular ballad
was soon manufactured, and peal after peal of laughter
echoed through the mountain-gorge. I must however
add, for the comfort of future aspirants to the noble
art of riding, that this same knight soon came to be so
much at home in the saddle, that he took to sewing
while riding, and actually made a fine cap-cover of
the "Havelock" pattern, which I hope he will long
preserve as a reminiscence of our rides upon the
Chamlù Bel.

Our direction was eastward. We rose higher and
still higher on the rocky path, and our pack-horse
dropped his load, thus delaying us nearly half an hour.
The rock, which had all along been a red conglomerate,
turned, soon after we began our steep ascent, to a hard
crystalline stone, resembling trap, but of a lighter
colour. I first considered it of volcanic origin; but
upon more careful and extensive examination found it
to be greenish shales hardened, probably by volcanic
agency, so as frequently to resemble trap on the one
hand, and serpentine on the other. The whole mountain appears to be composed of this rock, with the
occasional occurrence of a little limestone, and it extends
as far as the red sandstone and tertiary formations of
the Sivas basin. Its resemblance to serpentine in
places would lead me to suspect a closer affinity

between the two rocks than is generally acknowledged. My former experience of the fertility of soil formed from argilaceous shales was confirmed upon this mountain. For it is an unbroken forest, with artificial clearings, with the exception of a few circumscribed patches where the limestone occurs, and which are mostly barren. The natural beauties of the vegetable world were truly exhilarating. The pines were in full bloom, but the blossoms seemed shorter and rounder than usual. There was not much underbrush, and the occasional small clearings were covered with tall grass. After reaching a certain height we rode mostly upon an even level until we came to the *Yaila* of Emir Oghloo; *yaila* means a feeding-ground for cattle. It is a plateau at a great elevation on the mountain, cleared of forest, of an undulating surface, and covered with abundant grass, where the people of some of the villages below come up to spend several weeks of the warmest summer weather, bringing their flocks with them to give them better feeding and save them from the flies, while at the same time they clear their own persons of village vermin. The plateau is of a circular form, with a northern exposure; it has the summit of Kurju Dagh, one of the Chamlù Bel peaks, at its back on the south. There are two fine springs of water here, by the side of one of which still stand the booths occupied by the villagers during their residence. We preferred the vicinity of the other, "for obvious reasons," and pitched our tent under a spreading pine. We found a variety of mountain flowers, and, while wandering about, came upon a monster ant-hill, the largest any of us had seen in Asia Minor; it was built around the decayed stump of a pine-tree, and was made of dry pine-leaves. The occupants were the common black ants, and the mound measured 3 feet in height, and the same in diameter. Its size probably adapts it to the snows which lie long on this mountain. We had, however, as yet found no snow anywhere, nor was it visible on any of the heights in view. The little we met with upon this trip lay in a deep ravine under thick pine-trees; we came upon it the following day. These *yaïlas* each belong to the people of particular villages, whether by common consent or otherwise, I could not ascertain. They generally bear the name of the village to which they belong. Thus the *yaïla* of Emir Oghloo is the summer grazing place of the people of the village of Emir Oghloo. They live there in booths, which they repair when they go up. Hence villages are often found completely deserted by their inhabitants, who have gone to their *yaïlas*, or summer residences. This, however, occurs only when the occupation of the people is chiefly pastoral. In some cases a portion of the inhabitants go to the mountain, while others remain to watch the neighbouring crops. The nomadic Kurds have no *yaïlas*, properly speaking. They begin to move early, and get to the mountain plateaus by the time the warm weather begins. But they always live in moveable tents, and they are not permitted to intrude upon the village *yaïlas*.

Our sportsmen had left us early on our ascent up the mountain, and had gone round in various directions, "beating" the different ravines: they met us at the *yaila* in the afternoon, and reported that there was not a track of deer to be seen anywhere. The game had doubtless moved farther on, this portion of the mountain having already been invaded by woodcutters and herdsmen, whose foot-marks were but too evident. We therefore decided to move on without loss of time. We struck tent accordingly and started off at 5·45, going south over the crest of the mountain, and descending on the other side through primeval pines into a deep ravine. We had not gone far before we came upon fresh tracks of stags; those of wild boars occurred at almost every step. Having reached the bottom of the ravine, we went up on the other side to the *yaila* of Geuveshmeh, lying in a position very similar and parallel to that of Emir Oghloo. Ali had left us before going into the stream, and had taken to the right, following the fresh tracks of the deer. We reached the *yaila* just in time to hear the report of his gun, and to see two fine antlered stags running up the hill at the top of their speed. They had unfortunately got the wind of the sportsman, and they were already too far when Ali saw them, and sent them a random and ineffectual shot. Our *yaila* is a fine undulating plateau, covered with tall grass, and furnished with good springs of water. No booths remain in sight. The evening being very cold, and gnats abundant, we

dragged together several pine-trees which, having long
been cut, were very dry and full of pitch, and lighted
four great fires, which were soon roaring, and burned
vigorously throughout the night.

June 1st.—We were very warm in the tent, but there
being no room for our faithful Carabed, he dared not
lie down on account of the cold, and kept on his feet
all night. The other men slept by the fires. In the
morning we divided our forces into several parties, and
all started off at five, taking different directions, to look
after the long-sought game. I went with Ali upon the
tracks of the deer he had missed the evening before.
We were at first enveloped in a thick fog, but managed
to make our way through the dripping trees and wet
grass, meeting many tracks, some of last night. We
also found a fresh bear's track going up a bank; the
wild boars' tracks were very abundant. Went over
much ground, mostly through the forest, and up and
down steep ravines, and breakfasted by the cold brook
on bread and cold chicken. Returned to the tent at 10,
empty handed, and found that the rest, like ourselves,
reported only tracks. We concluded that last night's
shot, and our blazing fires, had pushed the game farther
back into the mountains; indeed, the fresh marks of
flocks and herds were already seen among those of
game, so that we had doubtless only come upon the
very last of these. The sun had now come out quite
hot, and we made our preparations to leave for home.
This place is said to lie ten hours from Tocat by the

route we have pursued; there is a more direct and shorter road over the mountains, by which we propose to return; we shall save one hour, in spite of all the irregularities of the ground.

June 2nd.—Saw for the first time the *Salep* plant, which is now in bloom. The root is about an inch in diameter, and irregularly globular; it is much used throughout Turkey made into a drink, being hawked about hot in every city early in the morning during the winter. There are regular salep hunters, who collect it in the mountains at certain seasons of the year; it is dried and reduced to powder, and makes a mucilaginous and sweetish drink, which is deemed beneficial to sore throats.

I had stopped to pull up salep roots, when the young men of the party, impatient to get on, pushed forward and proceeded across a barren *yaila* where several Koordish tents were pitched close to the road. We heard barking and voices, and, hastening forward, found our companions had been set upon by a number of splendid watch dogs, which paid no attention to the whips but appeared determined to fight. One of the largest bit my boy Willie in the foot, his teeth going through the stout leather. Seeing their owners indifferent, and having even heard some of them exciting and setting the dogs on, I hastened forward, and in the thickest of the "mêlée" shot one of the finest animals in the leg. The people then poured out of their tents, and showered imprecations upon us; but they were all women and old men; had the young men

been at home, we could not have got away without
trouble. Ali and the other natives soon came up
and resorted to the usual device of making up a
story that I was a great Consul from somewhere;
so the matter was "quashed." All the people who
own dogs in this country think they have a right to
allow or even encourage the creatures to worry
passers by, as much as they like; for if a dog is
killed they may claim a fabulous price for it from
the nearest authorities. As we had two dogs with us,
we were liable to continual annoyance, especially on
entering a town. In some cases, when out upon the
road, we frightened away the dogs by running our
horses at them, or even firing a random pistol shot.
But we finally adopted the expedient of tying a long
and powerful leather thong to the end of our whips,
and as soon as any dog came in sight, we took the
aggressive. Our horses became so used to it, that
they ran at a dog as soon as they saw him; and our
dogs learned to take shelter among the horses; we
found that no dog, however savage, would stand more
than one well-laid blow from such a whip.

After three hours' riding we passed under the ancient
fortress already described, which lay on our right, and
reached the bridge at 5·30, when we came to the road
by which we had started on this trip. On reaching
Tocat we had the gratification to find a bulky mail-bag
waiting for us; my own share consisted of sixteen
letters, besides newspapers.

CHAPTER XIV.

Career, cruelties, and tragical end of Icherly Oghloo — Corrupt
practices of Government officials — Unsuccessful bear-hunt —
The Mufti's country house — Erection of chapel and school.

TOCAT, *June 11th.*—I learned to-day the tragical
close of the infamous career of Icherly Oghloo,
the noted chief of banditti, who has for many years
past been the terror of this whole region. It is
truly worth recording as characteristic of the state of
the country. He was quite a young man, not over
twenty-five at the time of his death, a fine-looking
fellow, extremely powerful and athletic, but brutal and
often the worse for liquor. He belonged to a wealthy
and highly respectable Turkish family of Herek, the
chief town in the Tash Ova. The Turks of the Tash
Ova are noted for their fanatical hatred of Christians
and Jews, as well as for their spirit of independence,
and the Government have never succeeded in destroying
their old habit of constantly carrying arms upon their
persons; even boys of ten and twelve have a loaded
pistol in their belts; nor are they loth to use them
upon the slightest provocation, whether real or imagi-

nary, particularly towards the unarmed Rayahs. Icherly
Oghloo has had it all his own way in that entire district
for many years past; he has not allowed the Government officers to collect the taxes, and has made it up to
the people by levying contributions at his option. He
had a band of eighty to one hundred men, perfectly
devoted to him and skilful in the use of arms, with
whom he roamed about, stopping travellers, and punish-
ing with death the slightest resistance. At the same
time he usually resided in his own fine house in Herek,
and outward appearances were kept up by his fre-
quenting the Mejlis or Provincial Council, of which he
had been appointed a member on the usual principle of
the Turkish Government of courting the goodwill of
offenders too strong to be punished. The Muslems
generally had a high opinion of him; for he professed to be a bigot himself, and exercised his heartless
cruelty mostly upon Christians.   Several Pashas had
been sent with troops against him, but he had always
succeeded in either avoiding or bribing them. He had
for some time past felt unusual security from the fact
that the post of Pasha of Sivas, upon whom depends
the district of the Tash Ova, was held by his own
uncle, who favoured him in secret; this had given him
greater boldness, and the country was groaning under
his yoke. Among the many well-authenticated deeds
of cruelty related of him, the following will serve as a
specimen of the monster. He was married, during
our residence in Tocat, to a young girl of very

respectable family, and well do we remember the
rejoicings and feastings on the occasion. Yet he soon
got tired of her, and kept a paramour, who, wearied
out by his brutality, succeeded in escaping to parts
unknown. Ho heard that she was secreted in a Greek
village; this was not true, but he suddenly made his
appearance in the place with several of his band,
during the absence of the men, who had gone to
reap some fields situated high on the mountain. He
immediately ordered a search in every house, and as
the person he sought could not be found, he wreaked
his vengeance upon the defenceless Greek women by
ordering his bandits to seize every one of them, and in
his presence horribly mutilate them! Their husbands
and brothers vowed revenge, and obtaining from Constantinople a firman authorizing them to kill the
miscreant wherever found, they had for a whole year
watched and waylaid him for the purpose; but he
kept so thoroughly upon his guard, that they finally
gave up the attempt.

In 1861 he came one day to Tocat, though perfectly
aware that he was an outlaw. He very coolly called
upon the Governor, Mejlis, and principal people of the
town, who dared not receive him otherwise than with
marked attention. The whole military force of the
place amounted to about a dozen *zabtiehs* or police
officers, and it was known that his band held all the
roads leading out of the town, and were determined
to pillage it or even set it on fire upon the slightest

offence to their chief. An Armenian friend brought him to me and introduced him, hinting that in such a land, it is well to be on good terms with such people; I could not appreciate the force of the argument, but, yielding to curiosity, received him with attention and had a long conversation with him. He seemed stupefied by drink, his eyes looking dull and heavy, and it was difficult to make him talk. He finally, however, awoke from his lethargy, and closely questioned me respecting the possibility of escaping out of the country. He had with him a young man whose eye was sharp and restless, and who is reported to be a first-rate marksman. They both wore suits of scarlet broad cloth richly embroidered with gold thread, and were thoroughly armed. He tried hard to get possession of my Colt's revolver, but I declined parting with it. I proposed to sketch his portrait; he sharply asked, " Do you intend to send it to Constantinople?" I said, " No, I shall send it to our friends in America, in order to let them see what fine-looking men there are out here." He was evidently pleased with the compliment, and was immediately upon his feet, ready to be sketched. When he was taking his leave, I asked him for his cane as a memento of his visit, and he readily gave it; it is a club of hard wood, ornamented with an inscription bearing his name and commending him to the Divine favour; there is no doubt it has seen service.

Icherly Oghloo finding himself constantly watched

and waylaid by men who sought to avenge their wrongs, resolved upon a pilgrimage to Mecca. He therefore, as is customary in such cases, sent out criers to inform all who had money claims upon him, to come and get their pay. He was riding one afternoon in the plain of Niksar, when his companion, the young man we had seen with him at Tocat, laughingly observed that, now he was going to be a Haji, he must reform somewhat. He did not relish the remark. They stopped that night at a village hut, and while his companions were lying asleep around the fire, he drew his pistol, and placing the end of the barrel upon the young man's temple, blew out his brains. He never went to Mecca.

Upon the accession of the new Sultan, Abdool-Aziz, he talked of surrendering to the authorities in the hope of being treated with greater leniency; but before he accomplished his purpose, if he ever really contemplated it, he was apprehended in the following manner. A new Pasha having been appointed to Sivas, he charged with the business an old experienced *zabtieh* who proposed to employ craft, assuring the Pasha that force alone would be unavailing. He went to Herek with some documents which needed the signature of the Mejlis of that place, of which Icherly Oghloo was still a member; at the same time, he engaged the services of a number of resolute Circassians, settled near by, who were *accidentally* to be present in the Council Chamber at the same moment, armed as usual, under pretence of a claim which the Council had already refused to recognise. The Council met, but Icherly Oghloo was in his house. The *zabtieh* explained his business, and the members of the Mejlis there present put their scals to the documents as desired. Icherly Oghloo was sent for; he came in hurriedly, alone and unarmed, and sat down near the fire-place. By this time the Circassians had broached their matter, and receiving an unfavourable answer, they began to argue and became noisy. The *zabtieh* made them a sign, and they fell at once upon Icherly Oghloo; he immediately saw through the business, and snatching the heavy tongs, dealt a hard blow with it upon the *zabtieh's* head; but the Circassians quickly secured him, and the rest of the Mejlis and attendants, supposing they were all equally the objects of the Circassians' anger, fled at the top of their speed. The bandit was brought here, and Yahia Bey, the Koordish chief, conveyed him to Sivas, where he was confined in prison for more than a year. He frequently attempted to escape, but was unsuccessful; a servant long watched for him near the prison with a horse ready saddled; but the man was apprehended, fined 8000 piastres, and allowed to go only upon giving a security that he would not be seen there again. The Mejlis got a great deal of money from the culprit, by promising to exert themselves in his favour. In the meanwhile he was tried on many severe charges; but he managed through outside friends to obtain an acquittal each time by means of bribes. Finally, the widow of a relation of

his own, whom he had killed, arrived from Constantinople with stringent orders that justice should be done
her, and she demanded his blood. As she persisted in
refusing the commutation money (30,000 piastres, or
280*l.* sterling) he was sentenced to die. The fact of his
condemnation was concealed from him, for the authorities
thought so powerful a man could not be brought to execution by force, even after his long and painful confinement; they therefore informed him that he must be
taken to the Meïdan or largest square of the city of
Sivas, where his pardon and acquittal would be read
to the public. The account of his execution was given
us by a truthful friend of many years' standing, who
was himself an eye-witness. He stated that so great a
fear of him was entertained, that whenever he had to
be taken to the court, during the trial, he was bound
by a strong rope, each end of which was held by four
stout *zabtiehs*, just like a wild bull. On the day of his
execution, he was conducted in the same manner from
the public prison to the Pasha's Palace, where, instead
of his pardon or acquittal, he heard his sentence of
death read, and then they led him to the Meïdan,
followed by a great crowd. When he had reached
a small bridge on the way, he sat a few moments
upon the parapet, saying he had no strength left. As
he sat there, a man came up to him and reproached
him with having burned alive all his sheep one
by one in the fire-place. They reached the public
square, which was packed with an immense crowd. He

stood in the midst of a vacant space kept clear by
the police. He wore a handsome fur; his hands were
riveted together with heavy iron bolts. His arms
were bound with strong ropes, the ends of which were
held by *zabtiehs* on either side at the distance of several
feet. The Judge then came forward on horseback.
A fearful silence ensued, during which the sentence of
death was pronounced, and could be distinctly heard
by the crowd of spectators. Icherly Oghloo's wife then
advancing, kissed the Judge's foot and begged for mercy;
but he spurned her from him, and is said to have
kicked her in the face. The order was then given to
put an end to the scene. No one had been found
willing to perform the office of executioner, though
large sums had been offered. One of his fellow
prisoners, however, consented to do it on condition of
his own crime being forgiven. Icherly Oghloo was
then pushed from behind and thrown down upon his
knees; they tried to take off his pelisse from him, but
he would not consent, and they only turned it back,
baring his neck. The executioner, completely disguised, and wearing the costume of a Circassian, in
order to screen him from private revenge, lifting his
sword, struck the culprit on the back of the neck; he
fell forward upon his face, and the executioner, laying
the sharp edge of the blade upon the neck of the
prostrate man, pressed it down with his foot, and completely severed the head from the trunk. Thus ended
the career of a man noted for his heartless cruelty, and

his thirst for human blood, yet at an early age, probably not more than twenty-five.

13*th.*—We received a call from a young Frenchman, a graduate from one of the best Imperial colleges in France, who has been sent here by the Porte to examine the accounts of the Copper Foundry, respecting which doubts have long been entertained at the capital. It is ever thus; Turks always rob one another, and the Government most of all, and whenever any confidential or conscientious duty is to be performed they have to find some European who is willing to undertake it, but he must be one who has not been long enough in the country to become as corrupt or worse than themselves. It is notorious however that such a man, though he secure the respect of all, cannot retain his place unless he give up his honesty; for those who are interested in plundering unite to intrigue and get rid of him, because he gives them no chance. I fear this young man won't stay here long, for he seems bent upon a conscientious discharge of his duty. He says he has already discovered thefts to the amount of several thousand pounds, though he has only been a fortnight in the place, and is quite ignorant of the language. Speaking of items, he mentioned as a specimen that there are eleven horses in all, employed in the establishment, and yet the Government is charged 68 combs for them every year! There are five carts, whose cost *new* is 5*l.* a-piece, making an aggregate of 25*l.* Yet the Government

is charged 85*l.* a year for the repairs of these five
carts!

17*th.*—We had several times been told that bears
were unusually numerous this year in the neighbourhood; they are reported to have laid waste the vineyards that are planted on the western slopes of the
valley near by, not more than half-an-hour's walk from
our house. The owners of these vineyards have repeatedly sent to us to beg that we would come out and
kill or frighten away these disagreeable customers, as
they have been compelled to abandon their vineyards.
A few days ago one of these bears met with an accident
which put an end to his career and to further mischief:
t is supposed that he was trying to get at some honey
in hives lying upon a high rock at the Kemer, and that
he fell from a great height and was killed. As the
young men of our party were itching for bear experience, we finally promised to go and watch for Bruin
as soon as the moon was high enough; and now Ali
came and told us that three bears had made their
appearance in a vineyard and eaten off all the cherries
from several trees. So R—— and I went to Ali's
house at 6 P.M.; we had with us a French gunsmith,
M. Grégoire, from the neighbourhood of Marseilles,—
very fond of sport, but who, like R——, had not yet
encountered anything bigger than hares and partridges.
M. Grégoire wore a white linen blouse, and over it a
regular game-bag, while a long sword-like hunting
knife hung from his belt. We started up the steep

mountain side under the guidance of Ali's six-foot beardless son; the father having gone over to a neighbour to help to carry home, in an araba, a poor cow that had accidentally broken her leg. On reaching a considerable height we stopped and sat down to breathe and enjoy the fine panorama spread out before us. The hills on our side of the valley were in the shade; but those opposite were brilliantly illuminated by the setting sun. The valley was fast filling with shadows which grew longer every moment, and the town and opposite hills looked truly fine from this spot. We marched on through several vineyards until we reached two miserable huts built of mud bricks, one of which was occupied by a Turkish family. We went into the empty hut, and the owner on first spying us through the dusk evidently disliked our looks; but he soon recognised our honest-faced M. Grégoire, and received us cordially. Our tall Bekir now lighted a fire in the crumbling chimney, and we made ourselves comfortable and discussed our provisions. Unfortunately no one had thought of taking a tea-pot, for which M. Grégoire's hunting bag would have made a capital nest; so, after many "pourparlers," the *harem* in the other hut furnished us their whole "batterie de cuisine," every variety of cooking and feeding dish they owned, which mustered as follows:—(1) a long-handled coffee-pot, 2 inches high and an inch and a half broad; (2) a brass cup, without handle, 6 inches by 4; (3) a copper pan 2 inches high and 1 foot across; and (4) a brass non-

descript, 8 inches by 10. Oh! the tyrannical demands
of modern civilization! All this fuss for a single cup of
tea! But then we were unanimously of opinion that,
in this chilly mountain air, that cup of tea *was* worth
the fuss. After consultation, the feat was accomplished
as follows: we boiled our water in No. 3, and used
No. 1 as a dipper; we made our tea in No. 2, and
drank it by turns in No. 4; demolishing at the same
time twice as many cherries as the bear would have
eaten had he come in our stead. Several French songs
were repeated or improvised, chiefly at the expense of
M. Grégoire's delightfully cool summer blouse, his
convenient havresack, destined to carry all the bears
he would kill, and his spit-like sword, upon which he
might turn the steaks before the fire. At this stage in
the proceedings a man came in and reported that he
had been in the cherry-orchard which the bear had
visited last night, had lighted a great fire, and had then
run away; and he was congratulating himself upon
thus saving at once his remaining cherries and his
skin. We sent him back to put out the fire, and might
then have slept all the time till nearly one o'clock,
had not the place been already too thickly tenanted
by extremely lively and ravenous occupants.

At one o'clock after midnight we were groping our
way through vineyards and orchards, until we reached
a point higher up the mountain and entered a field
which occupies a narrow gorge through which the bears
have to come down from the rocky heights where

they spend the day. They could avoid us only by clambering over the rocks on either side of the gorge. We found half-a-dozen trees from which the bears had taken cherries the last night or two; this position was such as completely to command the pass. Three of us hid ourselves in a hole under one of these trees, so that our heads alone appeared above the ground; and even these were hidden by the trunk of the tree; M. Grégoire with his sword and fowling-piece went to the right; our party seemed to be a little apprehensive about which side he would take in case of a general mêlée with Bruin. In half-an-hour the moon sank behind the hills. Then the darkness seemed very great, and it took us some time to be able to distinguish anything in it. Ali was soon fast asleep, and snored so loud, I was obliged to punch him every few minutes, lest he should scare away the game. It was bitterly cold, and we could not stir to shake out our limbs. At 2 a hare hopped about in front of us; another nearly stumbled on the other party; M. Grégoire might have spitted him through with his sword had he not slept most of the time. Finally at 3 we concluded that Bruin was taking his supper somewhere else; we went over the hills into orchards and vineyards where he would be likely to call, and looked round for him, listening to every sound that broke the silence of the night. As we stealthily crept along by the side of a narrow gorge the watchmen on the top of the hill took us for a company of bears, fired off a pistol, and shouted

lustily after us. We passed by the tent of the chief
watchman and reproached him for not keeping his
word to meet us, and deserting us when we might, with
the aid of his experience, have met with some measure
of success. He apologised by saying that the *mufti*
was with his family in his country house near by, and
he was so frightened by the report of the bear's
approach that he would not allow him to go away for a
single night, and, moreover, kept several men firing
pistols all night around the house and bonfires burning.
We reached home about 5 A.M., and this is our adventure *about* Bruin, and "how we *didn't* do it."

This was not, however, our only attempt to make
the personal acquaintance of Master Bruin. The
frightened *mufti* had fled to town the very next
day after our mountain vigils. He entreated us to do
our utmost in order to rid the neighbourhood of so
disagreeable a visitor, and offered us the use of his
country house and of the cherries and other fruit we
might be so fortunate as to save from the clutches of
the bears. So we removed from town for the purpose
of a little change, and spent several days rusti-
cating, doing full justice to the poor *mufti's* white,
black, and red cherries, which we found "worthy of our
distinguished consideration." We indeed quite sympa-
thized with the predilections of the much abused animal,
who only deserved to be considered a gentleman of taste.
The hills on the east of the valley are called Komer,
and those on this side Kemal. The *mufti's* house is

probably the best building of the kind anywhere around here. It is an old style Turkish house, and shows many of the peculiarities they often exhibit. We give a sketch of the front of this dwelling, with its cool tank

The Mufti's country-house near Iznik.

and fountain, shaded by cherry trees. Soon after our arrival at the place we received a call from the chief watchman, or *bekji*, of the Kemal District; he is an old man, tall, bony, strong, but terribly out of shape, and with only one sound eye, which is never more than half open; it must be pretty sharp though, if but half of what is reported about him be true. He was accompanied by his two daughters-in-law, and three grandchildren, the eldest of whom seemed so much at home

in the place, that, without prelude of any sort, he at
once stripped and jumped into the tank of water for
a swim.

We spent the night of the 24th watching on a hill-
side, but to no purpose. And again, two of us spent
the night of the 26th under a shed commanding a view
of several trees which the bear had visited the night
before, leaving the marks of his claws upon the trunks,
and several broken branches, to betray his thefts. But
it was again in vain. About 1 o'clock a hare passed
within reach of my hand, hotly pursued by a weazel.
The latter, having missed his prey, stood some time
in full sight, evidently disappointed. Though we
failed of accomplishing our ostensible object, we found
in this delightful spot the change and healthy atmosphere we sought. I often went to town on business;
we rambled over the hills, picked and pressed flowers;
and the young men shot small game to their hearts'
content. The last night we watched for bears was
spent by Ali and the chief *bekji* in scouring the whole
region; and yet we found in the morning that Bruin
had visited a vineyard only a hundred yards from the
house we occupied, and had frightened the owner
almost out of his senses. Our experience of him,
therefore, fully sustains the reputation which he enjoys
for cunning and highly developed organs of smell and
hearing.

During all this time the erection of the chapel and
school was rapidly advancing. It had indeed progressed

so satisfactorily, and the native preacher and the
deacon of the church were so active and economical in
their superintendence of the work, that I resolved to
devote a few days to visiting Sivas, and the summit of
Star Mountain,—the latter being an object I had long
purposed to accomplish, but had heretofore been prevented by pressing engagements. This trip will be
described in the following chapters.

CHAPTER XV.

JUNE 30th. *Thursday.*—We left Tocat at 6 A.M.,
taking the summer road to Sivas, and going
through the narrow gorge on the east side of the
town, which becomes the bed of a powerful torrent
during a heavy rain; this we reached in five minutes
after leaving the last houses of the town. Went up
the steep ascent, with the song of the partridge upon
the craggy rocks around us. In the winter these birds
come down to the road to feed, and even enter the
gardens on that side of the town. We ascended a
narrow valley for about an hour, following and often
crossing a small stream of cold water, until we turned to
the left to climb what we have long called the Robbers'
Hill, on account of a trying adventure which occurred
here to our missionary physician, Dr. Jewett, and his
companions, and which I will briefly relate. A small
party of travellers had come from Samsoon to Tocat;

it was at the time of the Crimean War. The party consisted of an Englishman going to Diarbekir to purchase horses for the British Government, and supposed, though incorrectly, to be carrying plenty of money; with him was travelling the notorious braggadocio, Carabed Aghа, distinguished by the euphonious name of Zobaboornoo, or shovel-nosed, who very foolishly boasted all the way, in the most unguarded manner, that his belt was full of gold pieces. He actually carried some 200*l.* sterling belonging to different parties. They spent a night with us at Tocat, intending to leave the next morning for Sivas; but the Englishman felt too much fatigued to proceed, and as Dr. Jewett had to go that very day to Sivas, on professional business, he took the Englishman's place, and was, as a natural consequence, mistaken for him. The report that travellers, well stocked with money, were journeying almost unprotected, had brought together a number of Koords who are always ready to make the most of such a chance, and they chose as the best spot for attack the top of the ascent we had now reached, hiding themselves behind the rocks and among the trees. The ascent is long and steep. The robbers doubtless had their scouts out, and were notified of the travellers' approach. They rode up carelessly at a brisk pace, and in a body, and as their blown horses, now advancing at a slower rate, had nearly reached the top, several men sprang out in front of them from behind the rocks, while others all around presented the muzzles of their guns with a

shout. Resistance would have been impossible; for
they were but three besides the *surujy* or guide,
and only one of them, a *zabtieh*, was armed; while the
robbers were a dozen. Before they could look round
and comprehend their situation, they were hurled to the
ground, bound, and dragged to a secluded hollow near
by, where they were robbed of all their valuables. The
banditti were sorely disappointed to find that, instead
of an Englishman with saddle-bags full of guineas they
had only got hold of a doctor with a few surgical instruments; they were so angry that they pretended to hold
a consultation about killing their prisoners, which
frightened the *zabtieh* almost out of his wits. They,
however, only kept them until nightfall and then let
them go on to Sivas. The authorities of that place
made this affair an excuse for sending troops into
several Koordish villages to rob and plunder to their
hearts' content; but the victims of the robbery above
described got precious little redress.

Soon after leaving the Robbers' Pass, the vegetation,
which had been very abundant, presenting on every
side primeval forests, the resort of the stag and the
roebuck, began to be less profuse, as passing over a hill
we entered a narrow rocky valley running S.S.E., and
followed the course of a stream which flows in the same
direction. This is the first water we had yet met which
runs towards the Kuzul Urmak (Halys) on the south,
all we had yet seen flowing north to the Iris. We
reached the Bekjilik or guard-house at 10·30. The

house itself lies off to the right of the road across a swamp.

Travellers stop by the roadside under a booth near a spring of water, and are accommodated with coffee prepared by the guards. It is at this place that the Muslem convert K—— was overtaken by his pursuers; but he threw them off their guard, secreted himself until night, and went back to Tocat, reaching my house after midnight. We gave him refreshments, effectually disguised him, and sent him through by-roads to Samsoon and Constantinople—hiding during the day, and travelling at night. Had his enemies caught him they would have prevented the preparation and publication of some of the most effective attacks ever made upon Mohammedism.

We got into our saddles at 12·15. We went mostly up hill, through scattered pines, and ascending a steep declivity, reached at 1 the highest point of the Chamlù Bel upon this road, which I found by barometer to be 5512 feet above the sea. This part of the mountain is considered very dangerous to travellers, in case of a snow storm, on account of the drifts which obliterate the road, and the cold blasts which blow over the slopes on both sides of the pass, as well as at the pass itself. Nearly every year we hear of people buried in the snow, and a number of rude graves at the southern foot of the mountain affords ocular demonstration of the fact. Solitary travellers are also occasionally set upon and devoured by packs of hungry wolves. The view

is extensive and grand. The Star Mountain rises
like a cone: it is 3000 feet higher than this level,
but rises from much lower ground. Our descent
was rapid, and occupied 40 minutes. This side of the
mountain is nearly destitute of trees. We passed
the cemetery at the foot, and forded the stream called
Yavash Akan Soo, "the slowly-flowing water." It is
a tributary of the Yildiz Soo, the Star River. Being
interested in the question of the rise and flow of the
Star River, I made inquiries of the people of the
different villages which lie about here, and which I
visited at various periods. The result of my investiga-
tions is that the name of Star River is claimed, and
apparently with equal justice, by two streams, both of
which rise far up the sides of the Star Mountain, and
not distant from each other. One of them has its origin
in abundant springs which flow from the north side; the
other rises in the eastern declivity. The former takes
a circuit round, passing near the villages of Yoosoof
Oghloo and Doodooklitoon, and flows through the plain
on the west side of Karghùn. The latter encircles one
half of the Star Mountain, flowing near its southern foot
by the Star Village, and then taking its course westward
it unites with the northern stream, after which junction
they flow southward to the Halys. I have concluded to
retain the names of Star River as the denomination
of both these streams, and to distinguish them as the
Northern and Southern Branches. At 3·15 crossed the
northern branch of the Star River over a wooden bridge;

there was but little water, but there were evident signs
that the stream is sometimes very much swollen. The
shortest road to Sivas goes on south without crossing
the bridge, and travellers take it when they wish to
reach Sivas the day they leave Tocat. At 4 reached the
Turkish village of Karghùn, containing forty houses,
with one mosque, built upon the western slope of one
of the barren hills which surround the base of the Star
Mountain. The people here call it one hour to the foot
of the mountain; they probably have very indefinite
ideas as to where the mountain begins, for I am certain it is much farther. All seem to agree that the
best place to start from in order to ascend is Sarù
Yeri, the Yellow Place, a Turkish village about an hour
hence. The ascent to the summit is said to require
three hours. We have, however, ascertained that there
is a good ancient road from the Star Village quite to
the top of the mountain; it is said to go up its eastern
face; but as we cannot make the ascent now, and we
propose to do it on our way back to Tocat, we shall not
be able to try that road, none of our party being
acquainted with the way from the Star Village to
Tocat.

About two hours back upon the road, we had passed
some Turks who were working in the field, one of
whom, recognizing me as an old acquaintance, ran up
to us, welcomed us back to this region, and cordially
invited us to stop at his "room." As village houses
consist of but one room with an adjoining stable for

cattle, the roof of the whole being levelled even with
the hill at the back of the house—the name of " room "
has come to be the usual appellation for a house.   Our
friend directed us, on reaching Karghùn, to inquire for
the " new room " of Halil the Kiahaya, or head man of
the village.   It was readily found, and was probably
the best in the place.   Its roof was made of the trunks
of poplar trees, a foot thick, upon which had been laid
planks of oak covered with clay.   The whole was
supported by a row of five stout wooden pillars, with a
balustrade between, dividing off a portion of the room
for stores or servants.   The fire-place, cupboards, and
the rafter or shelf running around the room, were unusually clean and nice; but the earthen floor made no
deceptive promises of a good night's rest.   Our attentive host furnished us with two low tables, covered with
everything the village could afford.   We lounged about
till sunset in front of the " new room," carefully avoiding
the holes in the roof of the next house below us, which
formed the piazza of ours, lest we should fall through
and be landed upon the horns of the cattle in the stable
beneath.   The young men gave a variety to our fare
by shooting large numbers of the starlings which
fluttered all about, unconscious of danger.   An observation with the barometer indicated 4830 feet as the
height of Karghùn.

Friday, July 1st.—We rose at 3, but could not get
under way before 5.   The villagers here are not very
early risers, for a wonder, and we found it difficult to

rouse anybody to get us barley for our horses. At 7·30 stopped at a booth erected by the guards upon the road side, where coffee is offered to travellers. The rocks here stand upright, leaving but a narrow space between them and the river. They are perforated with holes of considerable size at an inaccessible height, which are used as nests by vultures. One of these holes was formerly tenanted by a species of hawk which was highly esteemed in the days of falconry, and the birds used often to be robbed of their young. They seem to have become discouraged, and have abandoned the place. A short stick is still standing across the entrance, placed for the purpose of making the spot more attractive to the bird by giving it a perching pole. It may, however, have been put there only to render a visit to the nest practicable, as it must be extremely difficult under the most favourable circumstances, owing to the great height.

While seated in the booth I noticed a skin spread upon the ground belonging to some animal we had never seen. Upon inquiry, I found it to be the skin of a wild mountain goat, killed in the neighbourhood two years before. This was the first I had ever seen, having never been able to obtain anything but the horns; and I esteemed myself fortunate to be able to make the acquisition. I had heard in Tocat of a large male skin being presented to the Sheikh of the Whirling Dervishes, for the purpose of saying his prayers upon it; for the Turks believe that the *carpet*

has much to do with the efficacy of one's prayers, and
the skins of the stag, the roebuck, and the wild goat,
enjoy the highest reputation in that respect. The one
now in my possession would seem to be a female, and
to have its summer coat. The hair is short and stiff,
fawn all over, except underneath and within the thighs,
where it is of a dirty white. There is a dark red line
along the back, extending through the tail; the hair
of the neck is curly. The legs are also dark red. The
whole length from the back of the head to the root of
the tail is 3 feet 5 inches; length of the tail 6 inches.*

Willie here shot some very pretty little birds, which
we agreed to call red-headed sparrows, from their
general resemblance to the common sparrow; their
habits also appeared very similar.

Soon after this the Star River turns to the right,
following the course of the valley; we part company
for the last time, for it now deviates considerably to
the right, falling into the Halys below Sivas. I was
thus glad to have had another opportunity fully to
ascertain the precise course of this river, interesting on account of its connection with the mountain of
that name, and Strabo's historical sketch of both. It
now only remained to ascend the mountain and ascertain the correctness of the statements of the natives,
who declare that the ruins of a castle exist on the top,

---

* Since writing the above, I have seen a male specimen of this
animal in the Zoological Garden at Amsterdam, together with one
of the *mouflon*, or wild sheep.

and that a fine spring of water issues not far from
the summit. Were this correct, we should have a very
striking corroboration of Strabo's account of the stronghold where Mithridates kept his treasures, which he
states was destroyed and the hoarded wealth seized
by the indomitable perseverance and energy of the
Romans. It was with great pleasure therefore, that,
having now obtained in the vicinity of the mountain all
the information we needed, we anticipated going up to
the summit on our return from Sivas.

After parting with the Star River, we crossed over a
hill through a narrow cut in basalt rock. Looking around
us from this point, we found a crest of basalt, forming a
pretty regular circle about two miles in diameter, the
central area and surface being smooth. Were it an
ancient crater it would not present a different appearance, and the Star River seemed to enter it at one
side, and to come out again at the nearly opposite
point. At 10·50 we came upon the Plateau of Melekon,
a barren waste, covered with calcined rock. There is at
first, *i.e.* at the north end, a little conglomerate, and
then a very little red sandstone; but it soon changes to
limestone, which, from its position, I take to be second-
ary, lying between the old red sandstone and the earlier
tertiary of the Sivas plain; but it has become hard
as flint by exposure to the air and sun. This effect
upon stone comparatively soft I have not unfrequently
observed in Asia Minor. In the present case the upper
surface alone is thus hard, for when you come to the

broken cliffs you find all beneath comparatively soft
and easily broken. Melekon has no water, and every
attempt to cultivate portions of it has failed. Ruins
attest the efforts of Government and individuals to
erect places of shelter for travellers; for in winter many
perish here, overtaken by snow storms, and losing their
way over this broad and even surface; and many are
frozen to death by chilling winds coming down from
the mountains on the north. I believe Melekon is
generally dreaded by travellers more than crossing the
Chamlù Bel. The attempt to obtain water from wells
is also said to have failed, probably owing to the
vicinity of the valley of the Kûzûl Urmak, which lies
several hundred feet lower, draining it of rain water;
and there are fine springs at the bottom of the cliffs
which form the boundary of the plateau. We reached
the nearest edge at 12·25, and looked down the precipice into the narrow valley which leads to the plain of
Sivas. This valley, about a mile in width, runs nearly
north and south; both its upper extremity and its two
sides are formed by nearly perpendicular cliffs, which
constitute the broken sides of the Melekon formation;
they present a limestone and somewhat chalky surface,
and constitute a cut into the plateau. The length of the
valley is about six miles, and the cliffs on either side abut
abruptly on the plain, into which it emerges. A powerful
stream of fine water pours out at the head of the valley,
apparently constituting the drainage of the plateau and
accounting for its barrenness. This stream rushes down

the valley, spreading fertility wherever its goes, and working several mills; it passes through the town of Sivas, furnishing it with good water in abundance, turning its mills and watering its gardens; and a considerable stream is left to flow into the Halys. The road down from the plateau is cut along the face of the cliff; and at 12·40 we reached a gushing fountain near the bottom, when there was an immediate rush of men, horses and dogs, to get the first draught of water; my own steed drank so long and so resolutely, that I began to think I had met with the same accident as Baron Munchausen, and succeeded in getting away only by leaping into the saddle and making use of spurs and and bridle. The rock of the cliffs presents very much the appearance of chalk, but it is harder. It easily crumbles and decomposes when exposed to the influence of the atmosphere at an elevated angle. The layers are nearly horizontal, the inclination being toward the south-east, indicating a moving force on the north-west. It is possible that this force may have come from the source which formed the old crater, already pointed out. In the valley, I found in one place considerable masses of tufaceous rock, sometimes highly crystalline; but these do not seem to be extensive. The bottom of the valley is generally homogeneous, fossils have been found in it, and in the cliffs some distance down, some of which are in my possession. They were given me by one of my old Tocat students, who followed with unusual interest my course

of lectures on geology, and has since attended somewhat
to the subject.

At 1·30 we entered the Plain of Sivas. The first
portion of it stands considerably higher than the level
of the alluvium, and it is formed of undulating hills.
It was probably at one time the bottom of the lake
or inland sea, whose waves beat against the limestone
cliffs I have described. When the water sank, the
limits of the lake became circumscribed to the present
broad alluvial surface, until running out completely,
they only left the Halys, which is fed from the skies and
runs unimpeded to the sea. Near the place where the
valley opens into the plain is a flour mill, where traces
of lignite may be seen in horizontal layers in the banks
which have been worn by the stream. Passed a short
distance from the Armenian convent, the residence of
the Bishop of Sivas; it contains several fine buildings,
and the whole area is well protected by a stone wall.
Just before entering the town we came upon a camp of
Turkish troops, occupying the ground which overlooks
it. Everything appeared clean and in good order. We
passed by the country seat of the Pasha, built high upon
the rising ground on the outskirts of the town, and went
directly on to our friends who had been anticipating
our arrival.

Saturday, July 2nd.—A former pupil of mine, now
residing at Tocat, had informed me of the existence
of petrified shells of a tertiary character in a lateral
valley on the south side of the Plain of Sivas, and we

started this morning at 6 to look for the locality, several friends accompanying us. There are gardens for vegetables on the outskirts of the town; the cold is too intense at this elevation (about 4500 feet above the sea), to allow fruit to come to maturity; the trees themselves, indeed, are mostly killed by the long and severe frosts; the only varieties we saw about the town were willows and poplars; there are a few others of stunted growth in protected situations in the gardens. We crossed the Halys, the Kûzûl Urmak, or Red River, upon a substantial but narrow stone bridge of twelve arches, an Abassidian structure, furnished with a good parapet. Instead of being built straight across the river, it makes a bend of nearly 40° in the centre, so as to present an angle to the current, which, however, strikes it obliquely. There is a similar bridge eight miles down the stream, which is considerably injured. We found a good deal of timber, mostly beams, lying in the river and upon its banks. It is cut in the mountains up the stream, and sent down the current to be used for building purposes; some of it is employed as fuel. Most of the fuel, however, is cut on the mountains, often several days' journey from Sivas, and is brought down upon sledges as soon as the snow allows; this wood is pine and fir. But the natives do not use much fuel for warming purposes. They build their houses tight, with very thick walls, often four feet, mostly of mud bricks dried in the sun; and the roofs are terraced with a heavy layer of clay. In the villages

the walls are of stone, and the houses partly under
ground; the occupants are moreover warmed by the
cattle, from whom they are separated only by a slight
partition or a railing; and as wood is more easily
obtained, the constant fire in the chimney ventilates
the place, for the foul air has no other means of escape
when the door is closed.   The hills we passed over are
mostly formed of gypsum, often finely crystalline, but
easily crumbling to dust.   Wherever watercourses have
cut through the gypsum, red sandstone appeared to
underlie it.   We descended into a small plain, which
has salt swamps in the centre, and is called "Bin Geul,"
the thousand lakes; salt is here obtained by evaporation; it is carried to Sivas to market.   Salt is obtained
in the same way in the Oozoon Yalla, a long plain,
lying to the south, and separated from the Sivas plain
by gypsum hills.   These two sources supply the whole
of this region as far as Kharpoot.   The salt marshes
in Bin Geul also point to the existence at one time of
an inland sea or salt lake, which we have already
suggested as being proved by the fossil remains found
in the adjacent rocks.   We left the swamps upon our
right.   Feeding in the marshy ground were large flocks
of golden ducks, which often rose in the air and sent
forth their peculiar harsh note.   There were also many
eagles, but we could not perceive what attracted them
to the place.   We reached, at 7·45, the small Armenian
village of Bin Geul, situated on the other side of the
plain, and upon rising ground.   It contains about sixty

houses and a church. The stones in the walls are mostly formed of deposits of sand and pebbles, with broken pieces of shells, doubtless formed on the shores of a lake of considerable size, or subject to the occasional flow of torrents. These stones are very compact, and so adhesive as to be broken with difficulty with a heavy hammer. We came, at 8·45, upon a considerable river running from left to right among high hills. As we could only see gypsum around us, we were beginning to despair of finding the object of our search, and had already proceeded some distance back when I discovered we had passed by the spot without noticing it. Right by the roadside, and running parallel to it, lay an elliptical hillock, 200 yards in length, 50 in breadth, and about 50 feet high, which contained so many shells as to seem formed of nothing else. This was doubtless a bank, where succeeding generations had lived and died, and left their tenements to form the basis of the houses of their posterity; so that now these shells are alone found here, mingled with coral, and the soil itself has disappeared. The shells are not petrified or altered, but preserved in their natural condition, except that they have lost their colour. We succeeded after much search in finding a little rock, which was marly and probably formed of minuter shells. I opened the only oyster we found entire, the valves of all the rest having parted. I found it filled with hardened sand. Most of the shells were oysters, though we picked in all some twenty different species of uni-

valves. We found several different species of coral,
some of them very fine, but all colourless; the coral
was very abundant, and may have formed the foundation of the bank.

I believe that what has already been described respecting the Sivas basin will make it sufficiently
apparent that it is a tertiary deposit, though probably
one of the older ones. Many have heretofore supposed
that this region belonged to the coal formation, and great
expectations have been entertained of the discovery
and working of coal mines. I confess I never could
enter into that view, from the few facts I had been
able to collect upon the subject. All attempts hitherto
made to find coal have proved abortive, and the little
that has been picked up from mere traces is bad lignite.
I have, however, in my possession almost pure bitu-
men in small particles, which is probably too rare to
prove of any use. I must add to the facts now related
respecting the Sivas basin, that there is a prominent
hill rising from the middle of the Sivas plain, and half
an hour to the east of the town, composed of a stone
sufficiently hard for building purposes. Slabs are
obtained thence for paving courts and sidewalks. The
stone appears to be sand united by lime, and corre-
sponds to the fossiliferous rock described on page 49.
I have been told that a number of interesting fossils
have been found in the rock taken from this hill, and
among the rest the head of a horned animal. My
efforts to obtain a sight of this valuable relic have been

unavailing. It may possibly be an ammonite. The only specimen I have been able to procure is the spine and ribs of some small fish.

A few words may not come amiss here upon the tertiary formations of the Peninsula of Asia Minor. It is said that such a formation exists in the vicinity of Cæsarea and Mount Argœus, but I never have visited the place. The tertiary beds of the northern point of Rhodes are highly interesting. They consist of sand raised to a height of about 200 feet above the sea, and slightly inclined inland. The sand is soft, and the weather and rains cut it down in steep banks, which reveal the secrets of the ancient seas. The shells are extremely varied, for I picked up 150 species in a short time, and many of them preserve their colours. This fact, and the species to which they belong, at once indicate the formation to be one of the most recent tertiary. But they are purely marine deposits. Those of the Plain of Troy probably belong to the same period in time, but they more nearly resemble the tertiary of the Paris basin, with which they may be contemporaneous. I have never had an opportunity to visit and examine this locality, but some fishermen have brought me the tooth of a mastodon, which they had picked up near the ruins of Troas; and the formation appears to extend to the vicinity of Ren Keuy. Leaving the bank of fossil shell and coral, we turned back the way we had come, paying closer attention to the rocks adjacent to this interesting deposit. The rock in the neighbourhood of

Bin Guel seems very much like the substratum of our
bank, only harder and without shells. It also lies
higher. It is slightly inclined to the south-west, and
as the result of all my observations, I conclude that it
underlies the immense deposits of gypsum which form
the hill country on the south and south-east of the
Sivas plain. The fossiliferous rocks on the north and
south sides of the plain probably belong to one and
the same set of layers, and once extended all the way
across, but have been broken up and washed away in
the centre, where we now find a lower level and alluvium. The cliff in the centre of the plain would then
be a remnant of this formation, being a connecting link
between the rocks on the north and those on the south
of the plain. However this may be, it appears sufficiently clear that the red sandstone underlies the whole.
It has a slight inclination to the south-east on the south
side of the plain, as we had seen on the other side,
still indicating a moving force on the north-west,
which is the nearest point of the Chamlù Del. There
are several questions respecting which I confess I am
much embarrassed; but whatever theory is adopted, I
believe that the main facts contained in the above statement will be found true on further investigation.

CHAPTER XVI.

TO persons who come from the shores of the Black
Sea, Sivas presents an appearance quite different
from the towns on the north. The latter offer to the
eye a mass of red-tiled roofs, and the houses are built
in great measure of wood obtained from forests not far
away. On crossing over to the southern slopes of the
Chamlù Bel, vegetation greatly diminishes: trees become rare, and then disappear altogether, and even
the bushes are few and assume a stunted appearance.
The country has been many times burnt over by pastoral tribes, for the purpose of increasing the immediate supply of grass for their flocks; and the consequence is that the soil, no longer supported by the roots
of trees and shrubs, has been carried off by the rain, and
has left the rocks bare and destitute of the soil requisite
to support vegetation. The scarcity of wood obliges
the people to build their houses of stone or mud

bricks. Poplars are planted near every watercourse, but chiefly in enclosed gardens, in order to obtain rafters to support the heavy roofs of clay. From Sivas down to the Red Sea and the Persian Gulf, houses are constructed in this way; and where stone can be found sufficiently soft to be sawn, the buildings are all made of regularly-shaped blocks of stone, with vaulted ceilings, as at Cæsarea, Aleppo, Beyroot, &c. Sivas presents the appearance of a flat-roofed town, with here and there a modern-looking tiled house. It occupies level ground, but some fine old stone buildings rise above the general line of flat roofs, and on a hillock there is an old castle, in a tolerable state of preservation, one of whose towers has a clock that strikes the hours. Poplar and willow trees mingle a little verdure with the dull colour of the town; a few vegetable gardens extend along the outskirts, but no fruit is produced here: it is all brought from Tocat. It is said that more wine and raki are made in Sivas than in Tocat, though all the grapes have to be brought from abroad. In the latter place the fruit is made into various articles of food, to be kept and used through the winter; this cannot be done when the fruit has been injured by transportation. A few of the streets of Sivas have lately been paved: but the greater part are extremely muddy in winter, and indeed at all times. The common sewers lie open in the centre of many streets, rendering the atmosphere both disagreeable and unwholesome. Uninitiated travellers generally enter the town involuntarily holding their hands to their noses. The climate of Sivas is severe, as might be expected from its elevation, which we found by barometer to be 4481 feet. Snow falls abundantly in winter, and lies long upon the ground; much of this is doubtless to be traced to the neighbourhood of the Chamlù Del. This place has been a missionary station for about ten years, originally occupied by two families, and for several years past by three. One of the members of the mission is a physician, who has acquired a high reputation as a skilful surgeon through the whole region. The climate of the place appears to be unwholesome for foreigners: for, during these ten years, three families who have resided for a time have been obliged to leave the country on account of ill-health, and the three now here are so feeble that they will also soon be compelled to remove. Thus it will be seen that the post has used up six educated missionaries and their families in ten years, making an average missionary life of less than five years: a period hardly sufficient to enable most foreigners to acquire the language and fully to enter upon their work. There is evidently a great call for a native ministry in this land, suitably educated and fitted to take the place of the foreign teacher; but the fear entertained by many lest the natives should learn too much renders the prospect of a speedy supply of well-qualified men dark in the extreme. The mission to Turkey has now existed thirty-seven years; and if we are not to-day raising thoroughly-

trained labourers for this most promising field, it is to
be feared that we never shall. On the other hand, the
idea of carrying on such a work chiefly by means of,
or under the exclusive direction of, foreigners, is one
which is sustained neither by analogy nor by the
experience of the Church. It is certainly clear that
such was not the system of the Apostles. They ordained
natives everywhere into the highest grades of labourers,
whatever that was: they even left the work wholly
in their hands. It may be that the moderns have improved upon the Apostles, and that we shall yet see
what does not now appear. At least, this is the hope
with which our souls have been fed. Nevertheless, I
believe that Evangelical doctrines will not triumph in
this land until they become indigenous, and cease to
be fed and controlled from abroad.

Monday, July 4th.—Some of our friends here have
insisted that they could give us ocular proof of the
existence of good coal in this neighbourhood, and we
started in the morning for the "coal deposits," said to
lie in the hills to the south of Sivas. We reached
the foot of these hills at 7. The first rock we met was
a coarse conglomerate, formed of pebbles of a great
variety of colours, united by a very strong red cement, immediately after which, and higher up the hill,
we came upon the gypsum-beds. The gypsum here
crumbles away wherever exposed to the air. Its dip
in this place is about 45° to the north-east. We descended into a narrow gorge, where we were assured

coal existed at the bottom. The sides of this gorge were steep and rocky, making our descent, without any trace of a path, somewhat hazardous. Found the red sandstone underlying the gypsum, and with the same dip. A small stream runs through the narrow gorge or watercourse, and here we saw traces of lignite, or bituminous coal, we could not tell which, so fine as only slightly to colour the soil. We could not find a particle large enough to pick up. The larger specimens brought to me from this spot, as it was stated, are *now* claimed to have come from farther down, and I have not heard that it has been discovered in any other locality than this; it occurs in the red sandstone which underlies the gypsum-beds. The spot in which we saw the traces of lignite lies a little west of the Diarbekir road, about two hours, or six miles, S.S.E. of Sivas. Though ill repaid in our coal-hunting, we found and brought away magnificent specimens of crystalline gypsum, the finest I ever saw. The amount of this valuable mineral existing here is stupendous; it would alone supply the wants of the whole world to the end of time. The natives understand its use, and plaster with it the walls and ceilings of their houses, often skilfully working it into tasteful ornaments, and even covering their floors with a thick coating of the same substance.

Tuesday, 5th.—Started upon our return to Tocat, with the intention of ascending the Star Mountain on the way. Left town at 6·15, and reached the booth opposite the guard-house at 11·30. Dr. West, of Sivas, and Mr. Burbank, a missionary residing at Bitlis, were to join us here, intending to leave Sivas a little after us, and they came up when we were lunching. While waiting for our friends we had an opportunity more particularly to examine the ledge of rock which rises perpendicularly near the river bank, of which I spoke on our way out. It is a fine specimen of tufa. It offers a smooth surface to a height of about 100 feet, thus exhibiting the internal structure to great advantage. There are layers of deposition which resemble strata, not made in exactly parallel lines, but rather by piecemeal. I suppose this to indicate that there were large masses of vegetable matter, which hindered regular deposition, the spaces of which were gradually pervaded by an infiltration of calcareous sand in solution. The structure of this rock seems to indicate that the tufa was deposited at distinct periods, the point of contact being marked by a margin of greater density and fineness, never smooth, but everywhere presenting the distortions common to tufa. It was easy to distinguish where a tree had fallen down; the calcareous deposit had collected around the trunk, the branches, and the leaves; this deposit hardened, and when the vegetable substance decomposed, it left its room quite empty, exhibiting its exact shape. The substance of the rock is highly crystalline, and perforated in every direction.

We left the main road just after crossing the little bridge by the mill, and turned up to the right into

a narrow lateral valley, directly toward the Star Mountain, of which we had, from this point, a very good
general view. It here appeared a regular cone, sharp
at the top, and covered from the middle up to near
the summit with a stunted growth of bushes, furrowed
by several broad lines of bare rock from the top
downwards, formed by the descent of rain-water and

Star Mountain.

the rolling down of stones and detritus. The hills
around were quite barren, with here and there a prominent rock, but generally covered with soil. The
little plain in front was carpeted with grass of a rich
green, and cut in two by the little stream which
runs down to the bridge by the mill, with bushes and
a solitary tree upon its banks. Our path seemed to be
taking us straight to the very foot of the mountain;

but we found, as it always happens, that when we had
passed the first hill there were others still separating
us from its base. All these hills were equally barren
of signs of vegetation, though mostly covered with soil ;
not even grass grew upon them. But we passed alluvial
flats, which were under cultivation, and where moisture
seemed to sustain a rank grass. We reached Sarù Yeri
at 5·30, a Turkish village of forty houses, occupying
the end of a narrow valley, and protected on the north
by a hill of considerable height. The people, as usual,
showed their inaccuracy in measuring time and distance
by insisting that it is just as far from the mill to
Karghùn as to Sarù Yeri ; whereas we found it about
twice as far to the latter place. It is also called four
hours from the Bekjilik to Sarù Yeri ; we made it in
three, but we moved at a rapid pace. There must be
about one hour's ride between Karghùn and Sarù Yeri.
The people of this village received us very kindly, gave
us the best lodgings the village afforded, and everything
they had in the way of eatables. They are rarely
visited by Franks, and are, therefore, more hospitable
and unselfish than those who live upon the great routes
of travel.

Wednesday, 6th.—The top of the mountain lies due
east from us. We propose to make the ascent straight
up from this point, no one in the village knowing anything about a road leading up to the top, of which we
had heard elsewhere. One of these people, an old
soldier, just returned home from Mossul, has offered to be

our guide; he says he has been to the top before, but his subsequent course proved either that this was false, or that he had failed to look about him. Not knowing whether he would prove to be a true guide or not, we made sure of his being useful by loading him with our instruments. We started at 5·30, the weather being beautifully clear and cool, with a slight breeze from the north. The observations already made with the barometer, and subsequently confirmed, enabled us to ascertain the elevation of Sarà Yeri to be 4957 feet, which is 120 feet above Karghùn, and not quite 500 feet above Sivas. Most of us were on horseback, intending to ride up as high as the ground permitted. Our course had to be zigzag, over somewhat unequal and undulating ground, with a rapid ascent. The soil was barren, or covered only with stunted grass, while we occasionally passed fine springs of water rushing by us. At 6·20 we reached a very fine, cold, and abundant spring, which issues out of the ground and rushes down the hill with great force. There is a place close by it where cattle are folded for the night during summer, while they feed by day upon the mountain-side. The enclosure is a rude stone wall. So far as I could ascertain by inquiries, corroborated by my own observations, this spring is the highest water to be found up the mountain. The spring on the other side may be higher up, but the statements of the village people are always inaccurate. They had told us, for instance, that this very spring was near the top of the mountain, whereas we soon found we had still far to go before reaching the summit. Indeed, there were but one or two of the people of Sarû Yeri who claimed to have been to the top at all. The water of this spring flows towards the north-west into the northern branch of the Star River. The loose statement, therefore, which we had so often heard from the natives, even in the villages not very far off, that "a river flows from the top of the Star Mountain which is called the Star River," is founded not on fact, unless employed as a figurative mode of speech, which is certainly not incompatible with the habits of the people.

Leaving our horses at the spring, we began the ruder ascent on foot. We had hitherto found little or no rock in place, but now had for the most part to climb on the face of the rock, amid•boulders and fragments fallen from above, with stunted bushes and flowers of great variety and unusual brilliancy growing among them. Higher up, grew dwarfish fir-trees, and our progress was impeded not only by the steepness of the ascent and by the slipperiness of the rock, but also by the thickly-matted bushes. After ascending the first steep acclivity we came to more level ground, and sitting down to breathe, we noticed that all the upper portion of the mountain was covered with masses of rounded boulders, varying in size from one to twenty feet in diameter, but more frequently of five to ten feet, of various shapes, but all having rounded sides and corners. These boulders were piled together to an

unknown depth in an irregular manner, and presented
the appearance of streams of loose rocks. The whole
mountain is formed of black granite, so that those
rocks must be extremely hard, and the force employed
in rounding off their edges must have been very great.
Then the question arises, whence came these loose
rocks. They cannot have been rolled down from the
top, for we are near the top already, and, moreover,
the very summit is piled with them. Nor can it be
admitted that they have been brought from some other
point, and heaped on this mountain; for I believe this
rock does not occur again for several days' journey,
indeed I am not aware of its being found either in
fragments, or in place, nearer than the region above
Yozghat. Moreover, had it been brought from elsewhere, it would not all have been piled upon this
mountain: some of it would be found scattered below,
or upon the neighbouring mountains, which is not the
case. The action of freezing water is the only explanation we can give to the facts and phenomena before us.
It cannot be supposed that these blocks were brought
here by an iceberg and dropped in so compact a mass,
for they would not all be of precisely the same rock
as the mountain itself, but most probably of some
different rock which the iceberg had taken up elsewhere. The whole surface of this granite cone was
doubtless smooth when first thrown up from the bowels
of the earth by the hand of the God of nature, and the
extreme hardness of the rock long kept it so.   But

cracks and fissures were in time made by the working
of the elements; the winter rains and snows entered
these fissures, froze, and by expansion, broke the
surface into fragments, chiefly toward the summit of
the mountain where the surface was not too steep.
Those of the fragments which lay on the declivities
rolled below; the others remained where they had
been broken. These boulders are every winter frozen
in together, and by the expanding force of ice rubbed
and crushed upon one another, thereby breaking off their
sharp angles and rounding them off in every direction.
This would account for their present appearance, and
account for it, too, without the supposition of any
change of place. The largest of these boulders were
nearest the top of the mountain, and the five hillocks
which crown the summit are completely surrounded
with them. I have thus far seen no evidence what-
soever of the action of glaciers or icebergs in Asia
Minor. The top of Mount Olympus is of common
granite, and offers precisely the same appearance as the
summit of Star Mountain, the blocks or boulders all
consisting of the same rock as that which constitutes
the mountain itself. This process is going on at the
present time on the tops of all our high mountains,
but may be particularly seen at any season of the year
on Mount Argœus, where the action of the ice has
such force as to break off fragments of rock from the
mountain and hurl them down its sides with detona-
tions resembling artillery.

Our course being as nearly straight towards the top as the nature of the ground seemed to allow, we were obliged to pass over several of these heaps of boulders; indeed, they often appeared to cover the whole surface in sight. We were obliged to jump from one stone to another, and even to scramble over them on all-fours, careful to avoid the openings between, where we might slip, and become wedged in. I kept by Willie, in order to choose the easiest path and avoid danger, as well as to restrain that youthful ambition to push too fast toward the goal, which he would reach in a state of perspiration that would ill fit him to stand in the cool breeze at the top. The rest of the party moved on more rapidly, and, by diverging to the right, found the ground less encumbered with loose rocks, and, indeed, before reaching the top came upon the ancient road, still in a good state of preservation.

We reached the summit at 9. We saw only the finely crystallized black granite all the way up the mountain, and, as far as we could judge from appearances, there exists no other rock here. This is remarkable, because I believe it is the only spot where granite occurs in all this region. But the same thing is met with at Sivri Hissar, whose rock is so precisely similar to that of the Star Mountain that it is impossible to tell them apart. We found at the latter place specimens in which the black crystals were large and beautiful. Grass is growing up to the very summit; here we also picked flowers, and Willie

caught a butterfly. The crest of the mountain consists of five hillocks or natural mounds in a somewhat curved line, running nearly east and west, the

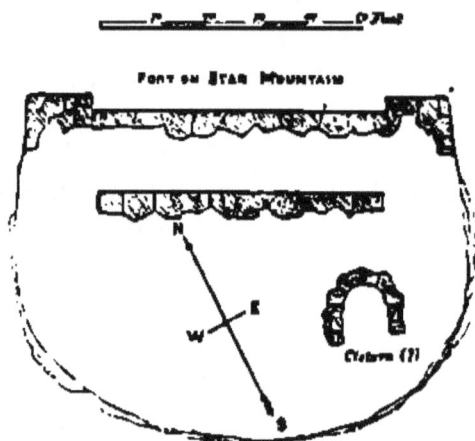

FORT ON STAR MOUNTAIN

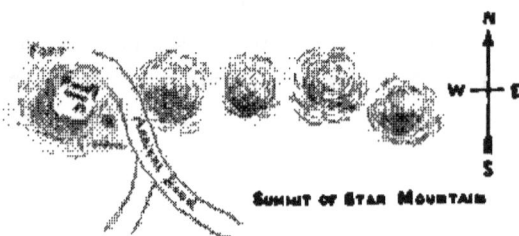

SUMMIT OF STAR MOUNTAIN

convex side being towards the north. The highest
of these hillocks is the farthest west, and it is
crowned with the remains of the fort, while its sides
are covered both with natural boulders and with the
hewn stone with which the fort was built. Judging

from the large quantity of stones, mostly granite, which showed signs of having been hewn by the hand of man, the fort must have been a lofty and solid structure; the latter quality must indeed have been an indispensable condition to its standing against the terrible blasts and storms of this high region. The foundations of the building have evidently been very thoroughly dug over, probably in search of treasure, so that but a small portion remains to point out the form of the fort. The part best preserved is a cyclopean wall forming the north-east face of the building, and running north-west and south-east; it measures 50 feet, and is flanked at each end by a solid square tower having a front of 12 feet, thus giving a face on this side of 80 feet. This is evidently the foundation of a wall, for it is level with the soil on the inside. It descends in front to a considerable depth, which cannot be ascertained on account of the mass of stone resting against it. Fourteen feet back from the outer face of this wall is another, built exactly parallel, extending only to the edge of the towers. Both these walls have but one straight face, the stones on the other being of unequal lengths and forms; and they are both level with the ground inside the fort. Back from the eastern extremity of the second wall stand the remains of a semicircular structure which must have been either a vault or a cistern. Outside the fort, and on the south-eastern edge of the hillock on which it was erected, is a cistern

in tolerably good preservation; it is built in the
shape of a broad well, and is now about 20 feet deep.
There are no other traces of foundation walls on the
hillock which offers a rounded appearance, the wall
now standing cutting off an arc. It is impossible to
say whether there was a ditch around the fort, or

Ruins of Fort on the summit of Star Mountain.

whether it was strengthened by an outer wall, for the
ground is heaped all around for a considerable distance
with large blocks of stone, mostly hewn, but injured by
the weather, though the hardness of the granite has
doubtless enabled them to resist longer than other
stones. The ancient road is distinctly visible, passing

in front of the fort, and going south; it then divides
into two branches going east and west, evidently following the easiest slopes of the mountain. The western
road was followed during a good portion of our descent.
There is a considerable quantity of mortar lying about
the ruin, as well as bricks. We also found a number
of hewn blocks of tufa; it must have been brought from
below, and was probably preferred for some particular
purpose on account of its lightness, and can have been
used only for the less solid portions of the structure.

We were fortunately joined at the summit by an old
shepherd from the Star Village, who pointed out the
various objects that are visible from this giddy height,
and gave us otherwise valuable information. A carefully made observation with the barometer gave me the
height of the top of the Star Mountain as 8556 feet
above the sea. The day was fortunately beautiful,
and the horizon clear. There was a slight breeze
from the north-west, and the thermometer stood at
67° Fahrenheit in the shade. I was able to take
valuable bearings of all the important objects visible
from this point, which materially aided me in construct-
ing the map of this region. We could distinctly see
with the spyglass the Armenian Monastery, one hour
from and opposite Tocat; the town itself is hidden in its
deep valley, and we thus ascertained its precise position.
In the direction of Sivas we could distinguish the road
over Melekon, the town itself being hid by the plateau.
Mount Argœus, near Cæsarea, appeared towering above

the horizon; we could just make out the Black Sea
near Samsoon; the shepherd told us he could sometimes very clearly distinguish it. The distance is 50
hours, or 200 miles. The shepherd also pointed out
the two branches of the Star River, which flow
around opposite sides of the mountain and unite near
the mill.

The view from this summit is truly striking as well
as extensive. The mountain is wholly detached from
the Chamlù Del range, although it does not lie far to
the south of it. It has already been seen that, geo-
logically, it is quite distinct from that range, whose
only volcanic rock, as far as yet ascertained, is trap
rock or trachyte. There are several summits in that
range which attain a considerable height; but none
will compare with the Star Mountain, which, in its turn,
is but one-half the height of Mount Argœus. From
this elevation the whole region around us, though
mountainous, seems almost level, yet no plains of any
size are in sight. Even the great Kaz Ova lies hid
among the mountains, and its place seems a deep gully
running east and west.

I have, thus far, given myself wholly to the
description of this interesting locality and have kept
old Strabo in the background. I shall now simply
report his language, and leave the reader to judge
whether we are on the spot he describes. He says
(Lib. xii. cap. iii. p. 39), speaking of the province of
Cabira, which Hamilton has shown (see ' Researches,'

vol. i. p. 347) to be the modern Niksar, that "here also is the so-called New Post."* He describes it as "a barren and isolated rock, distant from Capira less than 200 stadia (24 miles). There is a spring at the summit whence pours forth much water, and a river flows in a deep ravine around the base. The rock above is of stupendous height, making the fort impregnable. It is a wonderful fortress, yet the Romans destroyed it; the surrounding region is so wooded, mountainous, and destitute of water, for a space of 120 stadia (14 miles), that military operations are out of the question. Here Mithridates kept his most valuable treasures, which are now laid up in the Capitol, where they were consecrated by Pompey."

There is no need of any comment, but simply to mention that the Star Mountain is hardly 28 miles from Niksar by the present Turkish roads, which are no roads at all, but mere tracks made by passing over the ground; it is not hard to suppose that under Mithridates, or rather his Roman successors, the distance would be four miles shorter. The Star Mountain has, indeed, no forests immediately around it; but they are not far off, and as the hills have plenty of soil and have been under cultivation, the probability is that the whole surrounding region was once an unbroken forest, like the Chamlù Bel; while the great steepness of the Star Mountain itself, causing the soil as soon as formed to

* In the language of modern Asia Minor this would be Yeni-keuy, the new village; a hundred places are so called now.

be washed away, makes it difficult to suppose that
many trees ever grew upon it. On the whole, Strabo's
picture is not only correct, but vivid and characteristic.
Indeed, one can easily understand that the wily Mithridates would keep his most valuable treasures in such a
place as this. The access to the very base of the
mountain is defended by narrow gorges, some of which
were strongly fortified in ancient times. The passes
through the Chamlù Bel at the Bekjilik, and from the
Art Ova, as well as the Sivas Bekjilik, and through
the Kara Dere, could each be defended against large
forces by a handful of men. The whole region around
is arid, and furnishes no supplies for an army. The
mountain itself is difficult of ascent. A besieging force
must lie exposed to the inclemencies of the weather;
and the position of the fort is such that it could only be
taken by starving out the garrison.

We were but an hour descending from the top to
the spring where we had left our horses. We found
quite a group of villagers there, attracted to the
spot by the sight of our smoke and the flavour of a
sheep which was being roasted whole, turning before
a blazing fire upon a wooden spit. It was a grand
meal, seasoned by wholesome exercise, mountain air,
splendid water, and merry companionship, and full
justice was done to it by all the guests. The thoroughly
picked skeleton was set upon a pole, and several fine
eagles were pecking at it before we were out of sight.
We reached the village at four, and the friends who

had joined us from Sivas started immediately upon their return home.

Thursday, 7th.—Left Sarù Yeri at 5·30 A.M., forded the northern branch of the Star River. Both the branches I have observed to be low and easily forded during the summer months. But during a great portion of the year fording is dangerous, and travellers have been drowned in attempting it. They have to be crossed at the bridges which stand upon all the principal roads. The Star River was here 10 feet wide, and ran from right to left through a small plain, at the other side of which lies the village of Boolookhtoon, which we reached at 6·25. The top of the Star Mountain bore from this place a little south of east. We travelled among forests of pine, and reached the highest point at 9·30. Rock—green shales, often assuming dark shades, almost like jaspar. We descended from the summer *yaïlas* of the Koordish tribes and the pine forests, through which we had been travelling, to a more varied and luxuriant vegetation; passed the summer dwellings of the people of Semorji Keuy on our right, which overlooked a deep and beautiful valley, and came upon the Sivas summer or post road a little above the Robbers' Hill. We reached our house at Tocat at 5·15.

CHAPTER XVII.

Circassian music — Bishop Kcabish Oghloo — Dedication of new
chapel — Start for overland journey — Praying places — Villages
of Seungut Keuy and Pazar Keuy — Fountain of Chermook —
Farm of Haji Boghos Agha — Khzbllash labourers — Swamps
of the Kaz Ova — A pair of somersaults — Village of Yeghin
Musulman — Spirits of Turkish saints — Village of Chiflik —
Village of Enren.

TOCAT, *Saturday, July* 16th. — Some poor Circassians in rags have been performing music and
dancing in the street before our door to-day, in hope
of obtaining a present. One of them played upon an
iron flute of the kind called *naï*, while another kept
time with an instrument I have never seen before.
It is made of square pieces of board of equal size,
fastened together like the leaves of a book, and is held
by a handle, and jerked up and down, the boards
clapping at every motion. A little boy danced to the
music very much as do the Bulgarian peasants, taking
off his cap and throwing it up. The *naï* was small
and the tune monotonous.

Last Sunday the newly appointed Armenian Bishop
of Tocat made his triumphal entry into town, accom-

panied by some 200 horsemen, comprising all the
principal Armenian gentlemen of the place. They
were all in great gala, and his holiness rode a fine
horse, handsomely caparisoned. On Monday he went
to the Conak, where his firman was read before the
council and chief citizens. This Bishop is none other
than the well known and notorious Keshish Oghloo,
Vartabed of the Armenian convent at Dizeri, whom
the people despise for his infidelity, priestcraft, and
ignorance; but he is cunning, and has shown much
skill in managing Turkish officials; the most influential
Armenians here, therefore, have declared him to be
the man of their choice—for the place has been some-
time vacant. They accordingly sent a petition to the
Patriarch, who obtained the necessary firman from
the Porte, and the wily priest is now fully installed
Bishop.

The work upon our chapel and school has so far
advanced as to be very nearly completed. What little
remains to be done can safely be entrusted to the
pastor and deacon, who have already so cheerfully and
usefully accomplished the most important task. It was
moreover time that we should be setting our faces
westward on our long overland journey. The pastor
elect was therefore duly and publicly examined as to his
faith and qualification for the pastoral office into which
he had not yet been fully installed. With the approval
of all present, as well as of the representatives of the
Sivas Mission, and of the Evangelical Church there,

the ordination services took place on Sunday, July 24,
as well as the dedication services of the newly erected
chapel. The audience was large and interested, and
the sacramental services of the afternoon were perhaps
still more impressive. It was, indeed, hard to part
with this little flock, left comparatively alone in the
wilderness. But their situation was far better than
in 1861, when we had left them before. They were
now perfectly harmonious: had their own pastor
regularly ordained over them, and a valuable and
popular teacher in charge of the school. The chapel
and school were all that could be desired, and gave
to the Protestants there a feeling of security against
the apprehension of some day being left at the mercy
of their enemies, with no option but to get recon-
ciled as best they could with the Armenian Church
ecclesiastics. They had the elements of growth within
themselves; would ere long be able to support their
Christian institutions, their pastor, and school-master,
and would cease to require further aid from abroad.
I should probably have felt differently could I have
foreseen that the teacher, broken down by inadequate
support, his salary being cut down to a mere pittance,
and reduced below that of a common day-labourer,
would sicken of typhus and cerebral fever, and when
feeble in mind and body would be persuaded by his
friends to make his peace with the old Church, and
accept a competent support from them for teaching
their children as he had taught those of the Protes-

tants. There were other sources of anxiety, too, from which we then were free. But enough.

Wednesday, July 27th.—The house was early filled with friends who had come to see us off; men, women, and children had a last word to say, and "salams" and "parevs" to send to the absent ones whom we hoped soon to meet. A number of friends accompanied us out of town, riding on horses and donkeys. We started at 9·30, having been delayed even in the streets by many who stood upon their doorsteps to bid us good-bye. We took the usual road through the *meïdan*, between the great stone khan and the marble mosque, by the ruins of the ancient palace of the Abassidian khans, and under the tottering battlements of the old castle, and proceeded through the gardens and vineyards along the left bank of the Iris. We stopped to lunch at the ancient Muslem praying place, a handsome marble structure two hours from town. It is hard to say what the purpose of these praying places, so called, could have been. The one which lies just outside Tocat, on our present road, has a sort of indication of a Kûbleh. It seems much more probable, from their position at important places by the road side, that they were intended as stations for a police force, or for custom-house officers. The one upon the hill opposite the town, however, must have been a mosque. Our friends had parted from us just before we reached this spot. We were again on our way at 1·15, and passed the Turkish village of Seungut Keuy, "the village of

the golden duck," situated on the slope of a hill almost
entirely surrounded by swamps. A great variety of
ducks frequent this place in the winter season, and
cranes are said to live here altogether, and to breed
their young in the tall grass. But I have never seen
more than three or four of these birds here at once.
They are said to be extremely hard to approach, and
when pursued will run with great speed. They are
doubtless of the same species as those which perform
their distant migrations twice every year; but the
natives distinguish these as "yerli," indigenous. The
river is spanned by an old and steep bridge of four arches,
a Muslem structure, whose perforated sides are peopled
with wild pigeons. At 3·20 we came to Pazar Keuy, a
large Turkish village built on the edge of the plain, and
surrounded by extensive gardens and vineyards, water
being very abundant. A weekly market is held here
for the accommodation of the villages of this part
of the plain. It is the residence of a Mudir and Cadi,
whose authority extends over the whole *sanjak* or
district of the Kaz Ova. The village contains several
shops and stores; it has lately received the accession
of a number of Circassian families, who are said to
be very troublesome, helping themselves to their
neighbours' property wherever they find it, instead of
working for their own support. Instead of passing
through the village, we took a more direct road
through the gardens on the right, and then, leaving
the common highway which passed along the plain,

and is now very hot and dusty, rode upon the bluffs which skirt it on the left. These bluffs are well cultivated and shaded with trees. We turned into a side valley, or gorge, beautiful with gardens and orchards, with a fine stream coming down from the mountain, and passing through the Turkish village of Farno, continued along the slope, until at 5·30 we passed the Fountain of Chermook. This is a spring whose waters rush out with force from beneath a ledge of limestone rock some 30 to 50 feet high. It is well shaded by poplars and willows. Over the spring stands an old bath, whose well-worn stones indicate that it has been in use for centuries past. The water is supposed to possess medicinal properties, and is resorted to even from distant places. The name indicates this, for Chermook means a mineral spring. We could not, however, perceive that it differed from ordinary water, either in taste or in temperature. There was once a village here, for there are ruins of houses and a decayed mosque. A garden is still cultivated: the place, however, seems to be feverish owing to the want of draining, which might be remedied at a trifling expense.

At 6·30 we reached the chiflik, or farm, of our Armenian friend, Haji Boghos Agha, from whom we had received a cordial invitation to spend a night with him. It is a valuable property, of which the arable lands extend across the whole plain to the mountains on the north, and even occupy both banks of the Iris, as it

turns northward towards Toorkhal. This gentleman is
possessed of great natural intelligence, and has enjoyed
the best educational advantages procurable in the
country. He has travelled in all parts of Turkey,
though hardly 25 years of age. Agriculture he loves
with passion, and practised it with success; but, as generally happens to the Christian subjects of the Porte, the
Turks of the whole region, envious of his prosperity,
have combined to ruin him. They obtained an order
from the Sublime Porte, requiring that all lands which
had not been sown for three years should be given up
to the Circassians. In this country where the system
of rotation in crops is unknown, where land is abundant
and labour scarce, a great portion of the arable land
necessarily lies fallow for long periods. The authorities of Tocat and Pazar Keuy selected the most
valuable fields on our friend's estate, proved by Muslem false witnesses that they had not been cultivated
for three years, and sent a band of stout and well-
armed Circassians to take possession of them. They
settled down only a mile from the very house occupied
by Haji Boghos Agha himself. And now there is no
end to the robberies and vexations inflicted by these
men. The rightful owner has already spent much
of his property in the vain attempt to obtain redress;
and he assured us he was only waiting for an opportunity to sell his estate without too great a sacrifice,
leave the place altogether, and purchase a farm in
the neighbourhood of Constantinople or Smyrna, where

he believed the Turks would not dare to treat him thus under the very eyes of the representatives of the European powers. There can be no doubt that such conduct on the part of the ruling race, even where it benefits them immediately, must ultimately end in their ruin; and it argues great blindness on the part of the Government authorities not to perceive it. Everybody can see that this large farm, under the skilful management of its present proprietor, brings a considerable revenue to the Government in the shape of taxes, while the wretched Circassians, who are put forward to gratify Turkish bigotry and envy, will, in spite of the fine lands now handed over to them, long continue to prove a burden to the Government Treasury. Thus does bigotry ever defeat and punish itself; and wasted and starved Turkey is already starving those who claim alone the right to be fed by her.

The people who work on our friend's farm are mostly Kùzùlbashes, whom he finds very laborious, less deceitful than the Christians, and more obedient than the Turks. They build their own houses, which are circular, with floors considerably lower than the level of the ground, and flat roofs. These people look strong and hardy, and belong to a peculiar race, probably one of the earliest that occupied the Peninsula of Asia Minor. They profess to be Mohammedans, but this profession is known not to be sincere, and the Turks themselves are fully aware of it, and thoroughly hate them for it. They do not believe in God, and hold to the trans-

migration of souls. In imitation of the Muslems,
they give their religious teachers the names of Hoja
(sheikh), and Dervish (religious devotee). We saw
here an old man said to be 90 years of age, but strong
and erect, who is called Dervish Hussein Baba. He
seemed quite gratified by the proposal to draw his
picture. I noticed that he had remarkably small
hands and feet. Though many of these people are
found in all the large towns of Turkey engaged in
every trade, and filling every office in the gift of
Government, yet they are mostly addicted to agri-
cultural pursuits: their women do not veil themselves
in the presence of Christians, but only of Turks.

Thursday, 28th.—The swamps of the Kaz Ova are in
full sight below us. They do not affect the healthfulness
of this place, because the wind does not blow from that
direction during the fever season. In winter they are
the great resort of ducks and wild geese, which give
their name to the plain; they are sometimes shot by
means of flat boats launched upon the swamp, in which
the sportsman hides himself under green boughs, and
advances stealthily among the reeds. There are three
places where the water is very deep. Our host thinks
they cannot be drained by a cut to the river, which he
believes too high opposite the swamp. It is generally
supposed that the intermittent fevers which prevail
among the country houses situated farthest west in
the neighbourhood of Tocat, owe their origin to the
miasma borne from this swamp by the westerly winds.

I cannot believe it to be so. The distance, seven hours at least, is too great. The swamps around Seungut Keuy are doubtless the origin of that malaria, and the two chifliks, which are near to the latter swamp, suffer most severely, while the Tash Chiflik is perfectly free from fever. The swamps of the Kaz Ova are the resort of numerous wild boars, which come out at night and waste the neighbouring fields of grain. They have to be watched for a shot; but as the people are Muslems, they are often left to rot in the field and breed disease, so that Government officers have to come and force the farmers of the neighbourhood to bury them.

Started at 7·15. Went over the hills to the west. At 9·30 saw the town and castle of Zileh; it is built upon a broad hill with level surface, the town lying at the foot of it on the south-east and north-east sides. We now had a good view of the plain of Zileh, which we were skirting; it looked yellow from the stubble remaining in the fields after the harvest, and the appearance, therefore, was one of aridity, though we know that it is very productive. But the villages, which are numerous, were surrounded with verdure. While travelling over a good smooth road, our pack-horse, which was going at a good round pace, hit his fore-foot against a stone, and had such a fall as I never yet saw a horse accomplish. He went down head foremost, turned a complete somersault, and came to the ground with his four feet up in the air, his neck twisted round, and the

whole load resting on his head. The thing was done so
quickly that the first we knew of it was the sight of the
poor animal lying on the ground in that dangerous
position, running the risk of breaking his neck if aid
was delayed; indeed, we did for a moment think his
neck *was* broken. The muleteer was just behind him,
riding a diminutive donkey, and in his haste to dismount
became entangled by the ropes, and went right over
as if in imitation of the brute's performance, feet up
and head down. In spite of our alarm, we all burst
into peals of laughter; a knife soon cut the cords
of the load and set the poor animal free, and he was
carrying his burden again in a few minutes as though
nothing had happened. We now entered a narrow valley,
which we followed along its eastern side. It is fertile,
and its little river flows north toward Zileh, supplying
several flour-mills along its course. Went over undulating ground into a plain, and crossing a small stream
entered the Turkish village of Yeghin Musulman
(Bigoted Muslems) at 12·30. We saw orchards and
gardens around the village, and found, upon inquiry,
that we might, for hire, occupy one of them. It
was surrounded by a mud wall, and thickly planted
with fruit-trees, which afforded a pleasant shade; the
only means of access was by a small door at the end of
a bridge, formed of a single plank over the stream, thus
affording us a good shelter from the intrusion of the
curious. There was, moreover, an immense stable for
our horses near by. In this delightful spot we pitched our

tent, and were soon quite at home. The tent stood near
the graves of three Turkish saints, over which grew a
vine; the Imam of the village, who had special charge
of the sacred spot, soon paid us a visit, and after many
preliminaries and much general talk, advised us, for our
own comfort, not to remain here. It was Thursday, he
said, and the saint was in the habit of coming out of his
grave, on the night of Thursday to Friday, to wash
his hands and feet and say his *namaz*; he was apt to
be troublesome to strangers upon such occasions (he
meant Giaours), and we had better keep out of his way.
I assured him that we were well acquainted with that
kind of people, and never allowed them to disturb us;
that the buzzing of a fly would awake us, that our dogs
never slept, and that our fire-arms comprised twenty-
five to thirty barrels loaded and primed; in case one or
two shots should miss the mark, which was not their
habit, one of the rest would teach any disturber of
our peace that we were not people to be trifled with.
" Oh! said the Imam, your gun will not go off if aimed
at *him!*" "Good!" I replied, " we shall run no risk of
treating him with disrespect, or of hurting his Saintship.
In case our guns do not go off we shall know it is *he*,
and we shall let him move on; but if the gun fires it will
certainly be a robber, and we shall fire again and again
until we kill him or he cries *Aman!* Our guns are
English; they never miss fire; you see they are very
different from anything you have ever seen." At this
speech he made a very wry face. It probably saved us

a nightly visit. Had we not felt too tired, and in need
of sleep, we might have expressed some fears so as to
secure a call from the tricky priest, and have given him
a fright he would have remembered the rest of his
life. He asked me the next morning, with a smile,
whether we had seen anything during the night? I
very gravely replied that we thought we had heard a
slight noise on the other side of the wall, and our dogs
had barked; but, seeing nothing, we had not fired. He
winked his eye and whispered it was *he.*

The elevation of this place by the barometer is
2760 feet. This result cannot be far out of the way;
but the weather was fitful and blustering, and such as to
cause the mercury to fall below its mean level. About
5 P.M. the wind blew for a while so strong from the
north that it seemed as though it would tear down the
trees of our orchard; the tallest of our poplars in
particular bent fearfully. The young men obtained a
considerable quantity of small game on the trees about
us, which seemed to be their favourite resort, especially
about roosting-time, and the Imam had an opportunity
of convincing himself that what I had said of our guns
was not a vain boast.

It may here be remarked that the weather has particularly favoured me in my observations with the
barometer. During all our journeyings the sky was
clear, except upon the occasions specified in my journal.
This is important, for the most unvarying and uniform
weather is indispensable to give perfect accuracy to

the barometrical observations by which heights have
to be calculated. The fact sufficiently explains the
discrepancies to be found in the calculation of heights
given by different travellers. But, with this reserva-
tion, it cannot be denied that measurements with the
barometer are quite as reliable as trigonometrical sur-
veys.

Friday, 29*th.*—We left this morning at 6·15. At
10·15 we entered the miserable little village of Chiflik,
and, crossing a little stream, entered and took possession
of a small orchard, thickly planted with fruit-trees and
poplars. We rested here for several hours, greatly enjoying the cool shade and the refreshing breeze; the
only disturbance we met with was from an old woman
who stood outside of the hedge, and for a long time
vented her fanaticism by cursing us in all the terms of
her rich vocabulary, for polluting her orchard with our
giaourship. As there was no fruit we could do no
possible harm, so we just let her enjoy the sound of her
own voice until she stopped from exhaustion. The land
all around is fertile, and seems to yield good crops;
but, at this season, it looks parched and dry. The grain
had been gathered in, and even the *harmans* had disappeared. The only verdure to be seen is in the immediate vicinity of the villages, which are uniformly built
near some spring or water-course, and are shaded with
trees, mostly poplars, walnuts, and willows. We had
heard last night, at Yeghin Musulman, that some
Franks had been there, and had obtained several of

those peculiar excrescences found upon the trunks of walnut-trees, which are used in veneering, and are called "loupes" by the French. From all accounts, these seem to be common, and of a valuable quality, in Asia Minor, for we have heard of their being sought for and taken away from all parts of the Peninsula by men who have come from Europe expressly for that purpose; it is said that some of these people have made their fortunes in this way. We left our resting-place at 1·45, and travelled in a W.S.W. direction. The plain gradually rose, and became contracted between the bushy heights on the right and left. We reached the highest ground on this part of our road at 2·45, and ascended to an elevation whence we overlooked the valley of the Chekerek Soo, a tributary of the Iris, which falls into it on the north of Zileh. The descent into this valley was very steep. At 3 we passed through a village built upon the slope, in which the chimney-tops were made of osier baskets. Riding over undulating and cultivated ground, which rose as it receded from the river bank, we passed several large villages, where we had intended to stop, but found that all the people were gone to their summer quarters or *yailas*. We went on, therefore, to the village of Euren, and selected a beautiful camping-ground on a high terrace overlooking a series of vineyards occupying the sloping hill in front of the village, shaded and partly protected on the north by a row of cherry-trees. There is a fine old fountain at the corner, with two tall

walnut-trees by its side. This spot was frequented by
turtle-doves, which were numerous, flying all about us.
While the tent was being pitched our sportsmen bagged
a sufficient number of the poor birds for a plentiful
supper; a spit was improvised, and the cookery was
worthy of the occasion. This spot is high and airy,
and a tented traveller could nowhere spend a more
agreeable or refreshing night. I recommend to our
successors the terraced garden of Euren, under the
cherry-trees, with a supper of turtle-doves roasted on a
ramrod.

CHAPTER XVIII.

SATURDAY, *July 30th.*—Started at 6·15. Ascending a gorge which grew narrow and picturesque as we proceeded, we came to cliffs of green shale and limestone, indicating a great perturbation. Started a fine covey of red-legged partridges on the bank of the stream. At 9·45 passed over the hill at the end of the gorge among the bold trachytic rocks, which have evidently caused all this disturbance and breaking up of the crust. At 10 came to a small village on the north side of a little valley, which runs off to our right. We were constantly mounting as we rode on. Having reached the highest point of our ascent, we at once began to go down into another valley, and travelled along the side of a narrow gorge, whose little stream runs down in a direction opposite to our own course. The hills on both sides are low; they bear only scrub oak bushes, and small wild cypress, completely shutting us in, so that the heat is intense, and very trying. We were glad to see ahead of us the Turkish village of Beyordoo, which we reached at 11·30, crossing the small stream upon a wooden bridge at its entrance. It possesses a stone mosque, and the whole population were in holiday attire engaged in the festivities of a marriage which is to take place to-morrow. As soon as we appeared in sight of the village a procession was formed to meet us. We were preceded by the *davool* (drum), and *zoorna* (hautbois); made a grand entrance into the village; and were led up to the mosque, around which the people were collected. They proposed that we should alight there, promising us all sorts of comforts; but, having spied a beautiful grove of tall willows planted in a circle behind the village, we passed through the *harmans* (threshing-floors), whose heaped grain at once indicated that we had reached a more elevated region, and alighted in the fine grove, which effectually preserved us from the sun's rays, while it allowed the breeze to reach us unimpeded. There is a fountain of good water close by, and the young men found a fair supply of turtle-doves to shoot—the hope of our larder in this region. As we went to our quarters, however, the music and the crowd followed close at our heels; and the only way we could get rid of the nuisance was to pay the customary *bakshish.*

We were again in the saddle at 2·15. Reached the highest point on the hills at 3·10, and here met the first camels we have yet seen on our jour-

ney. They are not unfrequently found in the Kaz
Ova, and the Art Ova, though in small numbers.
They are chiefly employed in carrying ore from the
mines about Kharpoot to the foundry at Tocat, and
thence the copper bars to Samsoon. But they are not
numerous in that region; they appear to avoid the
northern portions of the Peninsula, where the dense
forests, and the generally clayey soil, cause the mud
to remain longer on the ground, making travel dangerous to these animals. They are owned exclusively
by the Koordish tribes in Eastern Asia Minor, the
northernmost of whom roam over the country which
lies between Amasia, Chorum, Zileh, and Tocat. The
Avshar Koords occupy the country around Cæsarea,
chiefly to the east and north of that place. They, however, make excursions as far as the neighbourhood of
Karghùn and Gurun. They all have camels, some of
which are very fine. Farther west the Koords give
way to the Turkmen.

We now began to descend toward a very extensive
undulating plain, in which lie Keuhnch, Sorkun, and
other important towns. No high mountain appeared in
any quarter of the horizon. We passed over a series of
low hills, with neither tree nor shrub, most of which
have at some period been under cultivation. There was
fallow land enough for the Sultan to supply any number
of his Circassian guests, without robbing his Christian
subjects. Shallow valleys occupy the lower grounds,
and convey the waters of the region southward to the

Halys. At 3·45 we descended into a fertile valley a quarter of a mile wide, which runs toward the southwest. All the rock around here continues to be green shales. The height from which we had descended appears to form the watershed between the Halys and the Iris. Before we reached it all the streams flowed toward the Chekerek, which is a tributary of the Iris. We now found them all flowing toward a stream that passes by Keulmeh, and goes southward toward the Halys. Kiepert's map makes all these streams tributary to the Chekerek, which is a mistake; but the region appears not to have been examined before, as Kiepert marks the course of the streams only with dots. At 4·30 passed a village on our left, and by it an extensive and apparently ancient cemetery, with large blocks of rough stone to mark the graves. The plain now widens, the hills which enclose it continuing very low and rolling; it is well planted with wheat, flax, beans, and Indian corn, or maize. The water of the little stream is used for the purpose of irrigation. At 6·30 we passed through the village of Karûlar (women). From this we descended at 7 to a still lower level, a purely alluvial plain, which appears very rich. It will thus be seen that there are here several distinct levels, the highest being shown by the low hills of green shales, and the lowest being alluvium. We now came upon the stream, which we found about 10 feet wide: it is used to water gardens on both banks. We found upon the left side an encampment of Koords, whose flocks of goats and

sheep were feeding in the grassy meadow, guarded by
savage-looking dogs. There were several Angora goats
among them, distinguished from the rest by their pure
white colour, and the glossiness of their coat. Their
form, however, seemed more like sheep than goats.
These were the first specimens of this breed we had
met on this journey. I was disappointed to find them
so small; I inferred they were young, but subsequent
observation upon a large scale has convinced me that
this kind of goat stands a good deal lower on his legs,
and is smaller every way than the common species.

As we crossed the stream, a solitary camel of large
size was led along the road, majestically bearing a
very large *maffa* filled with women. It was handsomely rigged out, and appeared to belong to people of
wealth. They were probably coming to the hot baths.
These are situated near the right bank of the river,
the hot water issuing from a spot about 20 feet
above the level of the stream, and flowing into it.
Over this spring is erected a building, which consists
simply of a square enclosure of stone walls, 30 feet
by 20, and 12 feet high, of modern construction, with
a door near the south-west corner, and recesses in the
walls for stowing away the clothes. Timbers are laid
across the top, so that it can be covered with a tent-
cloth in the winter. The bath itself consists of a
depression, or oblong basin, at the north-east corner,
paved with slabs and 10 feet lower than the general
floor. The spring issues at the corner itself, and a

hole in the eastern wall constantly carries away the sur-
plus water, maintaining a depth of about 4 feet. The
basin measures 12 feet by 10, and there are stone steps
leading down into the water. I wished to obtain

Hot Spring, near Krubnab.

the temperature of the water, but my thermometer
marked only 140° of Fahrenheit, which the mercury so
quickly reached that I was unable to make an observation. The water is whitish, as though containing
some alkali, but it forms no deposit. In the basin
it felt quite warm; and it was almost impossible to
hold the hand in it where it issued from the ground.
The place is resorted to by many people from the whole

surrounding region, it being supposed to contain valuable medicinal properties; but it is said to be hurtful to remain long in it. The water which runs out of the hole at the eastern wall falls into deep trenches, which are lined with hewn stones. The lowest of these are large, and appear very old, arguing that the ancients made use of this spring. On the inner face of the northern wall is a Turkish inscription cut in the stone, probably placed there when the building was repaired. No fees are required, and no one appears to have charge of the place, although a small house, close by, is occupied by people who seem to sell refreshments or keep lodgers. The effect of the water upon the skin was found to be somewhat peculiar by those of us who went into it. As long as a limb or the whole body was immersed no particular sensation was experienced, but, when brought out into the air, the skin at once became extremely hot, and remained so for some time; it was covered also with irregular red patches. The general effect upon the system, after remaining even but a few minutes in the water, was drowsiness, hunger, and great weakness. A slight whitish deposit is left upon the skin, which, on rubbing, feels like soap. The water of this spring rapidly dissolves soap.

The hills from which we had descended were of green shales; but, when we reached the plain itself, we found that even its highest level was formed of sandstone, which, in some places, is quite red. But, at the spring, the rock is coarse granite. We found

granite also all the way from the spring to the large
village of Keuhneh lying directly north of it, about one
hour distant. The hillocks which bound the plain on
the west are all of the same rock, and boulders are lying
about, and are used as landmarks for the fields. The
soil around Keuhneh is level, fertile, and well cultivated.
We passed through the village, and found a convenient
garden on its southern edge, where we pitched our tent
under a cluster of trees.

Sunday, 31st.—We had a pleasant and quiet day of
rest; we spent most of it in reading and singing, and
had a refreshing little service by ourselves. In the
afternoon we had some interesting calls, among which
was that of a young Circassian officer in the Turkish
service, who has come here to take the baths. The
country around us is one extensive level plain, under
good cultivation, with here and there clusters of
trees, and bounded near the horizon by low hills, such
as we had passed on our way here. There are many
mares kept in these fields, and some of them appear
to be fine animals. We also saw a good many camels,
one of them white. The horned cattle, however, are
small, and look feeble. Keuhneh is at an elevation
of 3752 feet, which shows a considerable rise since we
left Tocat. We are, indeed, but 700 feet lower than
Sivas, while the climate appears to be much milder.
But there is no Chamlù Bel about here!

Monday, August 1st.—We had a ride of six hours
before us to Yozghat, and a rise of about 700 feet,

not to speak of the greater heights we might have
to encounter on the way.   We started at 5·30 A.M.,
and following a direction due west, soon overtook a
Koordish tribe, who were travelling, with all their
goods and chattels, in the same direction as ourselves.   There were long lines of camels loaded with
property; the men and women mostly rode horses and
donkeys.   Several carried hawks upon their fists,
and wore a thick glove for this purpose; all the birds
were blind-folded.   They had several dogs, but only
one seemed to be fit for sporting purposes.   The chief
rode upon a skeleton of a horse at the head of the
file; he was an old man, and proposed to give us the
hawk he was carrying upon his fist, in exchange for
one of our dogs.   We replied that *our* hawks, pointing
to our guns, were quicker, more obedient, and less
troublesome than his, so that we did not care to acquire
any of his birds.   The country all around here is weari-
some to the sight.   Neither tree nor bush relieves the
eye; the land has all the appearance of having
been formerly under cultivation, but there is a scarcity
of water in it.   Came upon the highroad from Amasia and
Chorum; it has lately been repaired in this part, and
is good for carriages.   It looked like civilization to see
the lines of the telegraph upon it.   Went over the hill,
and from the top obtained the first sight of the town
of Yozghat, which lies at the bottom of a valley running east and west, rising slightly upon the slopes on
either side.   Vegetable patches occupy the bottom of

the valley; there are some trees and private gardens about the town, and an isolated grove upon the slope of the southern hill. With these exceptions all is barren and parched. The houses are made of rough stones united with mud, or of mud bricks, and are all covered with red tiles. As we approached the town, we could distinguish some very good-looking houses, and one handsome mosque with a minaret. The size of Yozghat is about half that of Tocat. The rock at the bottom of the valley is sandstone, which, in some places, is of a deep red, like brick, and in others of as deep yellow an ochre. We reached the town at 11·30, and went to the house of the Rev. Mr. Farnsworth, an American missionary who is stationed in Cæsarea, and often spends the summer in this place. His house is situated upon a slight declivity, which overlooks the gardens at the bottom of the valley, and affords a good view of a considerable portion of the city. We could distinguish from this spot a wall about 10 feet high running around the town, though it is broken down in several places. Yozghat is a place of recent origin; its convenient position with regard to this portion of the country, has led to its being made the seat of government for the Province.

Tuesday, 2nd.—The native Evangelical Church and community have been very frank and cordial in their intercourse with us, and I am pleased with their spirit, and their earnest desire for instruction and improvement. I visited their prosperous school, and at their own request, addressed them in the chapel, respecting the condition of their brethren in different parts of the country. I found the elevation of Yozghat, at Mr. F.'s house, to be 4418 feet. This is equal to the height of Sivas. The climate of these two towns is said to be identical, but the position of Yozghat, in a narrow valley, must expose it to be visited by strong winds, while there may perhaps be less snow than at Sivas.

Wednesday, 3rd.—We left Yozghat at 9·30 A.M. We had been obliged to part with our faithful Tocat muleteers, they having engaged to come only as far as here. Their places were taken by two Turks, who came to us very highly recommended, but whom we immediately discovered to be quite ignorant of their business; longer experience unfortunately revealed so many other failings, that we seized the first opportunity of getting rid of them. Our road led us in a northerly direction, through a narrow gorge, which took us to the summit of the high hills, on that side of the valley of Yozghat. The steepness of the road, and the inexperience of our new hands occasioned much delay; for the load turned over several times, and once barely escaped falling down a precipice of great depth; as it was, one box rolled some distance down the hill. We had to set our own shoulders to the work of loading, and greatly regretted the loss of Osman Agha, our neighbour at Tocat and a member of the police force of that place, whom we had taken as guide as far as

Yozghat, and who had turned out the most accommo-
dating and useful fellow I ever had with me upon the
road; he was invaluable in always getting us the best
accommodation and provisions our resting-place possessed, acted as groom and horse-doctor on emer-
gencies, and was everywhere and everything; best of
all, he left us with evident regret, and was pleased with
very moderate pay. I believe that he and our muleteers would have come with us as far as our journey's
end, had not both they and we been afraid of the cost
of their return home; it is certain, however, that we
should have found it economical had we engaged them
at any reasonable price. We henceforth depended
upon the good will of the pashas and mudirs, and a
handsome bakshish, for a guide; tho man the Governor of Yozghat gave us knew so little of the road,
that he had to inquire about it as we proceeded, and
was constantly talking about his being very feeble,
and having just recovered from a long illness, and his
horse having just come from eating grass; he always
extended his hand for and expected the best morsels
at each of our meals, and could not refrain from helping us to get rid of our tea; he finally abandoned us
long before reaching the point to which he had promised to accompany us, saying he would utterly break
down if he proceeded any further; this was probably
a trick for getting a present, but it failed, for wo
took him at his word and summarily dismissed him.
Our progress was very slow, owing to the steepness

of the ground, and still more to the frequent turning
over of our loads, from the ignorance and inexperience
of our new muleteers.   Indeed they had to take several
regular lessons on loading before we could make any
head-way; and in order to do this, we ourselves loaded
our two pack-horses systematically before their eyes, as
we had learnt by long experience and travel; adding
sundry homely expositions of the philosophy and the
laws of balance, and the strain upon ropes. Fortunately
the men turned out less stupid than might have been
expected, for they finally got their lesson so well, that
we had no more trouble from this source, though we
soon had worse grievances to urge against them.

We now began to descend, and at 12·30 reached a
fountain, where we stopped for luncheon. After passing
over undulating ground we entered a narrow gorge
watered by a small stream; its careful cultivation
indicated the neighbourhood of human habitations.
This high region seems to enjoy a good deal of rain,
for water was abundant, and the richness and freshness
of the vegetation reminded us of the showery neighbourhood of Samsoon. We left the village of Dishek
on our left, when we suddenly turned with the valley
to the right, still travelling near the bank of the stream.
Came to a fountain of very fine water, and proceeded
through a charming valley full of flowers and fresh
green grass, the fields being covered with standing
crops of wheat. Harvest was just commencing. This
spot is called Kamishjy Boghaz, or the valley of the

reed gatherers, and reminded us of the rich and beautiful vale which runs south from Tocat. Farther down the land was not equally well cultivated, and much of it is covered with dwarf oaks. Travelling near the bank of a stream, we entered a gorge, which soon turned to the south, and became very narrow and precipitous, stupendous rocks frowning on both sides, while the stream roared among the fallen stones at the bottom. We could no longer travel upon the water's edge, but climbing over a rocky road on the right, passed above a mill, and proceeded on the bushy slope of the calcareous mountain, the stream flowing at the bottom of a narrow and deep cut on our left. The difficult pass we had just gone through is called Devrend Boghaz. The view at this point is grand and picturesque in the extreme, and the place could be defended by a handful of men against the largest army in the world. Our path now led us into a broad valley, but we could see on our left the continuation of the deep fissure, at the bottom of which the stream continues to flow. After riding a while upon this sort of plateau, we rapidly descended into the fissure by a zigzag path trodden in the soil; there was hardly room for anything but the passage of the impetuous stream, upon which have been erected three flour-mills, at different points. The rock now stands boldly up on both sides, rising to a great height, but huge fragments are hanging about or have tumbled to the bottom, giving the scene a character most chaotic. The fallen rocks finally quite

close up the passage through the gorge, so that the
stream escapes through a straight fissure, 10 feet wide
at the bottom and 200 feet deep in height, cut smooth
through the solid rock, as though by human hands. The
path now leads through an opening to the right of the
fissure, and the gorge slightly widens; then comes another
chaotic scene, as though Titans and giants of stupendous height had fought and tumbled over the mountains and the hills in their wrath. The stream with
difficulty finds its way through the cracks of this last
barricade, dashing and foaming among the rocks; it
then suddenly emerges into the great plain of Boghaz
Keuy, which stretches out to the very horizon, and its
waters henceforth sluggishly pursue their way among
the remains of ancient cities. Our own path through
this pass (Boghaz) lay among the chaos of rocks;
limestone of a crystalline character, shales, conglomerates, and trap-rock, seemed to stare in amazement at
each other, wondering what could have mixed them
up so. I do not remember any spot that has produced
a similar impression upon my mind. The northern
edge of the mountain cluster I have been describing,
from the Devrend Boghaz to the Lower Boghaz, near
Boghaz Keuy, forms a pretty regular wall, running east
and west, and constituting the southern boundary of the
level plain, whose broad and fertile fields, covered with
the fruits of man's labour, and studded with villages,
present a singular contrast to the chaos of rocks from
which we now emerged. I confess that while going

through the lowest part of the pass, I was constantly
thinking of the third picture in Cole's famous 'Voyage
of Life,' where the poor traveller is represented standing
up with clasped hands upon his shattered bark, the
guardian angel visible far away beyond the clouds,
while the rushing stream of misfortune is dashing him
onward toward fearful precipices, leaping into fissures
of almost immeasurable depth; the stupendous cliffs
hanging overhead, the chaos of shattered rocks, the
broken trees upon the bank, and the very bend in
the river, all was there; and far away, down beyond
the whole, I could see the smooth plain stretching out
to the horizon, occasionally darkened by the shadow
of a passing cloud, not unaptly imitating the ocean of
eternity, into which the little bark is soon to be ushered.
I involuntarily said to myself: Can it be that Cole had
visited this spot? So true it is that genius and nature
both tend to the same ends, and produce the same
glorious results!

As we came out of the Boghaz we landed upon a
plateau occupying the left bank of the stream, where
lie the remains of the great temple described by Texier,
and of which Hamilton has given a very good plan.
A minute examination enabled us to find only unimportant errors, referring solely to the internal commu-
nications existing between the different apartments.
It must have been a grand edifice, and its high position, with a slightly inclined and extensive square in
front, must have greatly heightened the effect.   Bricks,

broken stone, and pieces of mortar, cover the whole
plateau on the east and north, indicating that here lay
the ancient city of Pterium; while a wall, protecting the
temple on the south, extended as a line of circumval-
lation to the small forts on the west. The citadel or
acropolis occupied the top of a mountain opposite, in
a direction nearly south of the temple. It must have
been a place of great strength in those days. The
stream which comes down through the Boghaz, has
hardly entered the plain when it receives a small
tributary from the east, and running westward flows
on towards Sungurlu. The present village of Boghaz
Keuy, or Village of the Gorge, occupies both banks
of the stream, about 300 yards from the temple;
and there are here, also, many old walls and ancient
remains. Indeed, one cannot avoid the conclusion that
Pterium was once a rich, well fortified, large, and popu-
lous city. We crossed the stream over a bridge, and
went to the Agha's Konak, a large establishment, in
the old Derch Bey style, facing the west, which we
reached at 5. The Agha himself was not at home,
but his brother received us with marked attention, gave
us the best room in the house, and invited us to dine
with him. We, however, made the most of our time,
by immediately going over to see the ruins, which we
minutely inspected. But they have been faithfully
described by others, and particularly by Mr. Texier,
who has thrown into the inquiry so much learning and
acuteness, that I feel incapable of adding anything to

what has already been published upon the subject. I
shall, therefore, merely state such items as have been
omitted by my learned predecessors; for these ruins are,
perhaps, the most remarkable and important that occur
in the whole Peninsula of Asia Minor.

CHAPTER XIX.

Detailed description of the ruins of Pterium — Forts — Subterranean
passage — Carved rocks — Hypothesis respecting their meaning
— Arrival at Euyuk.

THURSDAY, 4th.—An observation taken on the
piazza of the Mudir's house enabled us to ascertain
the position of Boghaz Keuy above the sea-level as
3515 feet. This is 900 feet below Yozghat, and, as we
first went up on leaving the latter place, the descent
from the upper to the lower Boghaz must be more than
1000 feet. It is also worthy of note that Boghaz Keuy
is about 1000 feet higher than Sungurlu, as we shall
see by-and-by, when we come again upon the water
which flows by the ruins of Pterium, while the level of
the Halys at Diashkhan is about the same. We took
an old Turk for our guide, and started off at 7 A.M. to
see the *lions* of the place, sending on our baggage to a
village on the road to Euyuk. About one mile to the
south of the Boghaz Keuy, we saw the remains of two
small forts built upon isolated rocks, which rise from
the general level. The foundation-stones were all we
found in place, and these are regularly shaped blocks

of limestone and brescia, similar to those of the temple. We found an inscription upon the smooth and inclined surface of a rock in one place; the letters were about a foot high, but they were so badly injured that we could not distinguish their form. The ground here is more elevated than at the temple plateau, and the city wall, which passes along the south side of the temple, extends to this point. We now rode to the south, and passed over the first line of rocky hills which form the southern boundary of the plain, and which are much lower than at the Boghaz. There is here a small valley running east and west, and, following it eastward for some distance, we came to an entrance or doorway into a subterranean passage, which is built in a northerly direction toward the centre of the hill. The doorway itself is formed of three hewn blocks, two of which are set up perpendicularly, while the third lies across the top. Some building must once have existed here, as is evident from the great quantity of hewn stones now lying about in confusion. Having scrambled over these, we entered the passage formed of two side-walls of hewn blocks, set upright, but considerably inclined inward at the top, with flat stones for a roof. The height of the passage is seven feet, while the width is also seven feet at the bottom, but it narrows upwards. We advanced in this passage for a distance of 45 yards by measurement, when our further progress was arrested by a block which had fallen from above, and completely closed the way. Having examined the ground overhead, we thought it

resounded under foot for a distance of a mile to the
east, and it seemed to us that the stones over all this
space presented an appearance not unlike a vaulted
roof. Beyond this the hill comes to a stop, and we there
found the remains of a square fort by the side of an
old road, which skirts the hill from the entrance of the
vault. As no necropolis has been discovered near
Pterium, it may be worth while to inquire whether this
subterranean work, which crowns the hill on the south
of the town, be not something of the kind. At any
rate it would probably be not a fruitless undertaking
to effect an entrance beyond the point of obstruction we
encountered. This is quite a different excavation from
the one visited and described by Texier, and which lies
below, near the river, and in the old town. The square
fort we found by the road-side stands on the edge of
the hill, and a valley of some 300 yards in width
separates it from the acropolis. The hill of the acropolis extends to the Boghaz itself, of which it forms the
western flank. The ruins of the castle are visible from
below, but the ascent is steep and difficult, and we had
no time to spare. We therefore descended to the plain,
and, crossing the river, rode eastward to the Yazili
Kaya, or carved rocks. The place is about two miles
from Boghaz Keuy; it is a sort of offshoot of calcareous
rocks, which leaves the general line of the mountains
that form the southern boundary of the plain, and advances north into it. The carved rocks are found in
a recess in the north-west side of this limestone, and

are certainly highly interesting. There has been so
much doubt and controversy respecting their character and origin, that I shall abstain from "darkening
counsel by words without knowledge." This much,
however, I may be permitted to say, with all defer-
ence to those who know better, that the isolation of the
place and the very form and general character of
these extraordinary remains, gave me the impression
that the carvings are commemorative of some *one*
event that occurred in their vicinity; that this was
not a building, a place of gathering for often-recur-
ring rites, but a monument and memorial of an occurrence which the parties concerned desired to impress
upon the minds of their successors and descendants.
On the next page is a carefully drawn plan of the relative positions of the carved faces of the rocks; the area
enclosed by the lines is an empty and uncovered space;
it will be seen that its extreme irregularity precludes
the supposition of this having ever been either a
tomb or a chamber. This will be made clearer if
we remember that this recess is evidently formed
by the accidental throwing together of very large
blocks of limestone, of various heights, sizes, and
shapes, which no human power could ever stir from
their place, and of which the surfaces alone have
been slightly smoothed over previous to carving; or
rather, as these figures are in relief, the face of the
rock has been cut away just sufficiently to form them,
and the space between and around smoothed with

a chisel. There is not the slightest proof that a
roof ever existed; all the evidence is the other way.
Nor is there the smallest proof of a wall having ever
existed across the entrance, but rather the contrary.

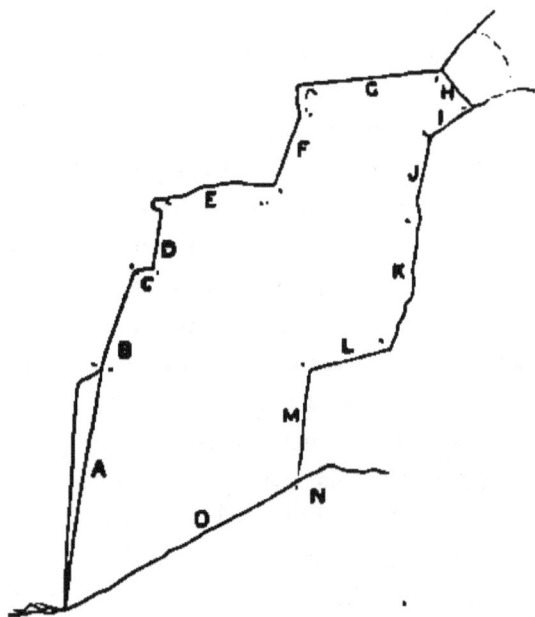

Scale of Feet

Plan of Position of Carved Rocks at Pterium.

Moreover the second passage is narrow and irregular;
and this, besides some interesting carvings, contains
rock-tombs. The following measurements will give an
idea of the dimensions of these carvings. The breadth
of the surfaces carved on these rocks by the hand of

man, at an equal elevation around the area, are lettered
on the plan, and measure as follows:—

A = 40 feet.	I = 9 feet.
B = 17 feet.	J = 14 feet 5 in.
C = 4 feet.	K = 20 feet 9 in.
D = 11 feet 1 in.	L = 13 feet 8 in.
E = 18 feet 4 in.	M = 14 feet.
F = 17 feet 10 in.	N = 4 feet only of chiselled
G = 23 feet.	surface.
H = 7 feet.	

Making in all 124 feet and 1 inch of bas-reliefs. The
line O, the entrance, measures 48 feet. The other
passage is nearly parallel to the side N H, but
branches into two: one portion turning irregularly to
the right, while the other comes round to the left,
and would communicate with the main portion did
not the rock H block the way. The smoothed surface and nearly obliterated carvings on the block H
are proof that it occupies its original position, and
has not fallen into its present place since these carvings were made.

I must say that Mr. Texier's drawings are much
more perfect than the original carvings, which are
greatly injured by time, and they produce a materially
different impression. He makes some clever guesses
on doubtful points, but it seems hardly fair for him to
make drawings of what he supposes carvings once to
have been, and give them to us as faithful copies of
their present appearance. It has seemed to me, therefore, that the reader would be glad to have a faithful

drawing, at least of the principal and most important figures in the group.

This is the central and principal group of the whole work. It evidently represents the meeting of a man and a woman, each of whom is followed by a long train of attendants, mostly of his or her own sex. The chief figures are represented larger than the rest, which is in accordance with both Assyrian and Egyptian custom. The King stands on what seem to be men with pointed caps, bending their heads forward while he stands upon their necks; the Queen and her son (?) stand upon panthers or leopards. Texier has figured a unicorn by the side of each; I did not succeed in making out what it was. I think the women all hold staffs in their hands. The double-headed eagle is worthy of notice here. This plate represents all the carvings upon the face marked G in the plan, and faces the visitor as he enters the area. It is also the converging point toward which all the other figures turn their faces.

Carvings on Rocks E and F.

The six figures represented on the previous page are carved upon the face marked F in the plan. The two in the middle appear to be women, but they are badly injured. The last would seem an important personage from his abundant millinery and the ponderous emblem of the Divinity which he carries like a helmet on his head. The lower figures occur in the centre of the surface marked E in the plan. It looks like two men carrying an ark or boat, but is very much injured.

Carving on Rock I.

The two women here reproduced are the best preserved portion of the right-hand or Queen's procession, which appears to be composed of women, wearing lofty tiaras, with long robes girded around their waists, leaning on staffs and carrying flowers in their hands. They occur on the surface marked I in the plan. The figures

on the surface at J are badly injured, and K is very much
broken down.   But the Pontiff occupying the surface
marked L, is the best preserved figure of the whole, and
I have taken special pains to reproduce it correctly.

Carving on Rock L.

He wears a cap of felt (?) with a turban around his
head, holds a sort of sceptre or staff of state in his left
hand, and a sacred symbol appears above his right. The
expression of his countenance is humble and devout.
His features, and indeed those of all the figures, are
regular and handsome.   They certainly have nothing
African about them.

The figures here reproduced cover the right side of
the narrow passages above described as nearly parallel
to the southern face of the carved recess, and almost
communicating with it at II. The left-hand figure is

Carvings on right side of passage.

doubtless the Divinity of these people; he wears their
cap, has their large ears, but features more marked and
harsh. His body is formed of four lions, the emblems
of strength, the lower two of which have the tails of
fishes. He is set upon a fluted pillar, and seems to
avert his face from his worshipper. The latter wears
an uncommonly tall cap, highly ornamented, and brings
a child or youth, around whose neck he has passed his
arm while he holds his hands within his. The emblem
is the same as on surface L.

I have reproduced with great care a sculpture

which appears to have been uncovered since Texier's
visit, occupying the left side of the passage, and nearly
opposite to the last figures. It is by far the best preserved of these bas-reliefs, and quite uninjured, having
apparently been but recently uncovered from the earth
which hid it, being very low down   I was informed by
our guide that it was uncovered by a Frank, who was
taking photographs, and whom I suppose to be Mr.

Carvings on left side of Passage.

Perrot, a young Orientalist of great merit. The want
of space, however, could not have allowed him to
photograph the carvings in the narrow passage. The
figures here represented are twelve soldiers, of whom
I give but six, as they are exactly alike.   Their
regular features, large ears, peculiar caps and swords,
like sickles, are the points which deserve special
notice.

It is certainly highly interesting and instructive to
be carried back so vividly to the men who lived here
so many ages ago, whatever hypothesis may be adopted
respecting the monument I have briefly described, and
which is worth a long journey to see ; especially if the
monument at Euyuk, which will presently be described,
is included. It may be added in further explanation
of the Yazili Kaya bas-reliefs, that the figures of
the King and Queen measure 4 feet 10 inches in
height. The other figures generally measure but
2 ft. 7 in. to 2 ft. 10 in. The figure of the Priest,
however, on the surface marked I, is 6 ft. 4 in. high.
The slab G contains seven principal figures and seven
accessory, 14 in all. The slab F, 6 ; E, 7 ; D, 6 ; C, 3 ;
B, 13. The surface A is smoothed over with the chisel,
but contains no figures. The surface H is indis-
tinct ; at I but 2 figures can distinctly be made out ;
J, 7 ; K (?) ; L, 1 ; M and N have no figures, though
they are smoothed with the chisel. So that this principal recess contains at least 59 figures ; the narrow
passage has 14 more. Mr. Texier's hypothesis is the
most probable I have met with. It does great honour
to his ingenuity and scholarship. He supposes the
introduction of the worship of Astarte, in Phrygia, to
be here represented. I cannot imagine that there is any
ground for the supposition that these carvings represent
the conclusion of a treaty, or a peace between the King
of Phrygia and the Queen of the Amazons, for all the
emblems of the latter are peaceful and religious, and

the Priest himself seems to preside over the whole
scene. The Queen presents a flower, and she rides
upon a leopard, the well-known emblem of the Astarte
of the Assyrians. In the King's procession, too, though
soldiers appear, yet there are, also, priests and religious
emblems. But it is singular that Mr. Texier should
have passed over in silence one of the strongest
proofs of the correctness of his theory, *i. e.* the
Prince, who follows the Queen, also riding upon a
leopard. He has an axe in one hand, but in the
other he holds up a figure (which may be the sig-
nificant emblem of an embryo). This Prince is no
other than Cupid following his mother Venus. We
must not be surprised, however, that Mr. Texier should
have overlooked this point ; for Mr. Layard has since
done the same. In his remarkable book on the remains
of Nineveh,* he has given us a copy of a procession, in
which priests carry the figures of their gods. He there
points out, on the left hand, the Jupiter of the Assyrians
seated upon his throne, and on the right hand Astarte,
or Venus. But he takes no notice of a little child also
seated upon a chair, which is borne behind the mother.
This tracing of the worship of Cupid among the Greeks,
as well as of Venus, to the Assyrians, through the
carvings of Yazili Kayah and the Nineveh procession,
was suggested to my mind by a carved gem or intaglio,
which came into my possession since our visit to Boghaz

---

* See Layard's ' Nineveh,' pp. 285-287, edition of 1807.

Keuy. It represents Venus, or Astarte, standing with
a robe girded at various heights upon her person, and
with her hands extended in attitude of adoration, while
in the sky on one side is a star, and on the other the
crescent moon. She wears a three-rayed crown upon
her head. A globe stands in front of her, and behind
her a partly veiled child is seated upon a chair with
his hands also extended in attitude of adoration. The
workmanship, I think, is Greek; but the figures are
evidently foreign, and the work probably dates to a
period but little subsequent to the carvings on Yazili
Kaya. It was found in the vicinity of Smyrna.

As to the other carvings. found in the lateral passage, they probably belong to a somewhat subsequent
period, although to the same nation, as is proved by the
features of the countenances. The image of the god I
believe to correspond to the Baal of the Phœnicians;
but he has the Phrygian cap, which shews him to have
become a national divinity. His worshipper is both
Priest and King, for he wears the cap of royalty and
bears the priestly emblem. He may be initiating the
child into the mysteries of the worship of Baal, but it
is more probable that the carving commemorates the
offering up in sacrifice of some youth of noble or royal
blood. There are tombs cut in the rock in this passage
or gallery, which were probably appropriated to the
highest of the priesthood.

The isolated and somewhat elevated nature of this
spot would favour the supposition that it was fre-

quented by the people of the neighbouring city for the celebration of the rites of Astarte, and, either at the same period or subsequently, for those of Baal. The ground in front of the carved rocks is a smooth terrace, which commands a fine view of the plain and of the site of Pterium.

The forenoon was nearly spent when we finished our sketches and notes, and we now proceeded nearly north down the sloping plain to the village of Yokbaz, lying half an hour or two miles to the east of Boghaz Keuy, with a small stream flowing westward through it. Our men and baggage were already here, and we rested awhile in the shaded verandah of the head man's house; a dozen little children of both sexes seemed in the height of enjoyment, tumbling into the water and rolling in the sand under the burning sun, all in a state of nature, and quite unconscious of the impropriety. We left this place at 1·30, and took a N.N.E. direction across the plain and over undulating ground, wholly destitute of trees or bushes, but generally under cultivation; the people are just beginning to harvest their crops. At 3·30 reached a spring of bad water; half a mile to the right lay a Koordish encampment of several black tents, with their flocks feeding around. This is their *yaila.* The ground rising, we were shown to the north the steep rock on which is built the castle of Karahissar; the natives who had seen it praised it as something very "antika." Hamilton does not think so, and accordingly we did not go out of our way to see it.

Reached Euyuk at 5·45; it is a small village built upon a little hill, which is a spur from higher hills on the north. The houses are like all Turkish village-houses in this region, *i.e.* a single room and a stable adjoining. We chose one with a wall partition; it was well tenanted nevertheless, but the nights were too cold to incline us to pitch the tent. We lighted a great fire in front of the house for such of our people as preferred to sleep out of doors. A small stream, shaded with willows, passes at the foot of the hillock close to the village, and makes an extensive swamp below.

The rest of the long summer's day was spent in examining, measuring, and sketching the remains of a building of great antiquity, to which I believe Mr. Hamilton was the first to draw attention.

CHAPTER XX.

Plan and description of the remains of an ancient building at Euyuk
— Sphinxes — Rock carvings—Conjectures respecting the origin
and design of the building.

EUYUK, *Thursday, Aug. 4th.*—I shall now proceed
to give our readers a description of the remains
of one of the most remarkable and eldest edifices to
be found in Asia Minor. I regret that persons more
learned in antiquarian lore than myself should not
have had the opportunity of attempting the difficult
task of tracing these to their real origin; but I shall
do my best.

This building covers the south-eastern edge of the
site occupied by the village. The whole hillock,
however, contains traces of ancient buildings; but
whether they all belong to this one edifice I cannot
pretend to say, not having attempted to trace the walls
beyond the immediate vicinity of the sculptures. And
first, it is worthy of note that while the monuments of
Asia Minor are generally cut out of rocks belonging to
the limestone class—such as limestone, marbles, and
breccias—this monument contains only black granite of
fine grain and great hardness. This accounts for the

remarkable and uncommon preservation of these sculptures, whose sharp angles have stood the wear of time
as well as the red granite monuments of Upper Egypt.
Another general remark should also be made; all other
bas-reliefs found in Asia Minor are rounded off at their
edges, however rude their workmanship, while these,
like those of Egypt, are angular. Some of these sculptures remain unfinished, and they show that the mode
of operation consisted in tracing out the figures and
cutting them down along the edges, which were allowed
to remain straight and angular. I feel warranted in
giving a full account of these interesting remains, as
I have nowhere seen them described. Mr. Hamilton's
visit was short and hasty, and I shall point out his
mistakes; moreover his drawings are not complete.

The plan on next page will give an idea of the
general form of the best preserved portions of this
building, as well as of their size. The first objects which
strike the visitor are two granite blocks standing erect
and forming the two sides of an entrance or gateway.
They are marked S 1 and S' 2 on the plan, and face
outwardly to the south-east, standing 11 feet 4 inches
apart, with a threshold rising like a step. These blocks
measure 15 feet in height, and 7 feet in width in
one direction, and 7 feet 2 inches in the other. Each
block has a large sphinx carved on its outer face
(*see Frontispiece to Vol. II.*). The sphinxes are 7 feet
3 inches in height, and 4 feet 7 inches in width.
They have been very much injured, doubtless by the

hand of man, the nose and mouth being entirely obliterated, but the minute ornaments of the neck and
breast are in a perfect state of preservation. The ears
also are well preserved. The head-dress is pure Egyptian.

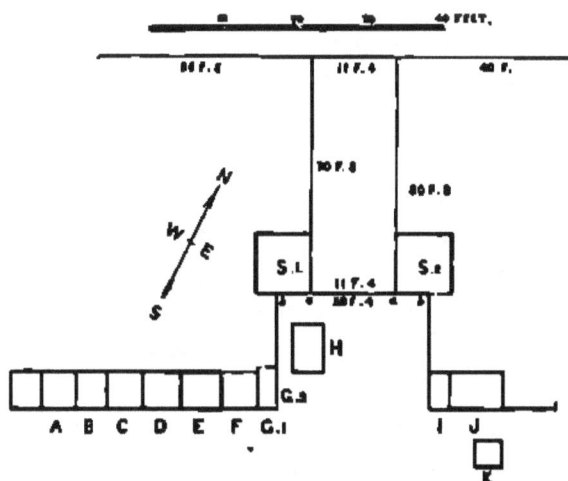

Plan of ancient building at Euyuk.

I can hardly account for Mr. Hamilton's taking them to
be "uncouth bird-like figures." I take it he was so
little prepared to find Egyptian remains, about here,
that it never occurred to him they might be sphinxes;
yet he acknowledges the sculpture to be "in a very
Egyptian style." It is worthy of remark, as an evidence
of inferiority in the artist who cut these sphinxes, that
one of the feet has five toes, while there are but four
on the other. The blocks upon which these figures
are carved, are single, the appearance of several pieces
upon the one, on the right hand, being produced by

a crack in the stone which does not pass through to
the other side.   It is, however, impossible to ascertain
the precise original height of these blocks, or conse-
quently the height of the door itself; but it was probably 15 feet.

As you enter the gate, there is on the right side, the
bas-relief of a double-headed eagle, upon whose heads
rest two human feet, while the edge of a robe is also
visible above.   This is a fac-simile of the double-headed
eagle of the Yazili Kaya; but I am inclined to conclude
from its appearance that it was put here at a later
period, and does not belong to the original work, which
is not the case at the former.   There was a similar
eagle upon the left side of the gate, which has been
almost entirely broken off.

It will be seen by the plan, that such portions of the
building as may yet be identified by their foundations,
had very much the appearance of an Assyrian palace.
Upon entering at the gate, you walk along a corridor
11 feet 4 inches wide, and 30 feet 8 inches in length,
at the extremity of which must have been an inner
door.   Here, however, we find the foundations of a wall
built across the corridor, probably a threshold, which we
can trace for a distance of 40 feet upon the right side,
and 26 feet 5 inches upon the left.   The remaining
traces of foundations have been removed by the villagers,
and they have erected their mud-houses and cattle-pens
upon the area once occupied by this costly edifice.

We now return to the gateway in order to describe

the remarkable bas-reliefs carved along the base of the wall which runs on both sides of it. The gateway with its two sphinxes occupies a breadth of 20 feet 4 inches, whence the two walls form a passage to the door, 15 feet in depth, both sides of which are formed of carved blocks of granite. There are then two sharp corners, and the two walls stretch out for some distance on both sides. The lower tier of blocks forming these walls is yet standing, and is covered with carvings; but it is impossible now to say whether there were sculptures upon the higher portions. I could discover none upon the many hewn blocks with which the ground is strewn. Let us now proceed to describe these carvings, commencing at the corner formed by the block G, and going to the left towards A. It is this row of stones which is the best preserved, and they are all lying in their original places, occupying a space 32 feet in length. These blocks measure 4 feet in height, as do all those which formed the lower tier of both walls. I shall point out the spots where blocks belonging to an upper tier are yet standing in their places.

I begin with the outer face of the left corner block marked G 1, for its bas-relief is evidently the key to the whole picture. This face measuring but 2 feet in width, represents the image of a bull set up on a stand or pedestal. The work is vigorous and characterised by that knowledge of the animal forms, which is so strongly marked in Egyptian and Assyrian sculp-

tures; the muscles and folds of the skin are well
delineated. The bull is proportionately too small to be
a representation of a living animal; besides, its position
upon the pedestal clearly points it out as an image.

Carvings at Eyuk (blocks F and G).

The hind-quarters of the animal are broken off, and the
face is somewhat injured; but the work is, otherwise, in
an excellent state of preservation, owing doubtless to
the extreme hardness of the granite. The next block
upon the left (marked F), is of the same height. An
altar stands in front of the idol, broad at the top,
and firmly set upon its widening base. It is divided
into horizontal strips, alternately smooth and barred.
Next to the altar is the figure of a priest or priest-
king, or high priest, the counterpart of the figure
already given from the Yazili Kaya, near Boghaz
Keuy. The head-dress is the same, and so is the rod

or sceptre (?) curved at its lower extremity, which he holds in his hand. The other hand is extended in the same manner, the fist closed, and the thumb stretched forward, but it holds no religious emblem or offering. The dress is also the same, but the lower part of the figure is hid by the soil. There are, however, points of difference, too important to overlook. The features of the Yuzili Kaya figure approach the Grecian type, while these are evidently Egyptian or African; the nose is flat, the lips protruding, and the chin extremely small. He wears an ear-ring, which is not seen on the Yuzili Kaya figures. Behind him is the form of a female; her arms folded and resting upon the end of a staff, the fingers of the right hand raised upward as if in the act of worship, as the Orientals hold them in making the "Temena." The head-dress is high, narrowing upwards and flat at the top. The tresses of her long hair lie upon the ear, partly covering the ear-ring, and fall along the back nearly to the feet. A garment is wound around the body. Again the features are very decidedly Egyptian. If the reader will place these figures by the side of those of Boghaz Keuy, he will be able with his own eye to detect the points of resemblance and difference.

The next figures upon the left are on the block marked E, which measures 5 feet 8 inches in length. They represent a priest leaning upon a staff, wearing a wide-sleeved gown, and leading to sacrifice a goat which he holds by the horn with his left hand. There

are three oxen following. The carvings on this stone
are remarkably well preserved, and their execution, espe-

Carvings on blocks D and E.

cially the animals, is superior to the other sculptures. This work appears to have been done by an artist of superior talent, for there is not only great truthfulness in the forms, but a spirit and life which does not belong to the others. The block D represents three priests in similar costume, long loose robes, with wide sleeves hanging from the shoulders, and the sleeves of their under garments turned up and lying in folds at the elbows. Their faces are broken, but it can be seen that one of them wears an ear-ring. The first appears to lead the way with a staff held in the left hand, while the right is raised in adoration. The second carries some instrument used in sacrifice, and in like manner holds up one hand, while the third lifts both. The feet of these figures are flat, the ends of their shoes turned upwards, and their legs are too small. It is impossible to say whether what is seen in front of each figure be a part of their dress or a distinct object, as a musical instrument. A block of the upper tier here lies upon the corner of the block D, and covers the whole of C.

The next block, C, is 4 feet 3 inches long, and represents a scene connected with the erection of this building. A man is ascending the ladder, probably a mason engaged in setting the stones in their proper places, aided by his companion below; while a third is standing with his back toward them, encouraging the workmen by playing upon an instrument very much like the modern "zoorna" (a species of hautbois, see vol. i. p. 248). They all wear short tunics tied around their waists with girdles

which fasten in a central knot; two of them wear
ear-rings. Their heads are shaved with the exception of
a curl which hangs in front, and in one case another
which falls behind. The musician, however, wears a
turban similar to those of the country farmers of the
present day, with the end hanging behind to protect the
neck from the sun. The features of all the three are
again decidedly Egyptian.

Carvings on blocks A, B, C.

The block B contains a continuation of the same
subject; exhibitions and music connected either with the
dedication or with the erection of the building. Even
at the present day, for public works such as a causeway,
a bridge, the erection of barracks, &c., every town and
village has to furnish a fixed number of workmen who
labour gratis; and in order to keep them in good spirits
while working without pay, the "davool," the "zoorna,"

and the bagpipe are called into requisition. When
heavy articles are to be dragged the movements of the
men are regulated by these instruments of music. The
same thing is represented on some of the Egyptian
monuments. In the present case we have two men
dressed like the preceding; their heads, however, are
too much injured to be distinguished. The right hand
figure holds a long-tailed monkey in his hand, and is
doubtless making it perform antics for the amusement
of the crowd. The other figure carries a snake wound
around his body, and is playing upon a guitar of a precisely similar form to that existing or found on monuments in Egypt.* Ribbons are attached to the end of the
instrument. The figures upon this block are finished,
but the stone has not been smoothed down between them,
indicating the steps of the process. It was evidently
intended to draw and cut out a third figure on the left
of these; but the work was left unfinished. It is also
clear from this instance that the carvings were made
after the blocks had been set in their places.

The last carved block on this side is A. It is a mere
outline of a bull carrying a chest upon his back with a
ring in front. The edge has been roughly cut out, but
the block has not been smoothed around the figures.
There is beyond the block A an additional smooth
block; it may have been intended to bear also some
bas-relief, which for some unknown reason was never
executed. We have now passed in review the whole

* See Wilkinson's ' Ancient Egyptians,' vol. i. p. 123, fig. 137.

row of figures from the corner of the block G; an important series which appears to throw light upon the whole work, and to indicate something of its origin and history. For, is it not the most natural conclusion we can draw, to suppose that the people engaged in this work were Egyptians, as the type of feature delineated clearly indicates, and that the building was in some manner connected with the worship of their god Apis?

But let us proceed to examine the rest of the sculptures. The portion of wall which extended from the corner of the block G to the left hand sphinx consisted of three stones: one of which, G, is in its place, another, H, lies in the passage way, and the third is lost.

Carvings on block G 2.

G 2 is the other sculptured face of the block which bears the image of Apis. It represents two soldiers, with short tunics, curled hair, and ear-rings, holding up

a standard. The forms are good, but the work is
injured. The other group represents a priest in his
robes holding an instrument whose form is too far
injured to enable us to define it, while a naked youth
stands before him, and holds his hand to his face. I
believe that a human sacrifice is here portrayed as
about to be consummated. I can see no other meaning
in the group. The Egyptians are known to have been
addicted to this crime in the earlier portion of their
history.

Carvings on block II.

The stone II, which has fallen from its original position, is 6 feet long, and represents six men marching in
procession towards the gate of the building; they wear
tunics, fastened by belts, in which are placed their
right hands, while the left is raised in the posture of
worship, the fist closed, and the thumb extended

forward. Their heads are shaven, and they wear locks
like the men at block C; their features are also decidedly Egyptian.

I have described all the figures lying on the left
side of the gate, which are by far the most important
and the best preserved. I now call the reader's attention to those on the right. The wall from the right hand
sphinx to the corner of the block I is broken down.
A prostrate block which may be seen in our general
view (*see Frontispiece to Vol. II.*), contains remains of
carvings, which are so badly injured that nothing can
be distinguished. Whatever figures may have existed
upon the southern face of the block I, have been totally
destroyed. The eastern face of the latter, and a block
adjoining, are now the only carvings remaining on this
side; they are much injured, and seem of an inferior
style of execution. It is not unlikely, however, that
the bas-reliefs extended as far on this side as on the
other. Indeed, the wall is better preserved here, both
in its extent and the elevation at which it still stands.
But the villagers have built on this spot a general
wash-room for the village, and bath for their women,
which begins at the edge of the block J. They have
taken advantage of the ancient solid wall, from underneath which a spring issues, and have erected against
it a square building of mud-bricks with a flat roof. We
were told that there were figures inside of the bath
upon the old wall; but as the place was full of women
and children, who set up a shout when we came too

near, we could not muster the courage to break the
laws of *Harem.*   We, however, obtained a good glimpse
of the inside in the early dawn, but what with the hard
usage the face of the wall had received, the thick coat
of soot it bore, and the darkness of the place, we did
not succeed in distinguishing anything.

Carvings on blocks I, J.

The width of block I is 2 feet 8 inches. It represents
a Queen with marked African features, seated upon a
throne, wearing a necklace, and her head-dress and
clothing generally bearing a close resemblance to the
left-hand figure of block F, holding up her right
hand precisely as the natives now do in making the
salutation called "Temena," while her left hand supports an object which may be a sceptre.   The execution
is inferior, as may be noticed more particularly in her
feet, which are entirely out of proportion.   The points

of her shoes seem to turn completely over, backward,
forming a ring; they rest upon a foot-stool.   The
next block J is 5 feet 8 inches long, and contains
three figures in tunics, apparently playing upon
harps, or other musical instruments.   These forms
are so much injured that the outline alone can be distinguished.

There is, however, one more work of the chisel of
the ancients which remains to be described.   Though
not possessing the interest of the series of carvings
already explained, yet, as a work of art, it is
certainly equal to any of them.   This is the block

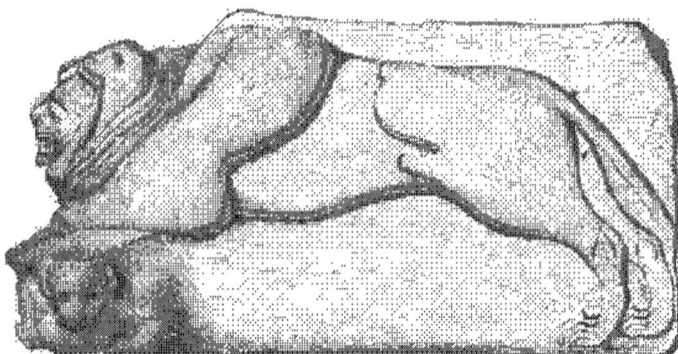

Side view of Carving on block K.

of granite which is marked K in our plan, and
measures 7 feet in its extreme length, while it is 3 feet
2 inches broad, and 2 feet 6 inches thick.   It represents a lion that has just sprung upon a ram, and
growls furiously, with his fore feet upon his prey.   The

body of the animal, hind-legs, and tail, are cut in bas-
relief on one side of the stone, while the front parts
are completely carved out. The hairy portions of the
body are represented by a greater thickness of the
stone, while instead of a mane it carries heavy folds of
skin. The work is original and striking. This block
is evidently out of its place. It must originally have
formed a corner piece, perhaps upon the summit of the
wall. It now stands set up on end so as to constitute

Front view of block K.

a support for the bath house. In order to draw the
front view, I was obliged to stand upon the roof over
the heads of bawling women and children, and to look
down upon it. It is worthy of notice that the emblem

of a lion *couchant*, resting his paw upon the head
of a sheep, is frequently reproduced by the ancients
in this region. There is a very bad one at the
village of Yozghat, west of the Halys, and several
occur at Angora. They are all of marble, however,
the position is different, and the workmanship in the
Greek style.

It is not my object to enter into a discussion respecting the probable origin and design of the remains at
Euyuk. I have endeavoured faithfully to describe
what I have seen, in order to furnish materials to others
who are more competent to adduce conclusions that
may be useful to antiquarian and historical research.
I cannot, however, avoid carrying away some impressions of my own from this examination, and these have
doubtless already leaked out during my description.
These remains have been considered as of the same
origin, and belonging to the same period as those
of Yazili Kaya. I am inclined to think that the
more they are studied the greater will appear the
differences between them. It has been thought that
the general form of the building proves it to have been
erected by the builders of the palaces of Nineveh, and
that they chose to adopt Egyptian figures and emblems.
Is it not more probable that Egyptians adopted an
Assyrian form of building? The turning point of the
discussion, must, it would seem, lie not only in the
sphinxes, but also in the features of the men, their
costumes, their deity, the monkey (an African impor-

tation), and the human sacrifice, if we are right in so interpreting the figures on the corner block. There are certain portions of the dresses of these figures which may, with truth, be disclaimed as Egyptian; we refer to the shape of the shoes, and the striped or striated appearance of the Queen's dress upon slab F; but it is worthy of notice that the same peculiarities are met with upon the figure of Sesostris, near Nymphio; of which Herodotus asserts the Egyptian origin, and the point is generally conceded by the learned. The reproduction of these peculiarities upon the Euyuk sculptures may, therefore, be considered as a proof of the truthfulness of Herodotus. The double-headed eagles on both sides of the gate were, in my opinion, carved at a far later period; they are superficial, and so the upper portion has been entirely obliterated. They are a perfect fac-simile of the double-headed eagle of Yazili Kaya with the woman standing over it.

I am of opinion that the building at Euyuk is of Egyptian origin, dating far back, to the earliest conquests of that people. The march of Sesostris, so far as we are able to trace it, followed the coast-line at a short distance from the shore. He passed by Nahr el Kelb, the Plain of Issus, the shores of Lycia, and the Passes of Tmolus, near Sardis; in one word, he pursued the same route as Alexander the Great, only in an opposite direction. This place may be considered as evidence in favour of some of the conquerors having made an

inroad, established themselves in Phrygia, and there
built a temple to the gods of Egypt. Their stay,
however, was short: they left their work unfinished,
and the people of the land dedicated the building
to the subsequently-introduced worship of Astarte.

CHAPTER XXI.

FRIDAY, *August 5th.*—We rose very early and
spent the morning in continuing our observations
and drawings of the interesting remains at Euyuk.
Left at 9·30, and went across the plain to the W.S.W.
In the afternoon our languishing guide took leave of us
and turned to the left into a lateral valley, which he
said would lead him by a shorter road to Yozghat. At
2·45 entered a narrower valley, thickly planted with
vineyards and orchards. Saw a hill where the standstone
strata were perpendicular. The rock possessing various
degrees of adhesiveness, the crest of the hill had become
curiously furrowed. Some similar hills, seen at a distance, presented the appearance of fortifications and of
ruins; but on approaching we perceived them to be the
effect of natural causes. About 6 P.M. we came upon
the town of Sungurlu, whose narrow and filthy streets
and dilapidated houses are erected upon a rise of ground

on the right side of the plain, and overlooking it. Sent
a man to the Mudir to announce our arrival and ask for
quarters, and promenaded about town visiting several
houses, the filthy condition of which discouraged us
from accepting the offer of hospitality. One of these
belonged to a prominent member of the Mejlis. When
we walked upstairs to examine the cheerless and dilapidated rooms, we found the proud owner of the mansion
sitting crosslegged on a carpet in the verandah, his feet
naked, too busily engaged cleaning his toes to look or
see who had come. We finally settled down at what
seemed a more respectable set of rooms, where we found
before night came on that we should have to fight
against three distinct species of enemies who were
determined to taste foreign flesh. It seems, however,
that our comfortless condition was not owing to any
want of goodwill on the part of the authorities. The
Mudir sent his chief officer to give us a welcome and see
that we had all we needed.

The feet of several of our horses are in a bad condition; the natives call it *arpalanmish*, and say it is
owing to the horses having no time while thus steadily
travelling to eat any straw with their barley; others say
it arises from their drinking while on the road; and
others again, from their stepping into water while their
feet are greatly heated and dusty. The fetlock is swollen
even with the hoof and first joint, and one horse is so
lame in all his feet he can hardly step. He was bled
this afternoon, but it seemed to do him no good. We

keep these horses as cool as possible, and give them grass to eat; for it is evident we shall be detained in this place for a day or two. Took an observation with the barometer at even; this, compared to several observations taken the two following days that we remained encamped in a garden below the town by the river side, gave me 2528 feet as the elevation of Sungurlu above sea-level. This is about 1000 feet below Boghaz Keuy, and nearly 2000 below the city of Yozghat. The respective elevations of Sungurlu and Yozghat very nearly correspond to those of Tocat and Sivas; and there appears to be much the same difference of climate, if one may judge from the productions of the soil.

Saturday, August 6th.—The Mudir himself called early this morning with a considerable retinue. He seems a somewhat intelligent man, and had many inquiries to make, as usual, about European news and the war in America. We requested him to procure us a good camping-ground in the vineyards; he gave us a guard, authorizing us to choose any place we liked. We went through a part of the Turkish quarter and down to the bed of the stream, which is now very low and can be crossed upon stones without wetting one's foot, and found an enclosed ground, where a vineyard had formerly been cultivated, and well shaded, close to the river bank and by a spring of good water. There were trees all around, and a thickly-planted orchard afforded fine shade for the hottest part of the day. We pitched our tent under a tree, having found that it is

not otherwise habitable in the middle of the day.
Orioles, here called "Sarù saudál," were singing in every
direction; and, desiring to be relieved of the never-ending
repetition of chicken boiled or roasted, we soon had
twenty-six of the beautiful creatures smoking on the
fire. The night was fine and refreshing, and oh! so
different from our lost in the Turkish Conak! The
weather continues charming; the moon is new, and we
shall have still to wait before we can travel in the night.
Our present day-travel at this season of the year is
trying, as the heat is sometimes very oppressive, especially when nothing green relieves the eye from the
sun's glare; but we have the advantage of studying
the country, which, in the brightest moonlight, we could
see only for a short distance around us.

Sunday, August 7th.—We have a fine refreshing
breeze from the north. Among the company who
called at our tent we had the satisfaction of seeing
several of the Protestant Armenians of the place. There
is a small number of these people here, and a preacher
is kept at this place by the Missionary of Yozghat; but
he is now absent at Cæsarea. I went up to the house
of a Protestant family in the Armenian part of the
town, and spent several hours with them. There were
twelve persons present in all—men, women, and children.
They were poor and ignorant, but appeared to take
great delight in the Word of God. In the absence of
their preacher I held the usual Sunday service, and
they were very attentive to what I had to say. They

have succeeded in purchasing a very eligible piece of
ground for a chapel, at the moderate sum of 10*l*. On
my way back to our tent I saw an ancient sarcophagus
of marble, of excellent workmanship, but badly injured,
now serving as a trough before a fountain. There is an
ox's head at each corner and in the centre of each
of the longer sides, with garlands of flowers between.
Later in the day several members of the Mejlis called
at our tent.

Monday, August 8th.—Two days' rest and a change
of diet having materially improved the condition of our
horses' feet, we started this morning at 5·15, and followed
the valley in a westerly direction. The only guide we
could obtain was a man who could accompany us no
further than to the next Mudir, whose head-quarters are
at a village ahead. We ought to have insisted upon the
Yozghat man continuing with us to Angora. At 6·50
passed the village of Chiflik on our right; it lies near the
river, and is surrounded by gardens, orchards, and vineyards. We continued to pass over alternate hillocks and
small valleys running down to the principal valley on
the right; the country is destitute of every green thing
—not a bush in sight, but only parched grass and soil, or
partly gathered grain. At 7·50 passed the cemetery of
Yorghanlû, which lies a quarter of an hour on our left.
The river flowing along the valley on our right is called
Delijeh; it is said to receive the waters of the Birdo-
ghassoo, at or near Sungurlu. Two villages were here
pointed out to us by the river side, called Yokaru

Ileshboonar (upper five springs), and Ashagha Desh-
boonar (lower five springs). At 10 we reached
Aghajù Koyoonoo, a respectable Turkish village,
lying a little to the right of our direct road across
the last-mentioned plain. We looked for a suitable
camping-ground among the vineyards, but as we did
not find sufficient shade, the hospitable villagers led
us to the piazza of their newly-built mosque, whose
northern exposure both afforded us shade and enabled
us to take advantage of a refreshing breeze. These
simple people seem to take great pride in the house of
worship which they had evidently raised by their personal exertions. It is a solid stone building of one
story, the interior woodwork unpainted; indeed there
was little within but a small pulpit and a platform near
the door. They showed no bigotry about our going in,
and the place being cool, we stowed away some fresh
provisions in it; some of our people even slept inside.
We could see no rock *in situ* between Sungurlu and this
place. The soil is reddish all the way, and the pebbles
are limestone and shales. But the mosque is built of
hewn sandstone, for the most part red, but some of it is
grey. We found two ancient pillars of brescia. The
red sandstone, being the softest, has probably decomposed and given its colour to the soil from here to Sungurlu, while the harder rocks have remained. The
public square of this village lies by the side of the
mosque, and here the flocks are collected every morning
and evening when led to and from pasture. We took a

stroll over this place after our mid-day nap. The
dogs were rather savage, but we kept them off with our
long whips. The wheat and barley are collected in
heaps (*harmans*), ready to be trodden by the cattle and
to be separated from the chaff by tossing up in the
wind. There are good horses here, and we particularly
admired some of the mares of Turkman breed. There
is a village stone mortar, of large size, by the mosque,
in which two women at a time pound wheat, previously
moistened, for the purpose of making " boorghoor," a
substitute for rice all over the interior, which they
cook in the shape of pilaf, soup with broth of sour milk,
or dolmas of stuffed vine leaves. It is considered very
good by those who like it. These women use a long
stick or pestle, for the purpose of pounding the wheat, .
which they do standing upright. They are dressed in
gay colours, wear long silver ear-rings which hang down
to their shoulders, and some of the younger ones are
not bad looking.

Tuesday, August 9th.—We slept well in the piazza of
the mosque, being incommoded only by mosquitoes and
sandflies, which we kept off by spreading our handker-
chiefs over our faces. A portable net, spread out by
means of a little hoop, or a couple of sticks, so made
that it could be hung up by tying it to a nail or rafter,
would certainly be a great convenience. Started at 5·45,
and soon came upon hills of gypsum, which extend
southward as far as the eye can reach, and doubtless
once formed the bottom of a lake. Passed Choghoon;

in this and other villages, we find that grain is stowed
away in a hole made in the ground, ten feet in
depth and six across; it is then covered with sticks
and earth. The soil must be very dry to allow such
a process to leave grain uninjured. These holes
are left open after the grain has been taken out, and
are very dangerous places for strangers. Went up
the hill, which is covered with a stunted growth
of green bushes, and a very interesting and striking
prospect broke upon our view when we reached the
summit. We were standing on the brow of a very steep
cliff, which continued of similar form toward the west.
At the bottom was a narrow valley, through the centre
of which flowed the Delijeh Urmak. This valley was
bounded on the north by a sea of red sandstone hills, whose
abrupt sides came suddenly down to the river. Right
under our feet were extensive salt-pans, into which flows
the water of a spring issuing from the gypsum hills on
which we stood. All the hills on this side being of white
gypsum, and on the other of red sandstone, the contrast
is very striking. The stratification of the sandstone
is very marked, but slightly inclined, and waving.
Came down the hill by a very steep road, having to
dismount for the purpose. We at once repaired to the
salt-pans, and found the process of desiccation going on
in the simplest manner. The salt was dried and piled in
the pans or shallow tanks nearest the dry land, and cause-
ways enabled the workmen to bring in the water and cut
it off for evaporation. Where undisturbed the salt had

formed very pretty crystals of considerable hardness.
The spring which supplies these pans issues from the
steep hill-side, only 100 yards off. The whole apparatus
is not extensive, and lies on the very edge of the river,
which must occasionally rise over its steep banks, if signs
we noticed are not deceptive. We stopped at a hut
close by, where the owner has his workmen and super-
intendents. A Government official also is here, to collect
a tax. The people were very polite and did all they
could to detain us; they informed us that 250,000
okes of salt are obtained here every year. This place
is said to be six hours from Sungurlu. We soon
crossed the river upon a wooden bridge, and perceived that the gypsum on the south side of it has
red sandstone lying beneath it. This is a repetition of
the formation of the Sivas basin, where, on the hills
south of the plain or valley of the Kizil Urmak, the red
sandstone is clearly seen to underlie the very extensive
formation of gypsum for which that region is remarkable. At 9 we came upon green shales, evidently underlying the red sandstone. Reached the village of Kara
Dekir, which had been hid from our sight by some projecting rocks. The stones and rocks here are all of
argilaceous shales, and very much tumbled about. We
climbed up into the Mudir's tall house, where we found
a number of Turks of high pretensions collected together. We took things in a very " sans façon " style,
however, made ourselves at home, had our luncheon
brought up, and occupied the sofas, to the evident

disgust of some of the anti-Giaour dignitaries, who
made themselves scarce as soon as they had stared
at our dusty party as long as their dignity would allow.
We found the Mudir himself was absent, having gone
off to the neighbouring villages to attend to the settlement of some Circassian emigrants. Our Sungurlu
guide had to leave us; but two men on horseback
were pointed out from the window, who were going
as far as the next village, and would show us the way.
The said next village was described as a charming
place for a camp, abounding with gardens, walnut-trees,
orchards, &c., enough to make our mouths water. Poor
innocents! I never could understand, however, what
object they had in deceiving us, unless some Frank
traveller had imposed himself upon them and gone
off without paying his bill, and they, thinking we
might do the same, used deception to get us off. I
think, however, it would have been hard to keep us
here; so we went off at 10·15, following the distant
scent of the two riders ahead. At 12 reached the small
and miserable village of Yaghlù, where we found a crowd
of *zabtiehs* and villagers at the door of a miserable hut,
whence we concluded that our hoped-for Mudir was
there holding his court. Without dismounting from our
horses I sent in one of the young men, whom the official
informed he had no man to spare, but that we might go
to the next village with the two guides who had led us
from Kara Bekir, and we should there find another Mudir,
who would furnish us a guide to go on. So we started

off again down a small hollow and up a hill through a
beautiful little oasis of gardens and vineyards, watered
from a single but abundant fountain. We now entered
a high plain or plateau, extending as far as we could see,
and shut out from the rest of the world by a slight rise
of the ground. The high rocky hills we had had on
our right from the salt-works receded and entirely disappeared. The soil seems very rich and somewhat
clayey, with very few stones in it. The crops have
been gathered in and heaped near the villages upon the
threshing-floors, so that all around us looks like a dreary
desert. Not a tree or a bush is in sight. We turned
slightly to the left, having long ago lost sight of our
two guides, who stopped at the fountain, and, being conducted by our own instinct and the plain road before
us, found the little village of Izeddin, containing a dozen
houses, built on the slope of a hill facing toward the
south. We asked the way to the Mudir's house, and
not finding him at home, took possession of his empty
quarters and occupied two comfortable rooms upstairs,
with a good piazza, putting up our horses in the stable
below. It was said this Mudir, too, had gone to attend
to the settlement of the Circassians. There was no one
to represent him but the Kiahaya of the village, who
had no power to act. As for the splendid gardens we
had been told of, there was not a bush or a leaf anywhere
in sight. No more was the *nalbant* visible, who was
to attend to the foot of one of our horses who had begun
to show lameness, having been badly shod at Sun-

gurlu, as it was thought. We were nearly starved, too, for no one would sell us anything; but the men being gone, we obtained several chickens from a woman by craft, for the poor creature thought we did not intend to pay her; so we shot them first, and then, to her agreeable surprise, paid for them at her own price. Tried to make a bargain with a man to serve us as guide, but his pretensions were so high that we gave it up, and I promised the party to conduct them safely on, which promise I kept as far as Angora, though I had never seen an inch of our route before. It is but fair to say, however, that the road was very plain, and there were so many people working in the fields that we should easily have been set right had we gone out of the way.

Wednesday, August 10th.—Started this morning at 5·10, without guide or guard. As for the latter character, which is the one principally claimed by these men, I have never found it of the slightest avail. In such encounters as I have had, or have heard of, with highway robbers, I never found *zabtiehs* to be of any use. They are the first to run away, and I have known several cases in which they were in partnership with the robbers, and have been the first to attack the party placed under their charge; not unfrequently they have themselves turned robbers and plundered the persons they were sent to protect. On the other hand, however, the mere sight of a *zabtieh* accompanying travellers produces the impression that the latter have friends of high standing and influence, who would punish any one who should attempt to injure them. Then, too, foreigners rarely pass through the country; extravagant ideas are generally entertained concerning them; the ignorant rustics are very much given to exaggeration, and while a lonely Frank traveller would be thought only a poor devil who may be plundered by all who meet him, a party with a police officer at the head is supposed to contain some consular or military dignitary. And again, the exactions of the *zabtiehs* keep the rural population in constant dread of them, so that one of these men will secure to you the best quarters in a village, and whatever provisions the place affords. You only need to see that everything is strictly paid for, and that the official takes no unwarrantable liberties with the poor people. On the whole, it is my decided opinion that when a European or foreigner has been several times over the same road, and is known to the natives, he will gain nothing whatever by encumbering himself with one of these men. But when he travels over a new road he will find it wisest to submit to the unpleasant necessity. The encumbrance is necessary; it will pay. But he should take a man from the capital of one Pashalik to another. As a general rule, these men, receiving monthly wages from Government to act as mounted or foot "gendarmes," or as messengers, are allowed to accompany a traveller as a special favour, the expedition being considered a holiday; the traveller

feeds them and their horse, and gives them a present
at the end of from 5 to 10 piastres a day: prices differ
in different provinces.   There are places, however,
where the whole support of the *zabtieh* is thrown upon
the traveller, and Government stops the man's wages
during the trip until his return; it thus becomes a
really expensive luxury which one should certainly
dispense with if he can.

On leaving Izeddin our direction continued west.
Passed a collection of black Koordish tents, whose flocks
were feeding in the low grounds; and were attracted by
the sight of two camels of the two-hump species feeding among the bushes and guarded by some men. Went
up to them and found them to be very fine animals,
both females, one of which had a mule colt of the same
breed.   The humps on the back were extremely high
and conical; the hair was longest at the top, and one
hump hung over on one side.   The men who had
charge of them said they were never saddled, but
kept entirely for breeding purposes, the cross of this
breed with the common one-humped camel being generally considered best fitted for Asia Minor.

This was the first time I had seen the bare back of a
double-humped camel in this country.   Having spent
by far the most of my time during the last twenty-five
years in the north-western part of Asia Minor, where the
camel is not a very common animal, all my efforts to see
the creature had proved unavailing.   I had fancied that
I might have seen him with his back covered over

by the pack-saddle, which hid his humps. But I was
now inclined to believe I had never met him before. I
had asked many Koords and other keepers of camels
about this species; they all professed to have seen it,
and several said that some of their own camels, now away,
were of that breed, but when I asked them what was the
difference between the two breeds, they only returned
evasive answers. Some said the males are all two-
humped; others, that they get two humps when
fattened and not allowed to work, &c. Since I examined
the two camels we now saw, however, I have had abundant means of judging as to the correctness of these
statements. This is the Bactrian camel, capable of
enduring the cold, and introduced into Asia Minor solely
for breeding purposes. A yearly supply of camels comes
from Mesopotamia; they belong to the Arab breed,
are tall, one-humped, short-haired, and of a light
colour. They are sold on their arrival for as low a
price as 7*l*. and 8*l*. apiece. But they are not accustomed to the cold of the climate, nor can they
travel in mud or climb mountains. The cross between
them and the Bactrian camel produces the best breed
for the climate, and has but one hump. This improved
breed reproduces itself, but is apt to degenerate, and is
renovated both by fresh importations from Mesopotamia
and the crossing of the Bactrian, which is kept in all
the southern portions of Asia Minor in small numbers
for this purpose. The Bactrian breed itself is kept pure
by means of a few females that are never loaded or

ridden. The notion, that the dromedary is the two-humped camel, used only for riding purposes, the two humps serving to keep the rider from falling in front or behind, while the one-humped camel is a beast of burden, was long ago exploded. The dromedary is any camel which is used for riding purposes; any camel may be made a dromedary or a pack-camel as the owner thereof chooses. But there is no more ground for dividing the camel into two species, one of which shall be called the dromedary, than there is for dividing horses into distinct species according as they are used for riding or for the pack-saddle.

A little further on upon this road a herd of common camels was feeding in the fields on our right, all bare-backed and one-humped. My attention was attracted to one of them, a female, whose single hump was extremely tall and conical, and hung half over on the left side. It presented exactly the same appearance as the humps of the Bactrian camel. It was evident this creature was allowed to feed, and had no burden put upon her. Moreover, it is a well-known fact that the common camels which are used as beasts of burden, when overworked, become thin and lose their humps by the month of March; their saddles lie flat upon their backs, and these are sometimes one continuous mass of sores, making the poor animal roar with pain when being loaded. I have sometimes seen the driver cut off pieces of flesh from the camel's back with his knife to keep it from mortifying. In summer, however,

the camels have more feed and suffer less from exposure,
and by autumn they get as great a hump again as they
ever had.   This lump of fat, or natural saddle, upon its
back, is one of those remarkable provisions by which
Providence intended to prepare this animal for the
service of man ; and so are the callosities upon his
legs, and the skinny cushion on the middle of his breast,
by which he is able to rest his weary body upon the
ground.   Those who deny such a Providential arrangement reject a most logical, simple, and beautiful explanation, for the sake of launching themselves into a sea
of doubt.

About an hour later we came upon the telegraph
line which passes between Yozghat and Angora, and
were destined to keep it almost constantly in sight until
we reached the latter place.   We now descended into a
fertile valley, where the fields were planted with cotton ;
this was the first sign we saw of the extensive cultivation of cotton which has been attempted since the price
of the article was raised by the blockade of the
southern ports of the United States.   These plantations, however, did not appear very promising, and
the expense of transportation to a sea-port must be
great.   We shortly reached some threshing-floors on
the side of this fertile valley, and stopped at a fountain
where several men were gathered to witness and help
in the shoeing of several oxen previous to their treading
the wheat.   This operation is rarely practised here ;
the cattle being small, the shoes, which are double, are

necessarily quite small. At 11·30 we came upon the
river Halys, last seen at Sivas; it there sweeps down
towards Cæsarea, whence it gradually bends its course
to the Black Sea, which it reaches west of Samsoon,
forming a long low and marshy delta, which projects
into the sea. It here runs northward. At noon we
reached the village of Diakhshan, built some 150 feet
above the level of the river and 200 yards from the
bank. It lies on both sides of a small hollow, and is
larger and better built than most of the villages we
have seen. Some of the houses have two stories. We
were taken to comfortable quarters, and took possession
of an ample piazza with a surrounding railing, where
we hung up our shawls and thus obtained excellent
lodgment for the night. Just before arriving here
we saw a jerboa run across the road; it moved with
great rapidity, and its leaps succeeded each other so
fast that it appeared to run instead of leaping. This
is the first I have met with except in the neighbourhood of Tocat, where, however, they are not common.

As we advance on our journey and come to regions
entirely destitute of trees, we are struck with the
measures adopted by the natives for providing themselves with fuel. We have been looking from our
piazza at some of the women collecting the manure
from the track which the cattle follow in going to
pasture in the morning, shaping it into round cakes
some 6 or 8 inches in diameter, by handling it as they
would a lump of dough, and sticking it on the walls of

their houses to dry in the sun. All the dwellings around
us are thus more or less ornamented. The women
seem to enter upon this duty with a matter-of-course
air, and conduct it with an artistic dexterity, which
proves that it is one of the accomplishments of the
housekeeper in this region. The fuel whose manufacture has been described, after being dried, is stowed
away in a store-room kept for the purpose. The
foundations of the houses are made of large stones,
but large mud bricks are employed for the rest of the
walls. The chimneys are made of the same, and have a
flat roof like the house itself covered with clay. Near
the bottom of the chimney, as it issues from the roof of
the house, there is on either side a triangular hole for
the purpose of allowing the smoke to escape. The
upper portion of the chimney is of course hollow within,
and must serve as a sort of reservoir for the smoke
which cannot immediately escape by the holes.

Yesterday morning, as we were getting into our
saddles, a Turkish woman came up to me with a string
in her hand, and asked me for something to hang to
the neck of her child, which was sick of intermittent
fever. Being in a sportive mood, and in a hurry besides,
I pulled off a single hair of my beard and gave it to her.
She said it was very little. I told her I could not spare
more, as it was very precious; and she went off much
pleased, holding it up high as something very valuable.
Though we found our way to this village without
difficulty, yet we experienced much backwardness on the

part of the people to furnish us with what we needed, there being no *zabtieh* with us. We now generally have to advance the money before the article wanted is produced. We are here informed that the distances this way from Izeddin (our last stopping-place) are as follows: From Izeddin to Balashuklu, 2 hours; Memetly, 5; Karajalù, 6; Kuruk, 7; Diakhshan, 8. The road we are following is not the one put down on Kiepert's map, for we pass south both of Kiskin Dagh and of Koorbaghùlù.

CHAPTER XXII

THURSDAY, *August* 11*th*.—Left our quarters at 5·10. Crossed the river and had considerable amusement at the expense of such of our party as were not much experienced in fording. Three boys were crossing on a donkey at the same time, and it seemed as though they would be carried down by the current. Our three-months-old colt, the pet and plaything of the party, went through mostly by leaps. He is growing so tall he can no longer pass under his mother, though he managed to do so for a week after we left Tocat, the mare lifting her back to allow him to do it. I have been giving him an oke of milk every morning and evening, of which his mother tries to get a share and sometimes succeeds. They both continue in excellent condition. No horse of the company can keep up with her at a simple walk; and as for the colt, he

would keep ahead of everything were he not so fond of
society.

After crossing the river, which we found to be
2571 ft. above the sea at this place, we went over a
high mountain and down into the village of Ku-
lüchlar (swords), then crossed a valley and went up
a narrow gorge on the other side ending in a steep
ascent ; we again gradually descended along the face
of a limestone hill, passed a fountain at 8·25, and after
riding on level ground for a mile, our road began
to rise. Continuing our journey, we pursued the
windings of a narrow gorge, where the sun's rays came
pouring down reflected by the barren rock around,
and went up a steep ascent still more trying to our
horses. Another narrow gorge now lay before us,
shallow in front, but growing deeper as it receded to
the right. The village of Yozghat is built on the
further or western side of this gorge. We went down
into it and found, at 9·40, in the yard of the only mosque
in the place, a comfortable shelter from the oppressive
sun. Of all dreary localities this is the dreariest we
had yet seen. The miserable dwellings are built over
each other on the steep hill side, the flat roof of one
house being a front yard for the next one above.
Nothing is visible around but barren and calcined limestone rocks. There was, to be sure, a fig-tree in the
mosque yard, and we rested well enough on the piazza
of that respectable building. There are here several
antique marbles, one representing a lion crouching,

and a rough altar with clusters of grapes upon it.
This place is said to be four hours from Diakhshan
and eight from Angora. Its elevation is 4100 feet,

Sculptured Lion at Yozghat.

being 1529 feet above the Halys at Diakhshan. Thus
it appears that the valley of the Halys is considerably
lower than the country on both sides of it. From
Yozghat we journeyed through an undulating region
and in two and a half hours reached two mills, whence
passing on we found the hills covered with dry grass,
but the valley fresh and green. The hills are mostly
of clay slate, some fine specimens of the argillaceous
slate used in Europe for roofing being occasionally met
with. Saw five very handsome Angora goats, whose
silken hair had not been cut, and almost touched the
ground. This animal is so much shorter on his legs
and every way smaller though stouter than any
ordinary goat I had seen, that I inquired whether

these were not young goats, but was assured of the
contrary. They were feeding on the edge of the plain
and not seeking the rocks as other goats do. We find
trees as we descend the valley, and now meet willows
planted in regular rows on the banks of the stream.
Passed a gushing fountain and the village of Lench;
it is eight hours from Diakhshan and on the right of
the road. The valley about here has many trees; the
people are engaged in carrying loads of freshly cut
grain to their *harmans.* At 6·15 crossed from the
right side of the valley over the stream, and entering a
narrow gorge, went into the miserable village of Orta
Keuy about seven. Willie's horse had been growing
more and more lame all day. The last hour or two he
brought down his nose almost to the ground every step
he took, giving the little fellow anything but an agreeable ride; but as no other arrangement could be made,
we went on, and the little rider bore it with remarkable
endurance. Our quarters at Orta Keuy were about
the worst we had yet had, nor were the people remarkable for their hospitality. What particularly struck
us here was the immense quantity of manure fuel
manufactured. It is made of two kinds, the first of
simple cow's dung, which the women are constantly
engaged in forming into cakes, as before described.
The other kind seems to be about 14 inches in diameter
and 3 inches thick; judging from its regular shape, it
is probably a collection of stable manure moulded on
the housetop as they make mud bricks. When some-

what dry, they turn them over. I noticed one of the
fair sex on a long roof of a house opposite, in an uncommonly brilliant suit, walking with apparent complacency
among vast quantities of the larger cake, probably
the fruit of her own toils, which she was turning and
arranging; I presume she was reflecting upon the
enjoyment she would derive the coming winter, or
the profit she should make by sale. We took up our
quarters upon the roof of a house, and ate our supper
by moonlight, but slept within, not venturing to expose
ourselves to the night air.

Friday, August 12th.—Started at 5·20, Willie's horse
still limping very badly on his forefoot. Recrossed the
valley and stream over the bridge we had passed last
evening. Our route lay along the northern edge of the
valley which becomes still better cultivated as we proceed, and we saw a number of Angora goats feeding on
the slope of the low hills on our right; they were
eating the dried up grasses with which the otherwise
barren earth is here covered, and many of which seem to
partake of the character of aromatic herbs. Entered a
road in the valley itself, which is lined and well shaded
with trees; orchards on our right and left. Saw a
Turk and his family gathering apples from the trees;
we called them, bought some of their fruit, and all fell
most ravenously upon it, having eaten nothing but
meat and rice for a long time past. We had been de-
prived even of bread after using up the supply procured
at Yozghat, for the thin cakes of the country were quite

raw, and after vainly endeavouring to accustom our
stomachs to this kind of bread, and finding it impossible
to digest, we had given up the use of farinaceous
food. At 7·30 crossed the river by a bridge of hewn
stone, and travelled awhile over a paved road in a very
dilapidated condition. Left the valley to our right,
and passing over a small ridge, obtained our first view
of Angora, the ancient Ancyra. As seen from the east,
it presents the appearance of a long and narrow hill,
whose flat summit is covered with walls and towers. This
hill slopes down on all sides except the north, where it is
precipitous, with the river passing at the foot of the
cliffs, embowered in leafy verdure. The town spreads to
the greatest distance on the western side, which was not
in sight. What we saw extended to the foot of the hill,
and ended in a well-defined outline as though there had
once been a wall there. The quarter of the city presented to our view is occupied by Turks, and appeared
for the most part in a ruinous condition. The Rayah
quarter is on the west next to the fortifications and
within the first wall; the lower part of the town on
that side is occupied by the markets and the Muslem population. Entered the town at 8, by the
south-east gate. It is made up of fragments of old
buildings, chiefly marble; a broken marble lion stands
on each side. Went up the steep streets paved with
trachyte to the open space between the upper part of
the town and the fortifications of the castle, and passing
over the brow of the hill, wedged our way through a

crowd collected by a fair, and reached one of the principal khans, a solid stone building occupied by merchants for business purposes. We had a letter from an
Armenian gentleman in Smyrna to one of the principal
Catholic Armenian merchants of Angora; we found he
was lying sick at home, but his son received us very
politely at his office and entertained us until our
quarters had been made ready in town. After an
hour we were conducted to a new wooden house that
had been hired for us; it is built on one side of a
small square or enclosure, which formerly made a
khan, but has since become a court with private
dwellings which are erected on three sides of it, with
a low wall and gate upon the street. Some of the
principal Catholic Armenian families have their residences here, and among them the person to whom we
were recommended. The houses of the Armenians are
built after the model of the Constantinople houses.
Ours has but one room finished; there is a small room
or kiosk on the top of the house whence we have a
very extensive view over this part of the town and the
surrounding country. Remains of ancient art and
splendour are met with at every step, more so than in
any town I have visited in this land. But they are
only fragments, while no building has resisted the
destructive effects of time. Our first concern was with
the outer man; we went at once to a Turkish bath,
and enjoyed greatly its healthful luxury. We then
called upon our host at his house close by. He was

lying sick in a bed spread out as usual upon the floor,
in which he received his visitors, sitting up wrapped in
a fur mantle, and smoking his pipe. The Catholic
Armenians of Angora are the most bigoted in the East.
They are chiefly the exiles of a religious persecution
waged against them at the instigation of their brethren
of the national Church, which they had abandoned for
the purpose of embracing the Romish errors, being
persuaded that they would thereby place themselves
under the French protectorate. The Turks wanted
nothing better than an opportunity to despoil the
Nabobs of Candilli, Orta Keuy, and Kuskunjuk of the
enormous gains they had been making out of the
simplicity of their Muslem masters. They exiled them
to Angora and took possession of their real estates in
Constantinople and its suburbs. It is the story of the
dispute about the oyster which the judge devours,
giving the shells to the disputants. But the priests have
had the skill to turn the dispute to their own account.
The Turks who were the real plunderers were deemed
to have done only what was a matter of course, while
the Armenians have been hated as the bigoted original
cause of their losses. Every effort has been made to
root them out of Angora, and with a great measure
of success. The Armenians of this city have very generally gone over to the Romish Church, unable to bear
the burden of the excessive *salians* (taxes) imposed
upon them by the Turks at the instigation of their
Catholic brethren. This effectual persecution has

nearly banished the old religion from Angora. Their
churches are deserted, and, individually, they are made
the objects of all kinds of vexation, so much so that
an Armenian must now have independent means not
to be starved out of his faith into Western orthodoxy.
The Catholics inveigh against the Armenians for their
former persecutions, and they are quite right; but they
are doing even worse themselves. The example of the
Armenians, however, is a fair instance of the natural
effect of religious persecution; it always fails in the
end of accomplishing its purposes, for it awakens a just
indignation from which there is but one step to a spirit
of revenge which brings punishment upon the original
perpetrators. There is no doubt the day of reckoning
will come with the Catholics as it has come with the
Armenians, until both shall learn that the battle of
truth can never be won by carnal weapons.

Saturday, August 13th. — Angora was inhabited
during the latter part of the seventeenth and throughout the eighteenth century by a complete colony of
English, French, and Dutch merchants, who carried on
the trade in Angora goats'-hair or Teftik. The article
was prepared in their warehouses and exported to
Europe for manufacturing purposes. The wars brought
about by the French Revolution, which put a stop to
most mercantile transactions everywhere, produced the
same effect here; but this most lucrative branch of
commercial enterprise, after lying dormant for a long
while, has, since the general peace, been again revived.

It is, however, now almost wholly in the hands of Greeks, who succeed in making very large profits; and by employing many hands in the business, as well as through their connexion with those who furnish the article, exert a very powerful influence over the affairs of this town and neighbourhood. Some of the houses originally occupied by the European merchants are still standing; they were very extensive, the lower portions consisting of magazines or vaulted rooms, where the *leftik* was prepared for exportation, with a separate entrance and courtyard for the use of the workmen. The premises inhabited by the family were entirely distinct, though built over the magazines. I visited such a house, which was once owned and occupied by one of my maternal ancestors. I roamed with intense interest through the now deserted halls and apartments, visited the parlour, stood before the fireplace, entered the private chamber, and looked around upon the spot where was planted the flower-garden, once, doubtless, the pet possession of the family, while my brain worked up a thousand images and fancies; I finally sat on the lofty terrace and refreshed my depressed spirit with the extensive prospect of city, plain, and hills, verdant with vineyards and orchards, and studded with country houses and villas. I searched in vain for some memento of the past, but only found in an inner chamber the date Jan. 19, 1779, and wrote under it my own name and the present date. This is the old Leidstar house, and my guide was the last

descendant of those European families, a gentleman
by name Leonardi, who has practised medicine here
for half a century. It is strange to find oneself
thus suddenly ushered into the past; and this trans-
ition was the more vivid in my own case, as I well
remembered the portrait of the old gentleman who
once occupied this mansion, and could distinctly recall
him to my mind in his Armenian costume, with a
great Calpak upon his head. In like manner the
European ladies, too, then wore the native costume, with
the broad belt composed of two large jewelled clasps,
fastening in front, and yellow slippers on their feet.
But what a contrast with the present! The house is
deserted and ruinous. It belongs to a bigoted Turk,
Shasùr Oghloo Sali Effendi by name, who lived a while
in it, but being surrounded by Christians, went away,
saying "he could not bear their smell." It has been
used only as a storehouse for grain since that time, and
is fast falling to pieces. Turks eminently possess the
genius of destruction. They envy their neighbour's
property, and get possession of it by every means within
their reach; but as soon as they have acquired the
coveted object, they childishly neglect and throw it
aside. The Santi house alone is still in a good state
of preservation, and now belongs, I believe, to a Greek
merchant engaged in the *teftik* trade.

I may here mention that though the European colony
has long disappeared, and an old man of eighty is now
its sole representative, yet I could perceive some signs

of Europeans having once resided there. As for instance, the wire-netting in the windows of many of the best Christian houses, a thing nowhere else to be seen in Turkey. There are also pigeon-houses protected in the same way, a very European object, which struck us as of evidently foreign origin. The little room on the top of many houses, called in Smyrna a kiosk, must have been introduced from that city, though all the Catholic Armenians have come from Constantinople.

There was a spot at Angora which I had a great desire to visit. It is a burying-ground lying by an old Armenian church and convent, built outside of the town upon the site of a temple of Jupiter.

We started on foot, and walked over the pavement of trachyte, and through narrow streets to the north-west gate. Saw on the way a number of remains of the ancient city, both lying by the roadside and built into the walls of the houses. The gate is of modern construction, but consists of pieces of marble taken from ancient buildings. The sides are made of fine cornices standing on end, one of which has the word ΚΑΙΣΑΡ cut in large characters. We left the main paved road, and followed a path leading us through gardens planted with vegetables. These are not divided by either walls or hedges, but only by well-trodden paths. The soil is alluvial and very rich, and nearly or quite the whole of the water of the stream we followed and crossed yesterday is used here for irrigating purposes. After passing the gardens we came to an open space, upon which are built very extensive barracks, now unoccupied, and rapidly going to pieces. Went down through fields to a small stream which waters other gardens. A number of people were encamped here under tents, most of them engaged in washing *teftik*. At the end of the gardens stands the Armenian monastery, on a gentle eminence. The church occupies the south-east angle, and is a very old structure of an octagonal form, built chiefly of brick, and very much in need of repairs. The people of the monastery, which we entered by a double gate, were very civil, and showed us the interior of the church, whose walls are completely covered with blue porcelain. We saw many ancient marbles and pieces of columns lying about in the yards. The cemetery is outside the monastery, in the open field; in the church there are no graves. The monuments nearest the building have inscriptions in Armenian, Greek, and Greco-Turkish. There is then an empty space, and beyond it, in an irregular row, are the graves of the former European residents. They consist of slabs of marble, just as they were taken from the ruins of the heathen temple, with a Latin inscription in memory of the deceased. One of them is the cover of a fine marble sarcophagus. Another consists of a handsomely-curved cornice, and another still was the capital of a pillar. I saw a heathen altar among them, which once bore sacrifices to idols, but now serves to mark the

resting-place of a believer in the one only and True God,
awaiting the morning of the resurrection. Another
altar, with its Greco-Latin dedication, covers the
remains of an Armenian or Greek, but bears no other
than the ancient inscription. Some of my readers
will, doubtless, be pleased to see the short list of the
names of the European residents lying buried here,
some of which point to families well known at the
present time in the Levant and even in Europe. It is
as follows :—

Joanna Dunscoit Addlevett, wife of an English merchant at
Angora, died 1750, æt. 30.

Henry Dain, English merchant, died 1708, æt. 47.

Peter de Lignelle, Dutch merchant, died 1693.

Theodore Leeker, Dutch merchant, died 1679.

William Black, English merchant, died 1684.

Paul Malbranch Leldenslortus, Dutch merchant, died 1704, æt. 87.

Jane Maria Leidstar, wife of John Justinus L., died 1767, æt. 57.

Francis Roboli, French merchant, died 1757.

Joseph Guieu, French merchant, died 1779.

D. Lewis Rossi, French priest, died 1768.

Bartholomew Edward Olaranychlus, French merchant, died 1737.

Anthony Joseph Santi, Venetian merchant, died 1702.

Leonard Polla Barbier, French merchant, died 1757.

Having accomplished our long-desired pilgrimage to
this sacred spot, we returned to town by the highway.
Found in many places the remains of an ancient paved
road made by the Romans, and crossed the river over a
bridge of hewn stone; the parapet is formed of blocks
once united with iron or brass ties, which the barbarians
have carried off. Received calls from several native
Protestants, who endeavour to maintain their ground

despite the plots and adverse influence of the Catholic
Armenians. These are, as usual, employing all the
influence they possess with the authorities in order to
prevent Protestantism from taking root in this city and
province. The Governor had imposed exorbitant taxes
upon these persecuted people, and one of them had
lain for some time in prison on this account. But it
was hoped that the authorities would finally be induced
to pay attention to the public orders received from the
capital, though it was suspected that they were
annulled by secret instructions sent to the Pasha. We
also met an old Constantinople friend, a Protestant
Armenian gentleman, sent here as agent of an English
merchant at the capital in connexion with the exportation of *teftik.* We were glad to learn that several
English merchants of the capital were again taking a
part in so profitable an enterprise; and there is no
doubt that, if wisely prosecuted, it will be highly successful. It has been very sultry here ever since our
arrival. To day the atmosphere was hazy and heavy;
but at 3 P.M. there was a sudden change produced by
a strong easterly wind, which made the thermometer go
down 15 degrees. These sudden changes are said to be
very common in Angora, and they make the climate a
trying one for delicate constitutions. I may also mention here the result of my observations during our
stay at this place. The barometer gives us 3334 feet
as the elevation of Angora; this is somewhat lower
than I had supposed; it is 1100 feet lower than Sivas

or Yozghat; and the region south of this city, in which
the Angora goat principally ranges, is not generally
higher, and often lower: Sivri Hissar is only 450 feet
higher, and well protected on the north by high hills.
It is also worthy of notice that the province of Karahissar, into which the goat has not penetrated, is
higher than the province of Angora, while the region
east of Angora, through which we had come, lies somewhat lower as far as Doghaz Keuy; but though we
had there first seen the Angora goat, the specimens
were rare; the owners highly valued them, and did
their best to increase their number. I think, therefore,
that a high elevation of the soil above the sea cannot
exert any marked influence favourable to this animal.
The only peculiar atmospheric phenomena which we
noticed, and which may have a bearing upon this question, are electricity and sudden changes in the atmosphere. We were more than once struck with the
amount of electricity in the air, and this, too, at a
season of the year when we should not expect it. We
could hear the sparks every time we combed our hair
or passed our hands over the dogs' backs. The sudden
changes in the temperature are generally acknowledged. How far these may affect the question of
teftik I would not venture to say, except that they do
have a powerful effect upon it, not sufficient perhaps to
account for the existence of the breed, but probably
enough to maintain it in certain conditions. It is
worthy of notice that in particular districts the

Angora breed *excludes* all others. Let it also be
remembered that while the Angora cat degenerates in
other places, it does not here. I must say, however,
that I did not see a single Angora cat during my stay
there. But I saw several dogs whose white hair was
long and silky, though they appeared otherwise of an
ordinary and valueless breed.

Sunday, Aug. 14th.—The few Protestants of Angora
are accustomed to meet this day in the house of a
helper sent from the Mission Station at Broosa, who
conducts services in the Turkish language. He is a
plain man, who has learnt all he knows from the
study of the Bible and of the few books published
by the Mission, having had no regular school educa-
tion. Such men accomplish a valuable pioneer work,
though there is some difficulty afterwards in re-
placing them by a higher order of labourers, which is
sure to be soon called for by the people. Having given
up their trade and business connexions, it is hard for
them to obtain a maintenance when they cease to draw
a salary. Some of our sorest difficulties have arisen
from the position into which these men have thus been
thrown, with perhaps a large family to support. The
natives have deeply sympathised with this class of
persons; they are considered to bear the relation
of servant to master toward the missionaries who
have employed them, and that relation has a patriarchal
character in the East which is unknown in the West.
A native always considers himself the servant of a

man "whose bread he has eaten." We here see men
who have risen to wealth assume the position of
servants whenever they enter the house of their
former master subsequently reduced to poverty. And
so a servant is never dismissed except for bad conduct ;
it is thought a virtue to cling to a master who can
no longer pay his servant's wages. It is true, wages
play a small part in the relation of master and servant ;
they generally consist of food and occasional presents,
and the servant has the power to leave without
cause, more than the master to dismiss him if without
blame. I believe we should study more carefully the
minds with which we have to do, and not endeavour to
force upon them a cut-and-dried system which our
theological studies and our Occidental habits have led
us to regard as the best for man in the abstract, but
which, after being settled upon these Orientals by dint
of hard pounding, will fall to pieces as soon as we get
out of the way. The institutions we introduce should,
like those of the Apostles, find so perfect a response in
the hearts and wants of men, that they will be sustained by their own inherent vitality after we are dead
and all pecuniary aid is withdrawn from abroad.

But to return to the Protestants of Angora. They
are simple-minded people, who bear persecution with
considerable endurance, and I believe there is a great
work to be done in that city ; the very opposition of
the enemy is an excellent sign for the future. We had
a religious service at 10 A.M., and twenty persons were

present. I addressed them in Turkish, and baptized
two little children. I took the opportunity to give
them an account of the condition of their brethren in
such parts of the country as I had visited, a subject in
which they naturally take a great interest. I shall
mention here a little incident illustrating some of
the annoyances to which the traveller in these lands
must prepare himself to submit. The helper thought
we should probably have a larger congregation than
usual, as was indeed the case. He occupies the upper
rooms of his house during the summer, on account of
their greater coolness. These being small, the service
was held in one of the lower rooms, which was large,
but had been little used since the warm weather set in.
The heat seemed greatly to have increased the numbers
of certain well-known lodgers, not to be named in
good society, but called by the natives wood-bugs, and
by a friend of mine B flats. Their appetite moreover
had become vastly developed in the absence of their
customary prey. Their head-quarters seemed to be
about the table that had been fitted up as a pulpit, and
a mattress laid upon some chests for the special comfort
and honour of the guests from abroad. As I proceeded
in my address, I noticed one and another of my fellow-
travellers fidgeting and changing his place, and began
to experience some strange sensations about the only
unprotected points, the neck and wrists. Still I per-
severed bravely, until, the very instant I closed, several
of my hearers rushed upon me and brushed off from

my clothes whole handfuls of most lively and slippery
enemies. Fortunately for me the services were sufficiently short to prevent any serious consequences.
This is not worse, however, than the experience of one
of my brethren at Marsovan, who could never preach
without first drawing a magic circle of insect powder
around him as he stood up in the pulpit, to keep off the
fleas. He, however, poor man, was peculiarly sensitive
on that subject, so that, when travelling, at the stopping
place for the night his good wife used to put him in a
bag and tie it around his neck.

An incident occurred in connection with one of the
Angora Protestants, which, though belonging to a later
date, may as well be mentioned here. There is in this
place a converted Turk who became acquainted with
Evangelical doctrine in Kharpoot, and was sent here
in exile two and a half years ago. He was first im-
prisoned, but as he was a very quiet and inoffensive
man, all fear of him was soon allayed, and he was
allowed to go free, though bound not to leave the city.
He lives in great poverty, endeavouring to support his
absent family by the labour of his hands, which is often
prevented by his enemies. I gave him some medicine
for an eruption of long standing which he had on his
hands, and two months after I received a letter from
the helper in Angora stating that he was quite recovered, and that he, himself, was suffering from a
similar malady, and desired some of the same medicine.
I forwarded some of the same homœopathic pills, and

after a while another letter reached me from the helper, saying he had used one half of the medicine and been cured; the other half he had given to a friend of his, on condition that, in case he received benefit from it, he was to present a copy of the Scriptures to some poor man. The present had been given, and as another person still desired some of the same medicine, I forwarded a supply, proposing to the helper that whoever was cured of his disease should follow the same good example, and present a similar thank-offering to the Lord. The matter stood thus when I last heard from them.

Monday, August 15th. — Visited the castle which occupies the top of the hill. There are three walls on all sides except on the north, where the place is protected by an inaccessible precipice. The many towers which support the walls are generally square, but those of the second or middle wall are of an unusual shape, projecting, in form like the bows of a ship. The third or outer enclosure is the most dilapidated of all, and appears the oldest; the ancient work is built of large blocks beneath, and brickwork above; some parts have evidently been patched up. The central towers by the west gate are sound. On the top of the hill is a small castle where powder is now kept. It is said there is also old armour preserved there. The highest part of the hill appears to be occupied only by Turks, and was silent and solitary. We saw several mosques made of fragments taken from ancient buildings. There are many old stones, several altars, some sculp-

tures, and inscriptions, in the walls of the fortifications
and the houses; I copied a lion resting his paw upon
the head of a sheep, which the reader may compare
with the Euyuk Lion. It stands near the brow of the

Ancient Carved Lion at Angora.

precipice on the north. The view from this spot, the
highest on the hill, is extensive and fine. A great plain
spreads out to the horizon on the south and west. On
the north and east the ground is hilly and covered with
vineyards and country-houses, to which a large portion
of the population of the city has now removed. Right
under our feet passes the stream by the side of which
we travelled the other day. Its narrow valley is fertile
in the extreme, and we can distinguish the people
walking or riding at the foot of the precipitous ledge.

Visited the Temple of Augustus near the south-
western extremity of the town, celebrated on account
of its inscription containing the list of the buildings
erected by the Emperor. It is very simple in plan,
as are most of these buildings; it is made of the finest
marble, with few but tasteful and highly finished
ornaments. The yellow on the outside of the marble
is not an effect of the atmosphere; it seems to me, as in
the case of the same tint on the Parthenon at Athens,
to indicate gilding. We also visited a solitary column

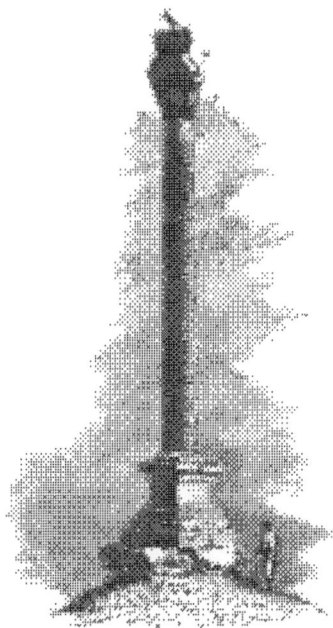

Ancient Column at Angora.

on the edge of the town in the same direction. It is
50 feet high, and of white marble. Most of the column

is made of thin circular pieces of marble set upon each
other. Much of the capital has fallen, and the rest will
soon follow. The storks have made their nest upon
the summit. This column was probably the centre of
the ancient market-place; and there are mounds in the
immediate vicinity which indicate that large buildings
once existed here.

CHAPTER XXIII.

Continuation of journey — Villages of Balû Kooyoomjoo and Chiflik — Petrified shells — Turkmen summer-houses — Sakaria river — Villages of Orta Keuy and Hortoo — Lazy muleteers — Black sienite — Village of Sivri Hissar — Dyeing of Skins — Trials of the Christian population — Physical features — Village of Dalahissar — Ruins of ancient buildings — The Angora goat — Ruins of castle and theatre — Sculptures — Night-travelling — Tents of nomad Turkmen — Turkmen village of Baghlija.

TUESDAY, *Aug.* 16*th.*—Our lame horse is unable to go on. We have tried to sell him, but have only been offered the worth of his skin. *Menzil* (post) horses are exorbitantly high. Having resolved to purchase an additional horse, we had a good opportunity of seeing the quality of Angora horses which generally enjoy a high reputation. That can be true, however, only of the Turkmen breed which is sometimes brought into town. What were shown us were a mongrel species, remarkable only for their extreme corpulence; the people about us seemed to think this a true measure of a horse's worth, and quite despised our thin steeds, though inured to hardship by a long journey. We finally purchased a small Turkmen horse, for which we were laughed at by the crowd of lookers

on, but which proved highly serviceable, and soon won
the affection of his young rider.

Wednesday, August 17th.—We did not manage to
get away to-day until 10·40, but succeeded this time
in obtaining a guide or *zabtieh* who was to show us the
way as far as Sivri Hissar. Our direction was nearly
S.W., and the weather very cool. Our course to-day
was entirely over an undulating plain which appears to
extend out of view from Angora in a south and west
direction. Its soil is generally rich, and nearly the
whole of it appears to be occasionally sown with grain.
About 4 the hills on both sides of us grew taller, and
at 4·30 we reached Balù Kooyoomjoo, a village built
in a kind of cove, with a tall palisade of trachyte on
the south, of a semi-circular form, out of which flows
an abundant stream that waters several gardens, and
willow-trees. We saw many Angora goats about the
village mixed with sheep. Our landlord seems to be
very well off; he is a shepherd himself, and owns 300
goats; he says that the goats give better and more
wool when they are not fed solely upon grass, but have
also the leaves of such trees as the scrub-oak and the
willow. He told us that some yellowish goats we
saw were brought from Koniah, the ancient Iconium,
where they have a goat similar to the Angora or
Teftik, but inferior in value. This importation occurred after a severe winter, which, three or four
years ago, killed many of their own goats, for the
true Angora breed is delicate, and cannot stand very

severe weather. The Koniah breed was thus introduced, and was crossed with the remaining pure
Teftik males. By persevering in this process all
traces of the foreign breed disappeared in two or three
generations. He assured us that this goat endures the
cold, but is apt to suffer from wet weather, and must
then be kept under shelter. I have noticed, thus far,
that this animal has the habits of the sheep far more
than those of the ordinary goat. Indeed the region we
are passing through would be very poorly adapted to
the latter, which is accustomed to climb the hills, and
feed on the leaves of bushes and young trees. The
Angora goat, on the contrary, feeds in the plain, and on
the slight hillocks which are somewhat rocky, and offer
them a scanty herbage; hence we generally see them
in the company of sheep, and indeed they cannot be
told apart at a short distance, owing to the simi-
larity of their form. This is especially the case just
now, when, the shearing season being but recently
past, their hair is still short. They are most readily
distinguished by their horns, which are bent backwards, while those of the sheep are outward and
forward. The high and cold wind has made us all
unwell to-day. I have an overpowering head-ache for
my share, and what seems like a touch of the intermittent fever. Balù Kooyoomjoo is six hours from
Angora, and there are said to be interesting ruins in
the neighbourhood. But I was too unwell to seek
them out.

Thursday, August 18*th.*—A bad night, with hard
cough and fever. Head better this morning. At
6 A.M. thermometer stood at 63°. Leaving at 7·30, we
reached Chiflik at 11·45. This, as its name imports,
is a farm belonging to a Turk, and contains a large
dilapidated house, as well as a large stable full of
horses, some of them very fine; there are also a few
miserable huts and a neglected garden, all built upon
the slope of a slightly rising ground. The master of
the place was there with a friend, and they spent their
whole time while we remained in drinking Raki. Everything about the premises showed the consequences.

We left Chiflik and its drunken masters at 2·30.
They seemed to be amazed that we, whom they called
English, should refuse to taste their beloved Raki,
and had no brandy to offer them. We picked up on
our road several loose bivalves, which had preserved
their form, while the rock that held them had decomposed. There were pieces of trachyte among them,
probably brought there from some ruin in the vicinity,
and too hard to change into soil. Ascended the hill,
and from its summit had our first distant view of the
sharp rocks of Sivri Hissar, behind which lies the town
of that name. As we came down the hill we picked up
more petrified shells, and soon came upon the ledge
which contained them. It appears to be a sandstone
which crumbles readily and covers the surface of the
ground with its débris. Came upon a dyke of trachyte
which has cut through the sandstone, and, after it, found

several beds of white marl. We still continued to descend until we reached an extensive plain upon which we noticed a line of mounds running nearly S.W. and N.E.; six of the largest certainly lie in this line, though some of the smaller ones appear to occupy a more irregular position. The ground soon became spungy though dry, indicating that it is swampy during a great portion of the year. We now had before us the *yaïla* or Turkmen summer-houses of Euyuk. They consist of houses open on one side, and containing a single room; and it was with difficulty we could find an empty one, which we occupied. It was separated from the rest by a small stream, with a wooden bridge consisting of a single plank. The soil was so clayey that we found it impossible to make the horses ford the little stream, and our effects were carried over the bridge by the men on their backs. We closed up the open side of our dwelling with a carpet lent us by the Turkmens, in order to keep off the innumerable mosquitoes and the sharp damp night-air. This place is occupied only in summer by these people, whose habits are somewhat nomadic. Their chief occupation is the rearing and tending of cattle. They have, however, several summer-gardens here, or rather *bostans* (melon-fields). They occupy a great portion of the region from Angora to the ridge of mountains on the north of which lies Baghluja, and many of them keep *Teftik* goats, though I believe that these generally remain in their villages, owing to the little

power of endurance possessed by that animal. I am
not quite certain of the fact, but I noticed few of
these goats at the summer camping ground as we
passed along; the greatest number were in the per-
manently occupied villages. The plain is drained by
the Sakaria River, and is swampy even now. In
winter it must be impassable. The several little
streams meandering through this district, some of
them very full, and one, 200 yards from our lodgings,
turning a mill, all flow into the Sakaria.

Friday, August 19th.—An observation at this place
shows that we have been rapidly descending since
yesterday noon; for we are 700 feet below the Chiflik,
and 1000 feet lower than Angora. We started this
morning at 7, the air being quite sharp and chilly.
Our lame horse finds it difficult to keep up, though he
has nothing on his back. The horses passed the night
out of doors, there being no stables; but the Turkmens
kindly tied carpets around them to keep them warm;
Master Colt cut a great figure with his night-gown on.
We very soon reached the Sakaria River, which here
flows through a low, marshy plain; its banks are
covered with reeds and coarse tall grass; its current is
very rapid, and the water whitish with the clay it takes
up as it moves on. It winds about a great deal, but
follows a general direction from the S.S.W. The soil
over which it passes is so clayey, that it must be quite
impossible to ford it, though the water itself is not too
deep at this season. We rode along the right bank,

going up the stream.   This part of the plain shows
no sign of cultivation; indeed, it is not susceptible of
it, as appears from the signs of inundation we see around
us.   The valley of the Sakaria here appears to have an
average width of about three miles.   There was, doubtless, an inland lake, which once covered the whole great
plain, through which this valley is now sunk like a
ditch or trench.   At 8 we reached the wooden bridge
over the Sakaria.   There is a small guard-house on
the right bank.   I took an observation, in order to
discover the height of the river at this place, and found
it 2387 feet.   We had come up 67 feet from Euyuk,
our last night's lodgings, a distance of about four miles.
While I took my observation by the guard-house, the
rest of the party crossed the bridge and found themselves among loose camels, to which some of the horses
were still unaccustomed; and thereupon followed sundry
interesting feats of horsemanship, which, I fear, the
Turkmens did not fail to see and duly admire.   It is
singular, that the horse has in every age, had an in-
stinctive dread of the camel, which habit alone can
subdue.

After going up a considerable hill, we descended
into a valley, which is watered by a small but strong
stream, running north toward the Sakaria.   We could
see the beds of gypsum on the sides of the hills, but
there are also many pieces of trachyte lying about.
Whole hills seem to be formed of disintegrated gypsum,
but the strata clearly distinguishable near the steep

summits have an almost horizontal position. Went across the valley and up the hill on the right to the village of Orta Keuy, which we reached at 11·45. A stream passes through it, and we went into a garden and took possession of a wooden platform, built over the water in the thick shade of the trees. This platform has a roof of branches resting upon the surrounding trees, and was altogether a most agreeable spot. Water appears very abundant here, but it is clayey, and we have to let it settle before drinking it. We found the people sociable, polite, and hospitable. Their houses are solidly built of stone, with flat roofs.

Stone Houses with roofing of Hay.

They pile hay upon these, by first setting a wooden frame upon the centre of the roof, which is made by four upright poles united with horizontal sticks. When the hay has been piled upon the frame, the whole thing is easily mistaken at a distance for a dome.

We have been rapidly rising since we left the banks of the Sakaria; for this village is 500 feet higher than the river. Started at 4 o'clock, and came right down into the valley again; it is well cultivated, and the banks of the little river are adorned with trees. The gypsum rock on the hill-side was trying to the eyes, but we found the green glasses surrounded with wire, which we had purchased in Angora, extremely serviceable. Some of us had blue ones; they offered but little relief to the eye: the green were invaluable, no traveller in Asia Minor should be without them in summer; many of the natives have adopted them.   But coloured glasses without wire netting are of very little use.

We entered at 5·30 the village of Hortxo, built on the slope of the hill, and commanding a fine prospect of the green valley beneath it; were kindly received and hospitably entertained by a well-to-do farmer, a Turk, whose house formed the lower corner of the village.   We had a comfortable piazza for our quarters, and an enclosed court before us, surrounded by stables, where our horses were put up.

Saturday, August 20th.—We were on the way at 6·30. Found that our two muleteers whom we engaged in Yozghat had given the horses no water either last evening or this morning.   Their conduct has been very unsatisfactory for some time past, they being excessively lazy, neglecting their work, and impressing the villagers to perform what they are paid to do themselves.   Moreover, it had been agreed with them at starting that they should ride only one-half of the time.   But they played us the trick of falling back, and then both riding constantly.   We had resolved to dismiss them at the first good opportunity, even before we had learnt their cruelty to our poor horses in making them go without water.   And now when we came to the stream they drove the horses through without allowing them to

drink, though the poor creatures tried hard to do so.
Their object was to push so far ahead of the party that
we could not see they were riding. The *zabtieh* turned
traitor on this occasion; he informed us of their conduct at the brook, and, when charged with their delin-
quency, they had nothing to say. The first consequence
was a whipping on the spot; next, the horses were
turned back and allowed to drink their fill. The men
were then made to walk, and the animals were led by
ourselves, not to allow them to lag behind. At 8·30
came in full view of the curious scalloped hills, behind
and at the foot of which lies the city of Sivri Hissar.
Passed on the left or east side of these hills, which stand
isolated. Our road led us among abandoned vineyards
and dilapidated country houses. This remarkable mountain is composed of black granite or sienite, extremely
hard, being decomposed very slowly, and producing a
sandy and almost unproductive soil. The vineyards
planted upon it seemed puny and withered, and the
rocky portions bare and black; this was especially the
case in the more elevated and steeper portions. As
we passed over the rising ground and turned north,
the town came at once into view. It lies at the
bottom of the highest hill, and is well protected by
the range on all sides but the west and south. The
rugged and black mountain behind it forms a striking
contrast to the white houses of the town, whose flat
roofs appear to lie in regular horizontal layers. From
this point the stratification of the sienite comes fully

into view; it is not far from the perpendicular, certainly
not more than 45°, the dip being toward the west, and
the hard strata forming ridges running nearly north
and south and making rugged crests upon the summits.
There appear, however, to be large masses near the tops,
which bear no signs of stratification. These crags are
so peculiar and marked that they are easily recognised
at a great distance; and I am told they can in clear
weather be distinguished from Angora itself. We entered Sivri Hissar at 9·30. It is a smaller place than
Yozghat, and in front of it lie very extensive burying
grounds, covered with upright stones. You cannot approach the town without perceiving that its principal
occupation consists in the dyeing of skins. The odours
which fill the air, and the coloured streams that flow
through the streets, as well as the appearance of the
shops—everything in the lower part of the city reveals
the employment of the inhabitants. We passed before
the door of the Governor's house and took a messenger,
who conducted us to the dwelling of a member of the
Mejlis, where we were furnished with commodious, but
not over cleanly, quarters. There are portions of
columns, and other ancient remains, lying about the
town. We took a ramble through the streets, but found
nothing of any interest. The domes of the mosques
are tall and pointed. All the women we met, even
small girls, wore a square carved ornament of silver
upon the tops of their heads; it appears in all respects
like a box, and is fastened to the head-dress. Strange

fashion, indeed, and as arbitrary as any I have ever seen,
Called on the Mudir, a very pleasant and well-informed,
and withal a quizzical gentleman, from Constantinople,
and met there a self-conceited young Cadi, who was
brought up at Bebek on the Bosphorus. We saw some
fine horses in the stable of the Turkmen breed. I
bought here a very fine skin of the *Teftik* goat, and
paid sixteen shillings for it. We had purchased some
smaller ones at Angora, for which we had paid from two
to three pounds, but they were both dyed and tanned.

I received a call from an Armenian who had heard
the Gospel preached in Angora by a native, and had
received it with joy. He has suffered much persecution
in consequence. He says there are twenty-five people
here who make the same profession. Though possessing no wealth or influence wherewith to resist the
assaults of their former co-religionists, they are well
thought of by the authorities, and protected from all
harm. The Armenian and Greek population of this
region is very small. They have been either destroyed
by the oppression of the conquering race, or have taken
refuge nearer the sea-coast, where the watchful care of
the European consular authorities afford them some
protection against their Muslem masters. There was a
large Christian population between Angora and Afion
Karahissar at the time of the Crusades, though the
Saracenic and Persian armies had already slaughtered
many of them. The Turkmen who followed were
far more numerous; and though many of them settled

down in the towns and villages, and assumed the
name of Turks, there are yet great numbers who
have preserved the nomadic habits of their ancestors,
and go by the name of Turkmens. It is said that there
is a small fort of great strength on the highest point of
the hill of Sivri Hissar, and in front of it a rock, whose
smooth surface is broad enough for a thousand horsemen to manœuvre upon it.

The barometer shows the elevation of Sivri Hissar to
be 3778 feet. This is 450 feet higher than Angora. I
cannot, however, consider the climate as likely to be
more severe, on account of the complete shelter afforded
the town toward the north and east by its great black
hill. The ground generally slopes down from it. The
country to the north and south of Sivri Hissar may be
described as a vast plain, without any mountains. But
this plain has been cut up by watercourses and slight
depressions of the soil, produced by trachytic dykes
breaking through rocks of comparatively modern origin.
I suppose it must belong to the cretaceous period
of Geology, though it is as yet difficult to fix its exact
age. From Angora there is a general depression,
extending as far as Euyuk-Yaïla, amounting to about
800 feet. Here we meet the bed of the Sakaria River.
From Euyuk the plain rises, probably under the
influence of the sienite of Sivri Hissar, until the up-
heaval amounts to 1400 feet, and 150 feet above the
plain. The latter then assumes a general elevation of about 3200 feet above the sea, until it ends at

the chain of mountains south of it, in the direction of
Baghlùja and Bayat. The upper town of Angora is
about 200 feet above this plain, leaving 3200 for
the plain itself. We have seen that, after making
allowance for unimportant depressions, the general level
as far as Sivri Hissar is the same. Balahissar has a
level of 3200 feet; and Baghlùja stands about 400 feet
above the plain, making the latter when it reaches the
mountains again 3200 feet. How far this formation
extends east and west I have no means of ascertaining;
but I point out the fact, not only on account of its
geological interest—indicating an extensive inland sea
to have once existed from Angora to Baghlùja—but
because it is well known that the region I have described
is the almost exclusive *habitát* of the *Teftik* or Angora
goat. It may be found that this has a good deal to do
with the successful rearing of the animal; and, at any
rate, in the present uncertainty of the question, I feel
it my duty to point out every circumstance which
seems to have a bearing upon it, however remote that
bearing may finally prove to be.

We were again in our saddles at 3·30 P.M. From
the higher points of the plain it appears level throughout in a southerly direction as far as some blue mountains in the distance. I can have little doubt that it
belongs to a single contemporaneous formation. If we
examine, however, this apparent level, we perceive
that the surface is often cut by watercourses, forming
valleys of greater or less width, and even lower plains

of considerable size. The denudation is sometimes so great, that isolated hillocks alone remain, whose summits indicate the original level of the whole country. Everything here is white with the friable limestone which composes the formation, and is now covered with a scanty growth of grasses, and short plants dried up by the summer's sun. Our way was first strewed with débris from the sienite hills. Passing over an undulating country, we came down into a narrow valley, and descended by a steep road flanked by limestone cliffs into the village of Balahissar. This is a small cluster of houses built on both sides of a broad street, which becomes a torrent in rainy weather. Ruins of columns and hewn marbles lie about us in every direction, and we can easily trace the foundations of ancient temples and other buildings long ago levelled with the ground. Many of these remains now mark the resting-place of the Muslem vandals who lie in extensive cemeteries on the hill-side. The Mudir of Sivri Hissar had given us a guide, who carried a long spear *à l'Arabe*, and was fond of showing his horsemanship by setting his steed to the gallop and brandishing his weapon. This spear is made of a strong but light reed brought from Damascus, resembling bamboo, but of a darker colour. This man led us to the house of the Kiahaya of the village, which consists of an enclosed court and large room, open toward the east upon the court. On both sides of the gate are blocks of antique marble, used as

scats. The main street of the village passes in front
of this door.

The sole occupation of the people here is tending
the Angora goat, with a few sheep mixed with them.
They are considered rich. Their houses consist of
two or three rooms with a flat roof, which are occupied in winter, and an open room like ours, for
summer use. The goats have large enclosures built
for them, with a stone wall, some 10 feet in height,
and extensive and good shelter, which can be kept
warm in winter, cool in summer, and dry at all times.
At this season of the year they are fed chiefly at
home. There is an excellent fountain at the east end
of the village, so arranged that the water runs through
90 yards of troughs laid in a continuous row by the
wall, on the side of the main street. These troughs
are principally of wood, but several of them are
ancient pillars hollowed out for the purpose. In
this way when a flock of goats comes up to drink,
which they do three times a day, every one of them
has immediate access to the water; and this can the
better be done because the goat does not soil the water
from which he drinks. The gate of our house being
near the fountain, every goat in the village passed
before us six times a day. The last time was late
in the afternoon, and then they went out to feed
upon the neighbouring slopes. I understood that they
spent the night out and remained at home during the
day, probably on account of the heat. We had thus a

good opportunity of watching the animal. I believe
that my sketch of it gives a correct idea. It must be
admitted, however, that at this season the hair is short,
so that we cannot see the length it attains. But this
disadvantage is compensated by our ability the better

Teftik or Angora Goat with Hair shorn.

to distinguish the form of the animal. I confess that
I began my study of this creature with a previous idea
that it was a near approach to the wild goat, of which
the domestic goat was a degenerated form. But I
immediately lost this conceit on seeing the *Teftik*
at home. His general form tends to that of the sheep.
I should say that he is the farthest removed from
the wild goat of any species I know, both as to form,
intelligence, and hair. He is the longest haired
goat I know; the hair of the wild goat is very short.

The *Teftik* is white, the other is reddish brown.   The
form of the latter shows a strength of sinew, an elas-
ticity of muscle, a quickness of eye, and elevation
of head which are more or less represented in the
whole tribe of goats.   But the *Teftik* is not made
for climbing any more than sheep, and like them
he keeps his head low, follows a lead, and makes
no attempt to feed by himself.   We certainly saw
some splendid specimens, especially of the males;
larger too than I had thought it possible, from what
I had hitherto seen.   Their bodies are compact and
broad; the male has long horns which are twisted
backwards, while the female, every way a smaller
animal, has also proportionately smaller horns, perfectly straight at first and then bending backwards
I noticed one male whose horns were the exact counterpart of those of a wild goat, only smaller; another had
them bending round behind his ears; while the horns
of a third turned gracefully forward and presented two
sharp points in front of his forehead.

It is curious that a place where perhaps the most
extensive ruins can be found in all Asia Minor, should
now be one of the most important spots where the
great staple of the province, the *teftik*, is produced.
But so it is.   Balahissar is old Pessinus, well known
more than 1000 years ago for its beautiful marble
temples and other public buildings.   The ruins are
comparatively in a virgin state.   A little digging has
taken place just outside the village on the south,

where fine marble slabs have been taken up to be used
for building purposes at Sivri Hissar. There cannot be
any doubt, however, that a rich mine of fine remains
lies hidden under the ground; but the difficulties of
transportation are such that no one is likely to disturb
them for centuries to come.

In our ramble about the village in search of anti-
quities we first went to the north-west, passed through
the cemetery which lies on the slope of the hill, and
ascended to the castle. It crowns the top of a hill
which is on a level with the plain above; the castle
hill is, therefore, somewhat difficult of access on all
sides but this, where the exposed part is small, and
seems to have been fortified by a strong wall. The
gate appears to have been near the eastern end of
this wall, and close to the road which goes down
into the village. We could easily trace the whole
enclosure around the citadel. There is a good general
view of the ruins from this place. We now descended
across the valley and found at the north-east end of the
village the foundations of a temple standing considerably above the ground. We proceeded thence to
a ravine which runs upward and eastward from this
point, and was once a side street running to the principal thoroughfare, there we found the remains of a
theatre. The portico must have been a handsome
structure, judging from the delicate carvings still remaining. A good deal of marble seemed to have lately
been dug up and carried off from this place. The seats

can be seen over a good part of the theatre, many of
them are lying loose above the ground, and some are
still in full sight in their places.   On our return by

Ruins of ancient Theatre at Prostua.

another road we came upon the remains of another
temple still in the main valley. We also took a ramble
on the south side of the village, and found the bottom
of the valley and all the eastern slope covered with the
marble remains of ancient buildings.   In several places
old foundations had been brought to view by recent
excavations. The sculptures were generally in very
fine taste and finish. One building stood on a slight
eminence nearest the village. It was very nearly of a

square form, and several stones had a representation of
boys supporting garlands made of bunches of grapes.
It was, perhaps, a temple dedicated to Bacchus, and
cornices and fluted and plain pillars lie all about it.
Every slight rise in the soil seems indeed to have been
taken advantage of in order to erect upon it some

Ancient Carving at Pambuus.

public building. The ground covered by the principal
ruins, beginning at the foot of the fortress, is about a
mile in length; but ruins of a more ordinary description extend a considerable distance down the valley.
The stone used is exclusively marble, which had to be
brought from a great distance; but there are also vast
quantities of bricks, evidently ancient, lying about in
every direction; most of them are red, but some black.
The village which now occupies the site of this once
rich and proud city is partially constructed from its
remains, but chiefly of common stone cemented

with mud. Here is seen the difference between the
ancient Asia Minor of the Romans and the modern
Anadoloo of the Turks, whose once destructive and
now crumbling empire is supported and propped up
only by civilized and Christian Europe. It certainly
looks very much as though neither civilization nor
Christianity had yet found its way into the politics of
Europe.

Sunday, August 21*st*.—We were isolated to-day among
this Turkish population with whom we have but little
in common in respect to our religious views. Our
landlord is hospitable, kind, and talkative; but he
appears not to trouble his mind with religious specula-
tions. We spent the day quietly under our roof with
a cool westerly breeze, reading or sitting under the
trees on the other side of the way. My fever has
nearly left me. But one of our number has been very
poorly for the last two days, occasioning no little
concern. He has fever, which may turn to either
intermittent or gastric, and it is hard to say which
of the two evils would be the least. One thing is
clear; travelling in the hot sun is beginning to tell
upon us. We must patronise the night more than we
have done, now that the moon has begun to favour
us with her light.

As E—— was much better at night I am inclined to
think he either had a touch of intermittent fever or
was over tired. We shall start in the middle of the
night, and trust we may fare better hereafter by less

exposure to the burning sun. Our *zabtieh* has gone back to Sivri Hissar, but we have found a man who will keep us company as far as Dervend, which is four hours hence, and six from Sivri Hissar.

Monday, August 22nd.—Started at 1·30 A.M. We at first greatly enjoyed the coolness of the atmosphere; and the moon shone bright over head. But when it set the air became so cold that we were glad to dismount and walk in order to keep warm. This being also our first trial of travelling by night, it was hard to keep awake; the regular step of the horses acted like the swinging of a cradle, and several of us nearly fell off the saddle. We tried whistling, singing in chorus, smoking, eating, all in vain, and had finally to resort to walking—the increasing chilliness of the atmosphere especially favouring this expedient. Our road was rather stony, generally passing along the ravines or valleys that are sunk in the plain at various depths. I could see in the moonlight that some of the rock we passed over was gypsum. At 3·30 we went by the village of Chiflik, and found the dogs wide awake and ready to salute us. At 5·30 we reached the Sakaria River flowing from right to left through an alluvial valley. This is called Dervend, and the river is here spanned by two bridges. Crossed over to the small village of Aktash, whose gardens and trees lie between it and the river. Stopped at an isolated two-story shed, the house of a Government official whose occupants were just getting out of bed, and where coffee was given us by a man

who spoke a little English and French and pretended
he was an Englishman; he had been a good deal on
board men-of-war in the vicinity of the Dardanelles.
Took an observation here and found the elevation of the
Sakaria River to be 2824 feet, or about 440 feet higher
than where we had crossed it before, a little above
Euyuk. Passed a Turkmen encampment where the tents
seemed to us better calculated for comfort than anything we had yet seen. They were rounded at the top,
and seemed to be made of pieces of felt spread over a
light frame of bent rods. The covering of the tent on
the side toward the wind, and from the sun, was raised,
and the opening was occupied by lattice such as is used

Tent of nomad Turkmen.

for the windows of
Turkish harems. The
lowest portion of this
aperture, however, is
closed by a board or
cloth to the height of

a couple of feet, preventing the reflection of the sun's
rays from the heated ground entering into the tent.
Having wandered off the road we passed by some threshing-floors, where we were directed to the first village on
the mountain. And at 11·15 we reached Baghlúja, a
Turkmen village considerably to the right of the main
road, built on the slope of the mountains at the end of the
plain. It is said our route will now pass over a mountain region, portions of which are wooded. The very
extremity of the plain, at the foot of the mountain, is

here occupied by the gardens of Baghlùja, and watered
from springs coming down the hills. Here ends also
the range of the *Teftik* goat, for as soon as we step
upon this sort of island, or continent, from the billowy
plain we have traversed, this animal is no more to be
found than fish upon the land; goats are plentiful,
but they are of the ordinary breed, with the usual
strongly marked forms of the animal, its varied
colours, and its active habits, climbing upon the rocks
and browsing on the bushes. The rock, of course, also
changes its character, and we now find ourselves among
primary limestones, conglomerates, and hard shales.

CHAPTER XXIV.

BAGHLÙJA, *August 22nd.*—As soon as one leaves the beaten track of Government messengers or *zaltiehs*, it is impossible to ascertain distances; for people keep no watches, and the only measure of distance known is the time it takes to pass from one place to another, a measure extremely unsatisfactory at the best, for no two men or animals move with precisely the same rapidity. But on the travelled roads the Government officials are obliged to fix the nominal distances in order to determine what is to be paid to the *menzil* (post). So now that we are somewhat out of the post road, it is impossible to ascertain our exact position. Some say we are just half way between

Sivri Hissar and Afion Karahissar; and others that
we are ten hours from the former and fourteen from
the latter, which seems to me more probable. I
ascertained our elevation at the upper part of this
village to be 3594 feet above the sea, which shows
that this portion of the plain has continued of about
the same height as the parts farther north, *i.e.* about
3200 feet.

Baghlùja is a Turkmen village, and we were glad to
find ourselves thrown familiarly among these people, in
order to study their manners. They were kind and
hospitable, and offered us the best they had. The
women, whether married or not, do not cover their
faces; they wear, however, a handkerchief upon their
heads, which hangs gracefully behind and on the
shoulders. They have a head-dress of great size, and
wear pieces of money hanging on both sides of the
face, as our ladies wear their hair. They also have
ear-rings made of long strings of coins, both gold and
silver, which come down upon the shoulders. They
wear bracelets around their wrists, and rings on their
ankles; but I was much surprised to see our host
treat his wife with familiarity and affection in the
presence of strangers, and show fondness for her society
and conversation. This is truly very *unoriental*.
These people appear to be well off, and their houses
are built so as to enable them to withstand pretty
severe cold weather. There were many mutilated
sculptures, and some inscriptions lying about or in-

serted in the walls, of which I copied the most
interesting. There must have been an ancient
town here.

Tuesday, August 23rd. —We slept all the afternoon, as well as the flies would allow, so that we
were better prepared for a night journey. Having
no guide that could be relied upon, we got all
the information we could from the villagers about
the road, and were in the saddle at 12·15. Although I generally con- sider personal narrative
a great bore, yet there

Mutilated Sculpture at Baghldja.

are luckless travellers, like ourselves, who do not
journey as " Milordos," scattering guineas as they
go, and surrounded by cavasses, guides, cooks, tent-
pitchers, and the other etcetceras ; but as *"particuliers"*
in more than one sense, who hold to the old proverb
that a man is his own best servant. For the benefit of
such, I shall continue to relate the misdeeds of our
muleteers and men of all work, the highly-recom-
mended Suleiman and Mahmood, against whose possible faults we thought we had taken every precaution,

when we obtained security for their good conduct.
We often rued the day we had taken these men with
us; and I am sure we should have fared far better, even
as regarded cost, had we made any, even the most
liberal arrangement with our well-known and trust-
worthy Tocat people to go on with us to our journey's
end. These lazy followers had, again, taken advantage of
us the preceding day, and had both ridden on the top
of the loads, so that the poor animals were completely
worn out. Indeed, one of them, a young but very promising creature, gave signs of breaking down; we therefore put most of our loads upon the other horse, and
allowed the men to ride the younger one by turns. This
would not suit "their honours'" humour, and they both
refused to ride, saying they would walk. So we let
them try it, purposing to stop somewhere and wait for
them. At first our road led us over a level surface, with
cultivated fields on either side; and the moon gave so
much light that we felt we could not lose our way again.
Here and there the people were lying by their heaps of
grain, or under a booth made of branches, the dogs
coming out to bark at us as we passed. We asked the
aroused sleepers whether we were going right, and they
always answered in the affirmative. We pushed on
with the same precautions for about two hours, when we
came to a deserted village in a hollow; the people had
removed their quarters for the summer to the top of a
hill on the right, as we could discover by the occasional
barking of dogs. After waiting some time, we grew

impatient at the non-appearance of our loads, and
leaving the rest of the party to take a nap in one of
the empty houses, R—— and I rode back half an hour,
firing signal guns. But to no purpose. Returned to
the party, and sent the *zabtieh* to the people on the
hill, where he ascertained that our wanderers had
passed that way and were gone ahead upon our own
road. We put our horses to a gallop, and when at
full speed on the stony ground, Carabed came down,
his steed almost turning a somersault. The horse
was hurt in the head, and his rider on the knee.
We however went on and soon overtook our loads.
The road now led us over unequal ground, covered
with bushes, rock, and hard limestone. Stopped by a
booth, and roused a woman and her children, whose dog
was barking frantically to defend his masters. She
told us we were all right. About 3, going over a
smooth road, we passed a village on our right, whose
canine population came out in a body to see who we
were, whereupon followed sundry canters, leaps, crack-
ing of whips, and howlings of said canines. We were
pronounced all right again, and proceeded to enter a
beautifully wooded series of hills, whose verdure was
truly refreshing to the eye. It was in the cool of
the morning, before sunrise. The trees were oaks, of
size increasing as we proceeded. About 4 we were in a
complete forest of pine and cypress; the latter were not
more than 20 feet in height, with spreading branches.
I know not whether we were beguiled by the beauties

which surrounded us, but we soon perceived that we were completely out of our reckoning. Indeed we found ourselves landed on the top of a hill, without the smallest trace of a path, or the least idea of whither we should go next. Fortunately we had kept our sumpter-horses with us. We had forced Mahmood to ride and load the other pack-horse, and Suleiman, who said he should keep to his feet all the way, was left behind to come on as he could. It was the last we saw of him until a day after our arrival in Afion Karahissar; and we had to do without his services on the worst roads we passed in our whole journey. We wandered about in search of information, and when obtained, it was anything but agreeable; we learned that we had failed altogether of reaching the main road from Sivri Hissar to Bayat, so that instead of making a four hours' ride from Baghlùju to the latter place, we had pursued a course which increased the distance to seven hours! We crawled down from our beautiful wooded heights into a finely cultivated valley, through which we travelled for an hour, and then crossed over the hills on the west side of it, which are almost entirely of flint, into another valley, both broader and flatter, in the widest part of which is built the town or large village of Bayat. This place stands upon what seems an artificial mound, about 20 feet in height, with a sharp projecting corner on the north side from which we approached it. We reached the place at at 8·15. Our horses were weary, the sun was growing hot, and we had a difficult mountain pass before us. . But having lost so much time, we could hardly afford to stop, and pushing on, entered a narrow rocky pass through which a torrent comes down in the rainy season. The mountains rose rapidly in height, and their steep sides were formed of broken and barren rocks. Further on, however, the slopes became less steep, and trees increased, so that we soon found ourselves in a forest chiefly composed of pines. We now made a steep and painful ascent through this forest; the face of the mountain is quite precipitous, and the road winds about between the rocks and among the trees. These mountains, on both sides of the gorge, offer as fine an example of metamorphic rock as I have yet beheld. It changes in appearance and colour every few steps of our ascent. It is often clearly serpentine, or pure clay slate, and other forms also present themselves in variety. Selenite is also seen. The trachyte appears to be the moving and transforming force. Dykes of it stand like palisades on the summit of all the mountains, on both the north and south sides of the pass; and we saw a hill of trachyte which looked as if it had but lately cooled down. Having reached the summit of the mountain in the midst of a strong and refreshing breeze, which in our heated condition was, however, not without danger, I fastened my horse to a pine tree, hung up my barometer to the branch of another, and found we stood at an elevation of 4838 feet, 1500 feet above the great

plain which we had traversed for several days. It
was with great difficulty that our poor pack-horses
accomplished the task of climbing up to this height.
Their loads fell several times, by knocking against the
trees and the rocks, and once they wandered off the
path among the precipices, whence they were brought
back with difficulty. Over the steepest portions two men
had to support each load on the sides in order to enable
the animal to go up. Oh! for railroads, or even for a
plain old-fashioned turnpike, where the poorest cart
might travel! I think I ought to entitle this paragraph
The Progress of Civilization in Turkey!

On the summit of the mountain we found ourselves at
once in the midst of a volcanic region, formed of pumi-
ceous stone beneath and overlying trachyte on the top.
The view from this point towards the south-west was
very striking and peculiar. We had before and beneath
us a vast and rough sea of mountain scenery, the foreground covered with pine woods, but all beyond bearing
only short though thickly-set bushes. And wherever
the mountain side was sufficiently steep, it was denuded
and white with the crumbling pumice stone. The
summits of the mountains were formed of dark-coloured
trachyte, generally presenting a precipitous front; but
under this the white rocks everywhere shone, and
their crystals glistened in the sun. The hill side right
opposite to us especially presented a peculiar appearance. At the first glance I thought a mountain stream
was coming down in beautiful cascades over the steep

bank into the valley beneath ; closer examination, however, showed that these apparently foaming sheets of
water, were only the worn fragments of the stone upon
which the rain, sunshine, and frost had alternately exercised their artistic power. Our descent was rapid, but over
a good road. We came upon some promising iron ore,
and went down into a deep valley, where the cattle had
taken shelter from the sun underneath a projecting
bank of pumice stone. This rock, even after decomposition into soil, is full of shining particles. Still
continuing our descent, we perceived the village of
Seïdiler, built under a high rock of selenite, so decom-

Village of Seïdiler, and natural Tower with Battlements.

posed by the elements as to present the appearance of a
castle with its battlements, windows, and gates, outstand-
ing towers and fortifications. This rock stands about
100 feet in height. Behind it is a level space, which

separates it from a second and similar fort of the same
height, but not so broad ; this is said to contain a very
extensive excavation.   These rocks crown the summit
of a hill, on the south side of which is erected a
miserable village, with gardens and vineyards below on
the edge of the plain.   As we approached from the
gorge, we had on our left an extensive area covered
with cones of pumice stone worn into the most fan-

Cones of Pumice Stone, near Seïdiler

tastic shapes by a freak of the elements.   Proceeding from this point we advanced between high banks
of selenite, resembling the walls of a city, and entered
the village through a natural gateway, which produces
upon the mind of the traveller the impression that he

is entering among the remains of one of the greatest
cities of the old world. And yet no ancient city
appears to have stood here. These are all the operations of Nature herself who seems here to smile in
disdain at the remains of Pessinus and Docimaeum, and
the boasted ruins that are scattered throughout the
length and breadth of Asia Minor.

We have descended rapidly, about 800 feet, and are
not much over 500 feet above Afion Karahissar and its
plain. Our horses are quite worn out. They travelled
ten hours to-day and eleven and a half the day before,
partly under the burning sun; it was all owing to the
blunders of our guide, who lost the way. The poor
young horse is pretty well used up, and we shall now
have to take him along without any load, and dispose of
him as best we can. We came to this conclusion in the
middle of the night; I could not sleep, and rising at half-
past eleven, went round to visit our poor beasts. The
exhausted animal seemed hardly able to step. I called
for the Kiabaya of the village and told him I wanted
a horse; he replied that everybody was asleep, and we
must wait till morning, and besides there were no
horses to be had in the village for either love or
money. I took a lantern, and putting the man before
me, went from house to house, rousing the inmates,
and showed him several horses I should take if they
were not freely given for hire. We finally secured the
horse of a man who was obliged to go to Karahissar,
having been ordered, by means of a surety, to deliver

himself up to the authorities for horse-stealing. We of course kept our eye upon him and his over-smart little boy all the way.

Wednesday, August 24th.—Started after midnight, at 2·30, and in two hours entered the town of Eski Karahissar. This place is celebrated for its extensive ruins, and seems to have occupied anciently the same important position in the province that Afion Karahissar does at the present time; hence its name of *Old* Karahissar. We had no time to stop, and we could barely distinguish some old massive walls and loose blocks in the moonlight. We here remarked the ceasing of spring water and the beginning of wells. In all the region hitherto traversed, wells were not a noticeable feature. Indeed they are extremely rare. I know very few in Tocat, and believe they are even less common elsewhere. People depend upon running water, which is sufficient to supply the wants of man and beast. We saw the first well at Eski Karahissar, and often met with them during the rest of our journey. They are everywhere of the antique pattern of a perforated stone forming the mouth of the well, with sides well worn by the ropes or chains which have gone up and down for centuries; the long pole is balanced on two upright posts, and the old " moss-covered bucket " hangs by a chain or an iron rod, not often by a rope. We saw the first of these familiar objects in the valley of Dayat just before reaching the village, and have often since espied with pleasure from a distance the long upright pole,

indicative of water, as we plodded over our weary road,
panting and thirsty under a broiling sun.

When daylight appeared wo woro travelling on a
plateau with boulders of limestone and trachyte lying
about us and cultivated fields on both sides of the road.
We gradually descended over undulating ground, and
among rocky hills, and at seven wo entered a very
smooth and level plain about four miles in width,
running nearly east and west, and bounded on the
south by high mountains. A stream flows through this
plain not far from its southern edge ; its water appeared
extremely muddy, and it runs between banks of clay
covered with reeds and high coarse grass. We crossed
it over a stone bridge ; there were evidences that much
of this alluvial plain is very muddy and difficult to
pass during the rainy season. The town of Afion
Karahissar is built upon the slope of a steep and lofty
hill on the south side of the plain. The buildings rise
from the foot of the hill to an elevation of 250 or
300 feet. The mountain itself rises boldly behind it,
frowning upon the town. A little in front of this
mountain, and somewhat to the right as you come
from the north, lies a steep and conical hill 300 feet in
height, with barren and rocky sides, crowned upon the
summit by a very old and ruinous citadel. The space
between this hill and the mountain is occupied by the
bazaars ; and the town spreads round the foot of the
citadel hill, as well as into a lateral valley running
southward. Among the buildings thirty-seven mosques,

with their lofty minarets, make a prominent figure.
We rode through a few gardens, traversed the crowded
bazaar streets, where whole rows of shops recently
destroyed by fire were being rebuilt, and entered the
best khan of the place, called Yeni Khan. The accommodations here prepared for the ill-fated traveller were,
however, anything but inviting; so leaving our horses
and most of our luggage here, we were glad to avail
ourselves of the proffered hospitality of two very agreeable gentlemen, Mr. Pharaon, and his brother-in-law
Mr. Pelozzi, at whose house, situated high on the hill,
we enjoyed good air and an excellent view of the town
and castle. Hard travel and exposure were telling on
all our poor horses, and we ourselves needed rest. I
had, for my own part, a slight touch of intermittent
fever; and so we remained at the house of our kind and
hospitable hosts until Saturday the 27th.

Thursday, August 25th.—We had, this day, our first
letters from home since leaving Tocat; they were of old
date, to be sure, being of the 9th and the 31st July; still
it would be difficult to conceive or over-estimate the relief
they afforded in circumstances like ours. Some of our
horses and both the men we took at Yozghat are giving
us no little trouble. As for our deserter, Mahmood, he
joined us only the day after we reached Karahissar, and
came to us as coolly as though nothing had happened;
when we asked for an explanation, he claimed to be the
aggrieved party. Both these worthies were dismissed
with full pay, but without the usual " bakshish," and

with a letter of introduction and recommendation in English to any luckless travellers they might meet to keep as far from them as they could. We took two other men to go as far as Smyrna; one of these stuck by the way, or rather we let him stick, for we found him a cypher in respect of work, but a hero in eating and taking his own case. The other did remarkably well on the road; but as soon as he reached the end of the journey, he stole a watch and several valuable articles of apparel, and went off no one knows whither. So that this additional experience confirmed our former conclusion, that we had made a great mistake in allowing our Tocat people, whom we knew well, and upon whom we had a sure hold, to leave us. As also with our horses. I believe it is an economy as well as a comfort to travel with one's own horses; but in order to do so they must be perfectly attended to. Our grooms ruined nearly all our beasts; so that these, as well as ourselves, would probably have fared far better with our Tocat people; but under the circumstances it would have been an economy to hire all our horses as we went along, with the exception of those we rode ourselves, upon which each of us could keep his eye and bestow especial care. It is a lesson for our successors. As for such as can afford to hire the post horses at Government prices, I have nothing to say to them. But had I the money, I should never waste it in such a way, for it would be subjecting myself, at a great expense, to the tyranny of Govern-

ment officials.   The pay for a post horse is at the rate
of 3½ piastres for every hour's travel, say threepence
per mile: an extra horse must be taken for a messenger
to carry back those you hire, at the rate of one horse for
every four, besides 2s. present to the messenger for his
day's work.   Hiring horses of muleteers is decidedly
cheaper; the price is 30 piastres a day near the sea-
shore, and 10 piastres in the interior, and you pay for
no extra horse or rider.   You can also load up to 120
okes instead of 60, allowed by the *menzil.*

We called on the *Caïmacam,* at his own invitation,
and found him a more enlightened and intelligent man
than any official we had yet met with.   Karahissar
being considered the second place in Asia Minor in
respect to Muslem bigotry—Konia being the first—he
certainly can meet with but little encouragement in
his efforts to reform the present condition of things.
It seems, however, that he keeps neutral in all matters
that affect the Muslem religion, and makes improvements which have no direct bearing upon it.   The
reconstruction of the bazaars is going on under his
care, with better ideas of hygiene than before.   He
has also built a new prison, which contains an infirmary,
a yard, and a distinct department for the worse class of
criminals.   The prisoners are made to work, and are
paid from 1 to 1½ piastres per day.   He told us he
is engaged in the construction of several roads, has
succeeded in settling the Circassian emigrants in villages erected in woody districts, and is now labouring

to introduce the culture of the mulberry tree, for which
the climate of the place seems to me altogether too
severe. This plain has an elevation of not less than
3700 feet, which is higher than the mulberry is ever
found in Asia Minor.

The cultivation of the poppy from which opium is
extracted, is very extensively carried on here, though
we were unable to see anything of it, the season being
already passed. Indeed, the town derives its name
from this drug, being the place where opium is chiefly
collected for transportation to the sea-port at Smyrna.
Afion Karahissar means the Opium Karahissar, and the
latter name signifies the Black City, a favourite title
given to towns by the Turks, though it is generally
hard to discover the reason of it. They have many
Black Mountains and Black Capes; some of their towns
certainly deserve the name of Black City, Diarbekir for
instance, which is built of a dark basaltic stone; but
the capital of the opium district presents no such
appearance, being built of mud, or of the rock of the
place, which is a feldspathic trachyte, of a light colour,
in which pink predominates. I could not discover that
the Karahissarites were more addicted to the use of
opium than other people in Turkey. But they are
exceedingly fond of the nasty oil which is extracted
from the seeds of the poppy, and will pay 10 piastres
the oke for it, while olive oil, though brought from a
distance, is sold for but 8 piastres. It certainly is
very disagreeable both to the taste and the smell of

the uninitiated. I was also assured that the effects
upon the system are decidedly deleterious. The Christians have long fasts, during which their food has to
be cooked with oil, butter being forbidden; and they
use poppy oil almost exclusively. It is said to produce
eruptive diseases, and particularly a kind of itch.
Hence many individuals are distinguished by the
surname of *Mangy* (in Turkish *Ooyooz*).

The Turks here are extremely fanatical. Their
Dervish establishment of the order of the Mevlevi
(Whirling) is next only to that at Konia, which is the
head-quarters of the sect, a representative of which from
the latter place enjoys the privilege of crowning every
new Sultan, if such a term may with propriety be
applied to the peculiar ceremony performed at his
installation into office, for it consists not in putting
a crown upon his head, but in girding a sword around
his waist. The building in which these fanatics reside
here is certainly very imposing; it may well be called
a palace, while the Governor of the city occupies
quarters miserable enough. The Sheikh's income is
as high as 4000*l.* a year. I was told, however, that
the Government had recently taken possession of the
property of the sect, with the promise of paying the
amount of the income instead; but they actually pay
just one half, to the great indignation of the holy
brotherhood and their partisans.

Visited the Armenian burying-ground, which lies
on the northern edge of the town, enclosed by walls,

with a porter's lodge at the gate. Saw there several
monuments of antiquity, slabs and sculptures said to
have been brought from Eski Karahissar, the ancient
Docimæum, the present town being of comparatively
modern origin. There were several pieces of marble
finely carved in panels, as the ancients ornamented
their ceilings. One sculpture represented men in
togas standing side by side; another, masks placed at
regular intervals, with festoons of flowers gracefully
hanging between them; it probably once ornamented
a theatre. The statues of females had lost their heads,
hands, and feet; but the drapery is well executed.
The best piece of work, however, is a Head of Medusa,
supported by two angels, which may have belonged to

Head of Medusa: Marble Sculpture at Afion Karahissar.

the same building which contained the carved masks;
this sculpture, too, has been greatly injured by the
ruthless barbarians who have so long held possession
of the country.

We remained in Karahissar longer than we had
intended. One cause lay in the fact of our host's

generous hospitality, which led him to employ every means to induce us to remain by multiplying our comforts. European beds are a real luxury after a long inland journey, and so is a well-furnished table, and especially good wholesome bread. We should, however, have torn ourselves away sooner from these allurements but for the touch of intermittent fever, which confined me most of the time to the house. It seems, indeed, wonderful that we should hitherto have escaped, considering that we are now in the fever season; I attribute it in great measure to the little bag of Peruvian bark we all wear on the pit of the stomach, suspended from the neck, so as to be in contact with the skin. Our servant, Carabed, far better inured to the climate than ourselves, is the only one of the party who has had a real attack of the fever; and we had neglected to provide him with this prophylactic, on the supposition that he was proof against the miasma. We have been looking over the route thus far pursued from Tocat hither, and what yet remains to be done. We find the whole distance by this route from Tocat to Smyrna is 202 Turkish hours. Our rate of travel has never been so low as four miles an hour; but we have generally done our task in shorter time than is usually reckoned, so that the whole distance may fairly be reckoned 810 miles.

Some of our party have ascended the high hill at the back of the town, and have brought me specimens of red trachyte, containing crystals of feldspar, which

is the same as the rock on which the fortress is built.
Indeed, I have seen no other rock about here, and
it extends nearly to Balmamood on the west, where
commences the formation of limestone or marl, with
underlying sandstone, which appears to extend as far
as the "burnt district" of Koola.

Saturday, August 27th.—We started at 5·20 A.M.
Passed along the edge of the plain, then between rocky
hills, and reached smooth ground again.   There were
many flocks of broad-tailed sheep in the plain.   Some of
them had the wool clipped in a peculiar manner, the

Caramania Sheep, as shorn at Afion Karahissar.

whole being shorn close, with the exception of the shoulders and hips.   The object is to allow the best wool to
attain great length, as its value is thereby much enhanced.   We also met on the road a young Albino
donkey; the mother was black, while the colt, fifteen
months old, was as large as its dam, and perfectly

white. It had pink eyes, and the light was evidently painful to them. Entered a narrow pass, where the road is cut down into the trachytic rock. At 8 we had before us the plain of Balmamood spreading westward; it was yellow with the ripened harvest. Reached Balmamood at 9 o'clock. It is a small Turkish village, with solidly built houses of stone, occupying a narrow gorge which unites two plains; the one extending towards the south, and the other to the north-east. I was not able to ascertain whether the latter communicates with the plain of Karahissar, or how far it extends. A small sluggish stream flows below the village toward the plain.

A good many flocks of the broad-tailed sheep are pastured here, and the breed raised in the district as well as farther south, is highly esteemed. It has been a matter of surprise to me that while so much attention has been paid in Europe to every natural production of Asia Minor, the broad-tailed sheep has not only been neglected but travellers have always spoken of it with disdain and ridicule. The poor, meek animal's burden—his ponderous tail—which in the eyes of the natives constitutes a most valuable prize, is spoken of as an unnatural excrescence; and it seems to be thought the animal is esteemed chiefly for his odd and unnatural appearance. I believe, however, that this creature constitutes one of the most valuable possessions of the people of this land, and should greatly regret to see the breed exchanged for

any other, not excepting the merinos. True, the wool
is not fine, and cannot be employed for the most delicate textures; it supplies, however, what is most needed
by the common people—a staple for manufacturing
cheap, coarse, and warm garments and excellent carpets.
But the flesh of the animal is superior to any other
breed on the face of the earth. Beef cannot be raised
here, as in Europe, for lack of abundant grass:
though the cattle of the interior mountain district will
compare well with those of Europe generally; and I
cannot doubt that when railroads reach those spots
now inaccessible to commercial enterprise—which they
will certainly do, and that at no very distant period—
the butchers' stalls of Smyrna and Constantinople will
be garnished with as good beef as can be found in most
large cities of continental Europe, surpassed only by
"the roast beef of Old England." But even in such
a case, the mutton of Asia Minor will maintain its
superiority to that of every other country in the world
as long as it is despised by foreigners. The natives
fully appreciate the economical value of the broad-
tailed sheep, and it has nearly supplanted every other
breed in the Peninsula. Fine rams fetch a high price,
and you see them kept in all parts of the country
solely for breeding purposes. Nor is the broad and
heavy tail the least valuable portion of the animal:
it is wholly composed of fat, which differs essentially
from tallow or any other fat excepting lard. Its deli-
cacy enables it to take the place of butter for culinary

purposes, and it is, in many respects, so far superior
—while also decidedly cheaper—that in most parts of
the country butter is not manufactured because it
is not needed; milk is there made into cheese only.
Moreover, "tail's fat," as it is called, is as much an
article of merchandise here as any other necessary or
comfort of life, and a market unsupplied with it would
be doomed poor indeed.   It fetches a medium price
between tallow and butter, and is almost entirely used
by the natives instead of the latter.   There can hardly

Caramania Sheep, unshorn.

be a doubt that this animal would succeed in Europe,
for it is hardy, and the best breed is raised in Cara-

mania, a high and cold district in the southern portion of the Peninsula. The wool, indeed, might be
improved by crossing with some other breeds, and it
would then recommend itself not only as the best
article of food of its kind, but as offering at the same
time a valuable staple for manufacture.

I give the reader two sketches in illustration of this
peculiar breed of sheep, the first of which represents
him as he appears when his wool has acquired its
greatest length. The form of the tail cannot be distinguished, being hid by his shaggy coat; but the
illustration below will explain the form of this part
of the animal's body. It is composed of two lobes,

Caramania Sheep, completely shorn, showing the form of the Tail.

the bone of the tail passing between them, and projecting like a small tail beyond them. It has been
supposed that this peculiarity is the mere product of
over-feeding; but there is no foundation for such a
supposition. Were it correct, this animal's tail would
be similar to that of any other sheep when in a low

condition; but this is not the case, for, whatever his
condition, whether fat or lean, his tail is always broad
and large, and resembles very much the mats or
cushions worn by the savages of some of the Pacific
Islands fastened to the girdle behind their backs, the
object of which is to save them the time or labour of
reaching out for a chair when they wish to sit down.
Only the poor sheep cannot sit upon their tails, but
must tug them after them wherever they go.* The
condition of the sheep has, therefore, very little to do
with the size of their appendage, and nothing at all
with its form. There is no doubt that this is only a
distinguishing mark of a particular breed, just as two
humps are of the Bactrian camel. This and all the
other peculiarities of the breed can be propagated by
the process of generation, and that alone. It is useless
to inquire how these peculiarities first originated, for
such an inquiry would probably lead to no practical
result. We must now take facts as they are. We
cannot, on the basis of a theory, set a train of operations in motion by which we may hope, in the course
of a few centuries perhaps, to convert a common goat
into an Angora *Teftik*, or an ordinary hack into a
thoroughbred Arabian. Just as hopeless would be the
task of making a broad-tailed sheep out of any other
mutton now in existence. It is a distinct breed, which

* We have seen a tail so cumbrous that it had actually to be
carried upon a little cart made for the purpose, and drawn by the
animal.

commends itself for many of its valuable qualities, and I believe other lands would gain much by its acquisition.

Being on this subject, I will mention a four-horned sheep, which I do *not* regard as a peculiar breed, but only as a *lusus naturæ*. It is occasionally seen in Asia Minor, as in other countries. These animals are regarded with a sort of veneration, or perhaps as curiosities, by the natives—it is hard to say which—

Four-horned Sheep.

and they are kept as pets. I saw a broad-tailed ram in a khan, where he roamed at liberty, and was petted both by the host and his numerous guests. Whether from lack of food, or owing to the experiments made by all these people, he had acquired the power to eat whatever was set before him; I saw him even eat tobacco with apparent relish. His horns were of various lengths, and the side ones could not have done much more than protect his ears from the attacks of an enemy. I have, however, seen even chickens with horns on their heads, and those, too, of considerable length.

CHAPTER XXV.

CHIFLIK, *Saturday Night, Aug.* 27th—We rested
for the middle of the day in the shade of the
piazza of the small mosque of Balmamood; the inhabitants were truly hospitable, and supplied us with
everything we needed. The day was very hot; the
only breeze, and that a very light one, being from
the south. We started again at 2·45. The weather
was exceedingly oppressive, and the road very dusty.
We have, thus far, gained much in the change made at
Karahissar in the *personnel* of our company. The two
new ostlers are active and good-natured for the present,
and they get on well with the *caterji* of whom we have
hired our pack-horses. They started, at their own
request, one hour before us, and we did not overtake
them until 5·45. Haji Eumer was walking, and Ismail

was riding a donkey which he has brought along, and
proposes to sell for a high price in Smyrna. We have
in our company an old Arab of Baghdad, who travels
with us at the request of the Caïmacam of Karahissar.
He is a fine old fellow, and very popular among all the
Muslems we meet. We feared he might be somewhat
of a leech, but find him of an altogether different genus;
he always chooses another stopping-place than our own,
both for himself and beasts, and settles his own bill.
True, his funds were exhausted shortly before we reached
Smyrna, and I advanced what he needed, but he paid it
back on our arrival. He travels with two fine white
donkeys, which he is taking as presents to a relative,
who is chief of the Smyrna police. One of these
creatures is very fine, and he told me he had paid 100*l.*
for it. The hair of its neck and tail is dyed with *henna.*
This he rides himself, and his servant, a good-natured
young Arab, generally bestrides the other; they have
no difficulty in keeping up with our horses.

At 5 we left the village of Duz Aghach (the Smooth
Tree) on our right; it is a place of considerable size,
and has some trees about it. The plain now narrows
into a valley. The sun disappeared at 6 by our watches
showing that we were considerably behindhand in our
reckoning. When we first came in sight of this plain
in the morning, we had noticed a smoke on the mountain south of it. It had been increasing all the morning, and as we passed opposite to the spot along our
path, it had become a great fire in the forest. The

sight was truly fine. We could see the tall and massive pitch-pines standing out in distinct relief in front of the flames, which were ever and anon bursting with devouring energy, and sending up clouds of black smoke or forked tongues of fire, which vanished in the air. We could sometimes distinguish the remorseless element leaping on one of those veteran denizens of the mountain, and twining itself, like a monstrous snake, around its venerable trunk and its hoary branches until it clothed it with a blazing and scorching garment. The fall of the aged tree was announced by the sudden rise into the air of a thousand sparks and a fresh outburst of smoke and flame. It is probable that the fire had already committed extensive ravages, for smoke arose from a very large portion of the mountain extending in a southerly direction; the smoke of this conflagration seemed to give heaviness to the whole surrounding atmosphere, and to render it oppressive, instead of producing a draught of air. There were a few clouds in the sky, but they were light, and the smoke gradually formed into a straight line, which, from our position, seemed to make directly for the setting sun. The western sky assumed a bloody hue, and the clouds above were painted with the most gorgeous colours.

The darkness of night advanced rapidly upon us after the sun had set. We reached the end of the plain, and ascended over broken ground, our horses stumbling in narrow gulleys and among rocks. It soon became so dark that each rider could only distinguish the tail of the horse that went before him, and not even that if he lagged a few steps behind. We let our horses have the reins, and went on like blind men, only guessing by the sound when we were passing through water, on dry land, or among stones. We finally saw lights, and found ourselves in the village of Chiflik; came to a door, and hailed; and, after being led a good deal hither and thither about the place, were finally ensconced until Monday morning in the upper story of a respectable building, with two tolerably clean rooms and an open piazza at our service—the holes in the boarding under foot not quite big enough to let us fall through into the stable below, and the window capable of being closed by spreading a blanket in front; and then a hasty supper, and "to bed, both man and beast."

Sunday, August 28th.—We were constantly rising yesterday, and have now attained an elevation of 4424 feet, which is more than 700 feet above the plain and lower portion of the town of Karahissar. This is the highest spot where we have lodged for the night, on our whole route from Samsoon to Smyrna, with few exceptions.

We had our usual Sabbath services this morning; but all the natives here being Muslems, no one could join us in addition to our own party. These seasons of Sunday rest, religious reading, and prayer, have been very refreshing all our long and weary way. I do not

believe either we or our beasts would have been able
to stand the wear and tear of the journey without these
regular seasons of rest. Many travellers lose much by
breaking the Sabbath, under the notion that a necessity
is laid upon them; that the Sabbath is no Sabbath at
all under such circumstances, and the like excuses.
Most unfortunately, the impression produced upon the
minds of the native population is extremely injurious.
They have an idea in consequence that all the "English," as they call Protestant Europeans, are infidels; for
they cannot conceive of a religion which has no outward
manifestations whatever; and infidelity in their view
is a stigma which annuls every other quality of up-
rightness, justice, and purity of morals, which, in such a
case, can be only apparent, not real. It often happens,
especially when travelling, that several men sleep in
the same room on the floor; and our native Church
members, in such a case, never hesitate to offer their
morning and evening prayer kneeling in the sight of
all present, though they abstain from "raising their
voices on high," as they do when alone. And they
are right. They reason that Turks, Jews, and other
religious sects, do not hesitate between kneeling in
the presence of other men and performing their devotions in an unsuitable posture; and I believe they
judge correctly. Outward posture means more in
the East than it does in the West or North. I have
often had occasion to go into a native brother's room
while engaged in his private devotions, and my in-

trusion has never made him do more than lower his
voice.

This village, so far as appears from our lodgings,
seems in a well-to-do condition. It appears of considerable extent, and trees, principally willows and
poplars, shade it here and there. This is the first place
where we have seen the poppy cultivated for the
purpose of obtaining opium. Unfortunately, however,
the crop has already been gathered in; there are fields
close to our house where it was sown, and seed-vessels
of the poppies have been left behind. The mode of
cultivation was described to me as follows :—The seed
is scattered broadcast in a field, which is carefully
enclosed. When the plant has attained a certain size,
each stem is tied sufficiently tight to prevent the sap
from rising higher, and an incision is made for it to
ooze out; the sap, indurated by the heat of the sun
and evaporation, constitutes opium. The flowers are
white or red. After extracting the juice in the manner
described above, the plant is allowed to bring its seed
to maturity by unfastening the tie; and this seed constitutes an important part of the value of the crop, oil
being manufactured from it, as previously stated.

The hills beyond this small plain are covered with
forests, which accounts for the houses' being wholly
built of wood. We have thus far found that in all the
villages from Karahissar westward the people make
hay, which they keep in heaps either upon the flat
roofs of their houses or upon the ground; in the

latter case it is preserved from the cattle by means of a
wooden fence.

Monday. August 29th.—Weather cloudy and threatening. Rose at 3·30. Our "new brooms" continue to
"sweep clean." Were in our saddles at 5·40, and, soon
after, met the finest Bactrian camel we had yet seen.
He appeared very gentle, had neither halter nor pack-
saddle; his majestic form was wholly uncovered; he
moved like a colossus, followed by two Turkmens, who
appeared to guide him in the direction he was going.

Male Bactrian Camel.

I asked them to stop so as to allow me the opportunity to sketch him. And he remained motionless
all the while I was drawing. The men told me they
belonged to the people encamped close by, whose
tents we could see; there were many camels feeding

in the neighbourhood. This animal they said was
never loaded, but kept solely for breeding purposes. His
humps were well marked, and so high that they both
hung over on the right, having a tuft of hair at the
extremity. Like all the camels of this breed he had
long dark hair on the top of the head, around the
throat, in front of the whole length of the neck, and
on the upper part of the forelegs. His form clearly
showed the distinction between the Bactrian and the
Arabian camel; the length of his body was very great
in comparison to his height. He was a heavy, mus-
cular, and powerful animal, the largest I ever saw of
the camel kind.

At 6·30 we reached an elevation whence we had a
very fine and extensive prospect. A heavy mass of
thickly wooded mountains lay in front of us, with a
very considerable stream flowing along on our right.
Underneath our feet were cultivated fields and a village
among them. The clouds which had hitherto hid
the rising sun were partly broken up, and thus light
and shade were cast upon the whole scenery, while the
summits of the mountains were enveloped in clouds
and rain. We had so long viewed the sky as brass,
and the parched earth had so long dazzled and strained
our eyes with the reflection of a scorching sun, that we
could not turn our faces for a moment away from the
refreshing prospect around us. We came down the hill
and passed an old Turkish fountain standing by the
wayside. It has four faces, and is supported by an

ancient pillar at each corner. At eight descended into
a valley watered by a small stream which runs westward. The rock had heretofore been friable marl, but
it now became more compact and less laminated, and
gradually passed to sandstone and conglomerate. The
hills on both sides of us were covered with pine trees
which, as the clouds disappeared, refreshed the eye
with their agreeable verdure. At 9 we reached a
dervend, or guard-house situated in a gorge, and found
in it two young men who acted as guards. This region
being occasionally infested with robbers, we had been
advised to keep near our loads, and had thus come
on at a slower rate than usual. This café is three
hours from our last stopping place. We remained here
for ten minutes to take the regulation coffee, and proceeded through the valley. Trees are scattered about
among cultivated fields, whose owners live in villages
out of sight from the main road. They are for the most
part walnut and wild pear trees, and I saw a few stunted
cypresses. The trunks of the walnut trees are short
but very thick. Soon the valley somewhat widened, and
we came at 10·30 to the village of Islam Keuy, and
passing through several of its filthy streets and by a
very plain mosque ornamented with a large wooden
minaret whose balustrade is of the same material, we
reached the Kiahaya's house where we stopped for
food and rest. Found here a Smyrna Greek engaged
in trade, and had the pleasure again of speaking that
language. You rarely meet in the Interior any Greek

who is acquainted with his native tongue, so completely have the ruling race succeeded in abolishing
it and substituting their own dialect. The weather
had been extremely variable all the morning ; but the
wind was high from the east, so that the mercury in
my barometer doubtless stood lower than it would
under other circumstances ; as it was, it gave me
3250 feet, which shows that we had descended nearly
1200 feet from Chiflik in the course of the forenoon.
Started again at 1·30, still keeping company with our
loaded animals ; entered an extensive grove of valonea,
which spread in all directions as far as the eye could
reach, even when we stood upon high ground. There
were a few bushes, but the soil was mostly planted
with fine trees of this species of oak, whose shape is
regular and graceful, and some specimens attain a
considerable size. The valonea acorn was only partly
developed, being in the shape of a ball of green leaves
two inches in diameter, the acorn itself not having yet
come through. The foliage was very thick so as to afford
a pleasant shade, in which we repeatedly avoided the
burning rays of the sun. At 2·45 we reached a fountain with a cemetery near it ; the water was warm and
brackish. The gravestones consisted of slabs of sandstone, calcareous marl, and metamorphic rock, all of
which it would seem are to be found about here.
Farther on we enjoyed a very extensive prospect, the
unevenness of the soil enabling us to look over the
forest of valonea oak, which extended for a distance of

five or six miles. Saw Koordish tents and cattle a
little distance off, and met a Koordish boy who was
engaged in watching a herd of cattle and busy, at the
same time, in spinning some of the coarse wool which
that people make into carpets. Spinning is the
general occupation of shepherds throughout the interior while tending their cattle, and the immense
flocks of sheep which travel from the region of Kars
to Constantinople are generally led by a man thus
engaged.

At 5 descended through a village into a rich
alluvial plain, and stopped under the fine pine trees
which skirt it to drink from a fountain that flows from
the rock. The view westward from this spot is extensive and fine. The ground slopes down to the plain
which though alluvial is still undulating. No valonea
is seen in it, which indicates that this tree requires a
dry soil, such as is produced by the decomposition of
the sandstone. In the plain are seen here and there
clusters of trees and verdure, and occasionally tall
poplars. The villages are mostly hid in orchards of
mulberry and fruit trees; we could see the minaret
of the village where we intended to stop for the night
shining in the light of the setting sun. We now ven-
tured to push ahead of our loads, and made the hour
and a half to Bozghoor by 6·15. This village contains
about sixty houses and one mosque, whose minaret is an
elaborate structure which does not at all correspond to
the style or appearance of the building to which it is

an appendage. As we entered the village I noticed
that the women went about quite unveiled, and without
appearing to show any feeling on the point, and that
this was the case even with the old and the homely.
One of these was walking quite uncovered straight
towards us, and when she noticed us she continued just
as before, only standing where she was, gazing with
the stare of astonishment and curiosity, but without
evincing a particle of bashfulness. Our inquiry for a
lodging place procured us rooms in the best house in
the village, whither some other travellers appeared to
have preceded us. It belonged to a wealthy Turk
who was absent. One half of the house was occupied
by his harem, a small door upstairs leading into it,
which was guarded by a powerful dog. All the apartments were in the upper story, the lower being occupied by the stables. A large verandah gave us air
and a good prospect upon the enclosed grounds and
the village. The room where we slept was spread
with two small carpets from the famous Ooshak manufactures, the delicate pattern of which was finer than
anything I had yet seen.

Tuesday, August 30th. — Rose at 3 and started
at 5. The plain is undulating and well cultivated,
studded with villages embosomed in gardens and
orchards. We reached Ooshak at 6·30. It is a large
town, of purely Turkish style, situated in a natural
hollow of the plain; the houses are of mud bricks,
only partially plastered over. Streams of muddy

water flow through the streets and pass under some
of the buildings. The mosques are mean, but their
minarets fine; there are some ten or twelve of them,
tall and well shaped. Many of them are fluted on
the outer surface, the fluting being made to wind
around the body of the minaret. The sharp domes of
all are covered with tin. We stopped at the principal
khan in the place, called as usual Yeni (or New) Khan,
a building with a narrow oblong court, lying not far
from the edge of the town, and gave ourselves the luxury
of fresh fruit, which is not to be procured in the villages.
We had the good fortune to have a letter of introduction
to a Sciote merchant, Mr. André Glisse, an old resident,
or we should have seen nothing of the place. He was
extremely kind to us, insisting upon giving us an
early dinner, and taking us round the town to see the
celebrated carpet manufactures. We were fortunate
enough to have an occasion somewhat to repay him for
his kindness by setting up for him a cotton gin which
had just arrived, the first ever introduced here. He
informed us that the crop of valonea will be ready for
gathering in about a fortnight; after picking the fruit
of this species of oak entire, it is left to dry until the
acorn becomes somewhat loose, when it is removed
with a nail. There are no shops, much less a factory,
for the manufacture of carpets, but they are made in
private houses, both Christian and Turkish. The
work is done exclusively by the women. There are
two kinds of carpets made here. The plain is woven

like ordinary cloth, but in patches, each colour by itself. In both cases the loom upon which the framework of the carpet is stretched from top to bottom stands on one side of the door entering into the yard of the house, and the women who do this work squat down in front of it. Little girls are busy bringing the woollen thread of different colours as needed. The woven carpet is made very rapidly, and is necessarily cheaper than the other, while it is inferior in appearance and durability. The Turkey carpet, as it is called in Europe, is made by a very laborious process. Every stitch requires a separate thread, which is tied with a peculiar knot to the perpendicular twine, which is laid regularly, up and down across a frame as wide as the carpet is to be. The ends of the thread are then cut off, but not close, another stitch is tied in the same way by the side of it, and so on. The stitches are thus made one by one in a horizontal line, and when the row is completed a stout strand of red woollen thread is passed three times across, interwoven in the perpendicular threads with the hand; they then press down that and the new row of stitches with a wooden comb, and cut all the ends of the threads smooth with a pair of shears from right to left. They appear to have the patterns in their minds, though they occasionally consult the finished portion which is gradually rolled up underneath. Some of the designs we saw were very pretty, particularly some flower patterns, and a small Persian design. I

was informed that these women are able to imitate any
pattern sent them, and a beautiful carpet had lately
been made for a gentleman in Smyrna, the centre of
which represented the arms of Italy.

The Rayah population of Ooshak consists of 150
Greek and 50 Armenian houses, there are no Papists.
The elevation above the sea given by the barometer is
3137 feet, indicating the continuance of the plateau
which occupies most of the interior of Asia Minor,
though there is a gradual descent as we advance westward. From Ooshak the plateau continues to diminish
in height, though we shall still travel upon it until we
have passed Koola.

We were again in our saddles at 2 P.M. and ascended
a small hill, from which there was an extensive prospect
of vineyards and orchards on our right. There are
several mill runs about here, and they are lined with
tall poplars. Further on cultivation almost entirely
ceased; but the hills were covered with a thick growth
of bushes, mostly of oak. We passed along some fine
bold ravines cut through by the stream we were
following, and which is the same as that which flows
through Ooshak. Rode on the right or northern
side of a narrow valley until about half-an-hour from
Geuneh. At 3 found some blocks of fine obsidian,
the first indication of volcanic action, which henceforth
multiplied as we proceeded westward. The rock, however, both here and for a great distance to the west
belongs to a formation of strongly stratified lime or

marl, containing impressions of shells. This stone
is sometimes quite soft and is easily decomposed,
forming a rich and fertile soil.

The strata are very nearly horizontal; it often alter-
nates with a conglomerate, having a basis of sand or
soft marl. This conglomerate being more compact
than the limestone occurring with it, the latter is often
worn away leaving the harder rock isolated in strange
and fantastic shapes, resembling somewhat the pinnacles
of Seidiler. Again the marl is worn away from beneath the sandy conglomerate, and leaves it standing
suspended in the air. In one place I found the rock
strongly impregnated with sulphur and copper, giving
it a yellow and green hue. There is considerable volcanic disturbance in some parts, and the occurrence of
obsidian points the same way. Sometimes also the
limestone assumes the appearance and hardness of
flint, probably from igneous causes. Masses or boulders
of other rocks are occasionally found, having probably
been brought hither by some convulsion of nature or
by glacial action. These parts are said to abound with
partridges, and people come from Ooshak to shoot
them. The ravines, however, are favourable to robbers,
and we subsequently learnt that a deed of blood had
been committed upon this road the day before we
travelled it. We reached Geuneh at 6, a most miserable, ruinous, and dirty village of half-a-dozen houses
standing, though there are ruins of many more. This
must have been an important town at some period, if

we may judge from the public buildings yet remaining.
There is a handsome mosque and minaret of considerable size. An isolated minaret of brick, without its
pointed spire, marks the spot where another mosque
once stood, and a third in ruins has lost dome and
minaret too. Our quarters here were decidedly the
worst we had yet encountered ; our host's boy attempted
to steal, and when reproved for it drew his knife. Fortunately, however, we were too many for him, and he
gained nothing thereby. We also had some trouble
with the *zabtieh* furnished us by the Governor of
Ooshak, who was to have gone with us as far as Koola.
He insisted upon having the best quarters in the house
for himself, was scolded roundly, and went off in a
pet to another place. Next morning we caught sight
of him as he was pursuing his loose horse among the
ruined houses, and he shortly after went back to Ooshak
without even calling for the customary bakshish. We
have descended nearly 900 feet from Ooshak, *i.e.* in a
distance of about 15 miles.

Wednesday, August 31st.—Started at 5·30 and at 6
reached a spot which has become famous for the highway robberies there perpetrated. It is a regular trap,
and so perfectly adapted to the object in view, that all
it needs is the living springs to work it. The robbers'
hiding-place is upon two small natural mounds upon the
outer edge of the road, where large stones are arranged
for the purpose of screening them from view. They
allow the caravan to reach a circular spot between these

mounds, and then effectually prevent their advance or
retreat—for the precipice on the right and the high
rocks on the left render flight quite impossible in those
directions. All the robbers have to do is to show themselves from behind their hiding-places and to give the
caravan the order to stop; in case of resistance, they
can shoot down the travellers without danger to themselves. At 6·15 we descended again into the Muzuk
valley, so called from a village of that name, which we
passed at 6·30, situated on the opposite or north side of
the valley. The valonea oak here grows abundantly on
both slopes of the valley, the lower alluvial ground alone
being cultivated. Yuruk tents were lying about among
the trees. It is in this valley we first came upon the
Hermus, which descends from a lateral valley running
up to the north-east. It is now 10 to 15 feet in width,
and but a few inches in depth. Our course hereafter
lies in a great measure by the side of this stream, though
we shall often lose sight of it altogether where its banks
are too rugged to leave a foot-hold for the traveller, or
where its lengthened windings render a shorter cut
desirable. The rich and promising soil lies mostly
unused, and the population is extremely scattered and
wretched. Going over a hillock saw the Chiflik house,
and stopped at the café at 6·45. It belongs to some
Greek gentleman, and lies in a pleasant position among
hills covered with valonea oak. Its cultivated lands
are in the valley below. We were hospitably entertained here, and left at 7·15. Came down again into

the valley of the Hermus, and the lands belonging to the Chiflik, which are planted with vineyards, flax, and grain. Continued on the same side of the valley and stopped a few minutes to shoot some partridges—which are said to abound here—for a meal. We were told at the Chiflik that a man had lately shot twenty-two brace in one day. The Hermus, along which we rode, had increased already to 20 or 25 feet in width. At 8·30 reached the village of Yenishehir, consisting of some houses mostly in ruins, built upon a slope facing the north-east, and occupying the foot of the pass over the stony and steep Chatal Tepeh or Fork Mountain, which is in full view, with the two rocky points which give it the name. The Hermus here turns to the north and finds further on a way round the obstruction presented by the mountain. The rocks in that direction have a very dark colour. Here mica slate has taken the place of the limestone. This village must once have been a place of size and importance, from its extensive ruins. The buildings, however, mostly of mud-brick, unbaked, are being rapidly obliterated by the rains, and it certainly is now the very opposite of Yenishehir, the New City. On the highest part of the slope it occupies are the ruins of the former residence of a Dereh Bey, consisting of a piece of ground, some 200 by 400 feet, enclosed by a stone wall 20 feet high, with a square tower at each corner. In one of these towers is an underground prison. The whole enclosure is divided by a wall into two portions—the part

toward the village being for the men, or the selam-
lùk, and the other for the women, or the harem; each
had its own outer gate, and there was a door of communication between the two.   Each also had its own house
and outbuildings, resting chiefly upon the north-west
wall.   The houses are quite in ruins and uninhabitable;
but much of the timber still supports the mud-brick
structures.   Most of the walls, however, are built of
irregular pieces of mica slate taken from the mountain
side, united only with mud.   This was once the residence of a Dereh Bey, or independent Muslem chieftain,
and his stronghold at the foot of the pass doubtless
enabled him to levy black mail upon the travellers who
frequented this important thoroughfare.   It was easy
to imagine the busy scenes which once occurred on this
spot, some centuries back; now, however, all is silent.
The yard has become a goat and sheep's pen.   Three
fine minarets, built of red bricks, attest, as at Geuneh,
the former existence of fine mosques; two of them have
lost their pointed spires, but the third has lately been
repaired, as well as the mosque to which it belongs.
The comfort of clean quarters and the hospitality of
our Turkish host made us forget the unpleasant ex-
periences of Geuneh.

Handsome minarets appear to have been the rage in
this region some two or three centuries ago, for we
found them not only in so large a place as Ooshak, but
in such villages also as Bozghoor, Geuneh, and here.
There is no doubt that these were once places of con-

siderable size; but their present condition not only indicates a striking diminution of the Turkish population, but also of the religious zeal of the Muslems. Indeed one is struck with the universality of these two facts while passing, as we have done, through the central portions of Asia Minor. We have not yet found a single town that presents indications of growth. New houses are extremely rare—ruinous ones very common. Fields lie uncultivated; vineyards and orchards are running wild and overgrown with grass and weeds. At Afion Karahissar the Government was rebuilding some of the shops; besides this, there were a few new villages built by the lately-imported Circassians, but they looked miserably poor and filthy. An observation showed the elevation of Yenishehir to be 1776 feet, or nearly 300 feet below Geuneh, our last stopping place. We left this village at 2·15, and went immediately up a very steep ascent. The road was mainly cut or worn among the rocks, and often so narrow and steep, that a loaded animal passed through with some difficulty. Our course was zigzag up the hill of mica slate, which was too steep to be overcome any other way. The dip of the rock has a strong inclination toward the south-west, and is greater on the western than on the eastern side of Chatal Tepeh. It seems that some efforts have lately been made to improve the road, for we found the rock had been blasted in several places. We reached the summit at 3·15, and began to descend. This was done very

gradually and along a comparatively easy road; and
in so doing we went round the mountain, skirting
perhaps one-half of its circumference. The view was
very extensive and picturesque. On our right was a
broken mountain region, with deep and rocky ravines,
apparently all of mica slate. At some distance west
and north-west beyond this mountain we could distinctly see the limestone formation in the valleys
below, the white marl cropping out from the verdure.
Where the soil has not been washed away the mountain is covered with grass, scrub oak, the wild acacia,
called Judas' tree, and some valonea oaks; partridges
must be very abundant here, for though we saw none
yet, we could hear them singing in every direction,
and the path was covered with their tracks. At 3·10
we again caught sight of the Hermus; it was dashing
among the rocks and narrow openings in the mountain,
coming down from the north to pursue again its western
course. As it leaves the mountain its bed widens,
although but a small portion of it is covered with water
at this season of the year. A valley opens farther west,
and we can perceive the black tents of the nomadic
Yuruks scattered here and there in it. We saw the
village of Tash Keuy, "stony village," on the mountain side below us on the right, and soon after at 4
reached a guard-house, situated upon an eminence
and commanding the road. There were two men
stationed here, and they told us they remain during

the whole winter upon this spot, the weather being sometimes very severe. Looking down from here, we could see the bridge, whose single arch spans the river; it appears very narrow and high. The undulating plain to the west has now come in full sight, and it is fertile and well cultivated. We continued rapidly to descend, and at 4·30 reached the bridge. Its main

Bridge over the Hermus.

arch is very long and high, and the river passes under that alone, except when it overflows its banks, in which case it runs also under the small arches on either side. The bank at each end of the bridge is high, but I suspect even that is sometimes covered with water.

The parapet is partly broken down, and the ascent
and descent over it is steep and narrow, the base of
the structure being much wider than the summit.   It
is a Turkish work.   The water of the Hermus is now
very low and everywhere fordable ; where we crossed it
the greatest depth was 1 foot 6 inches.   Some of our
animals found it so agreeable that they got away from
their masters and attempted to continue the journey
down the stream.   We now followed the right bank of
the river along a path which ran by the base of the
overhanging mica slate cliffs.   Large platanus or plane
trees grew here and there near the water, and our old
friend the *Agnus castus* lined the banks of the river ; we
had not seen it since leaving Smyrna, and it seemed to
give us the first welcome home again.   We soon ascended
a knoll and found another guard-house.   At 5·10 the rock
which had been mica slate from the time we had set
foot upon the mountain side at Yenishehir changed
again to friable and well-stratified limestone and marl ;
but the change was not sudden.   The mica slate began
to contain larger and more numerous pieces of quartz ;
the mica then became more rare, and at last totally
disappeared, the stone assuming all the characters of
what is called quartz rock.   Marl soon appeared to be
mixed up with the quartz ; the latter disappeared in
its turn, and we had reached the marl or limestone
formation.   We now moved along the plain where the
Hermus makes a bend to the left ; passed over some

harmans or threshing-floors, forded the river, and went up a steep and high bank on the other side to the village of Suriyeh, which is built on ground at a considerable elevation above the stream. We were taken to the Governor's house, who was very polite and attentive, and there our persons and animals were well cared for.

CHAPTER XXVI.

THURSDAY, *September 1st.*—An observation taken
this morning shows that we continue to descend,
though slowly, toward the western plains; this is also
proved by the course of the Hermus. I gave medicine
to a sick man last night, which did him so much good
that a number of applicants came this morning upon a
similar errand. My medicines, however, were packed
up, and I was ready to start, so that I was obliged to
decline the aid requested. We left at 5·25, and rode over
a hill into a valley. Before us extended a steep mountain,
formed of marl or soft limestone, its face washed and
worn down into deep gulleys and irregular forms. The
top of this hill appears to be a far-stretching plateau,
composed of a layer of lava about 100 feet in depth.
On our left, too, we had a similar mountain, so that we

were travelling in a fissure, about 1000 feet in depth, cut into the marl and its superincumbent lava. The bottom of this fissure, or gorge, forms the bed of the Hermus, generally too narrow to allow a road upon its banks. Our path led us over the detritus, which lies in masses of more or less elevation on the right and left. As far as we could see, the upper layer of lava appeared everywhere of equal thickness, and seemed from where we stood to have a columnar formation. Came down to the Hermus at 6·30 by a smooth little valley, an enlargement of the gorge. The river here flows in a south-west direction. We found mica slate in place at the bottom; above it lies the marl, and the lava on the top of all. Fragments of the last lie all about us, which were probably broken from above, and were too hard to be decomposed and washed away like the marl. It once formed, I am persuaded, a general crust over the whole limestone formation, and it continues to break down and fall from above as the underlying marl is giving way under the influence of the weather and the river. We crossed the Hermus, and going up the steep bank on the other side reached the guard-house at 5·50, where we waited for our loads to come up. We had been told that there were forty Turkmen robbers in this pass; but we, certainly, saw nothing of them. We at first kept by our loads, but left them to come on behind us in the vicinity of the guard-house. This is built upon a hillock which commands a view of the road on both sides for a considerable distance. The river passes at the foot of it and winds about in the chasm. The spot is highly picturesque, the nearer bank of the mountain being very steep, the marl worn into the most extraordinary forms of chimneys, minarets, domes, cavities, and honeycombs, and the whole surmounted by a broad line of black lava. The hillock on which we stood was of mica slate, which underlies the marl, and stretches out in a southerly direction. There are pieces of lava lying all about, however, and the columnar formation of the broad layer on the crest of the mountain is still more distinct than before. We took a man here to show us the way, and left the guard-house at 7·20. Passed among the tumbled rocks close under the overhanging cliffs, with the Hermus on our left. The partridges were singing on every side amid the echoes of the mountains; but they kept out of sight. As we rode along close to the foot of the cliffs, we had to pick our way among large pieces of lava which had tumbled down from the top; many of them showed the columnar form, which gave the appearance of ribs in their sides. These were quite smooth, each surface being about six inches in width; otherwise the substance of the lava is very uniform. As we looked up, in places, we could clearly distinguish the columns in the lava standing perpendicularly. In one spot, however, these were contorted.

There is a piece of lava as large as a good sized ship, which has fallen from above, and has alighted near the road; its shape and position is very much like a vessel

lying on the stocks, and the columnar surfaces well
represent the planking on the ship's side. This rock
has long attracted the attention of the natives, and has
given its name to the place; for it is called *Gemi Dereh*,
the Ship Gorge. We now came close to the bank of
marl, and saw the explanation of the fantastic shapes we
had noticed. The foundation is mica slate: then comes
a mixture of fragments of mica slate, quartz, sand, and
clay. It is the soil formed by the decomposition of
the mica slate rock. It is precisely like the soil we
had already seen lying upon a mica slate bottom, and
which we had farther on a still better opportunity of
studying. The quartz pebbles prevail in it; for they
are the hardest portions of the rock, and they longest
resist decomposition; though in the rock itself they
occur only in numerous veins, yet they prevail in the soil
into which the rock disintegrates. Above this species
of conglomerate, is a layer of clay or marl, of different
thickness in different places. Then comes a narrow bed
of sand and small pebbles, and marl again, thus forming alternate layers of gravel and clay, the former much
thinner than the latter. The weather wears away the
clay, while the gravel holds longer together, thus producing the fantastic shapes we see. At 7·45, came
quite down to the bank of the Hermus, at the ruins of
an old bridge, but continued to travel on the north side,
upon a narrow bank lying between the river and the
cliffs. The valley soon widens; we forded the stream
and went up a hill toward a village on the other

side. The Hermus now runs north-west, and we lose sight of it altogether. Rode over an undulating, sandy ground, which is simply decomposed lava, with large fields of melons and water-melons on both sides of the way. Found by the road-side two small stone enclosures, roofed with branches of trees, in which are kept jars of water, quite cool; and following the custom, as we were told, we stopped and took a refreshing draught. The hills lying to the west of us, and near our road, are of lava, regularly rounded and conical, presenting the appearance of extinct volcanoes; but their sides are smooth and under culture. The ground gradually ascends. We now entered a narrow pass, when Koola burst all at once upon our view. It seems to be a place of considerable extent, built upon unequal ground. The houses are all covered with red tiles, and there are some good-looking minarets. In front and on the right is a long line or wall of black lava, in broken masses, which has flowed out of the now extinct volcano on the north-east side of the town. It resembles a rough and surging stream, which assumes odd and fantastic forms. The old volcano which threw it out lies about two miles on the right, and the stream of lava can be traced down its western side; it is called Devlit, or the Inkstand, by the natives. No crater is visible from below: its form is somewhat irregular, and a narrow path can be traced ascending to the very top. The houses of the town are built of pieces of lava and mica slate, mud alone being used for cement. The walls are everywhere

of a very dark hue, resembling those of Pompeii. The
streets all have high side walks, made of slabs of mica
slate; and the portion left between for horses and cattle
is narrow and unpaved. This is made still narrower in
many places by the frequent crossings. We stopped at
a large but ruinous khan, where they gave us a small
room which we soon perceived was already tenanted by
a variety of vermin sufficient to satisfy the keenest
entomologist. But we were fortunately provided with
a letter of recommendation from our hospitable friend
Mr. André Glisse, at Ooshak, to a fine old bearded
Turkish merchant, Hadji Zadeh Ali Agha: we lost no
time in sending it to its address, and soon had the pleasure of seeing the kindly face of the gentleman of the
long robe himself, accompanied by a Greek merchant
of the name of Kutchuk Yanaco, Little John, who
took us to his house, gave us an excellent dinner,
and treated us with the generous hospitality of which
the dwellers of the interior of Asia Minor may so
justly boast. Walking about the town, we saw a
marble sarcophagus with its cover bearing an inscription in which is the name of the person whose remains
it once contained. It is now used as a trough for
a public fountain. We likewise saw at the door of a
public bath two lions holding the heads of bulls. As I
believe Koola is not built upon the site of any ancient
city, these must have been brought from the neighbourhood, where there were many towns in the olden
times. The position of Koola (2412 feet) is much

higher than the Hermus, which passes round to the
north of it.

Town and Volcano of Koola, with public Well.

We left Koola at 3·15. The soil is quite sandy, but
seems abundantly to remunerate the labour of cultivation. After twenty minutes' ride came to a well,
where we stopped to water our horses. I took here
the accompanying sketch of the town; but the greater
part of it is out of sight, the banks of lava standing
as a high wall in the foreground, so as almost completely to conceal it. The extinct volcano appears to
fill the centre of the picture, while a black stream of
lava runs down its side toward the left, and then
advances again to the front and right. There are no

fountains at Koola; the water is all obtained from wells,
and is drawn up in an iron bucket, attached by a chain
to a long pole, which has a weight at the other end.
A small platform is built of stone round the mouth of
the well, whose worn edges attest its age and usefulness.
I have taken this opportunity to delineate our party,
not forgetting our faithful dog Ira, who has rendered
herself very useful all the way in assisting to provide
for our table during the day, and keeping faithful
watch at night. I have only left out our pack-horses
and the mare and her colt.

Here we were joined by the mounted guard which
the Governor had provided for our safety. We accepted
the proffered escort; not that we placed the slightest
reliance upon such people in case of danger, but solely
because no one in our party was acquainted with the
road as far as Cassaba. There is, however, this additional motive for taking such people along when travelling in the country: in case of meeting robbers and
suffering loss by them, the Government officers succeed
in throwing off all responsibility, unless it can be made
to appear that this precaution, which they always
recommend, has been taken; and even then it often
occurs that the robbers have partners in the Mejlis, or
Provisional Council. The ground now gradually rises,
and we had, further on, an excellent view of the city,
with its volcano and stream of lava flowing from it
to the town, which appears, indeed, to have been built
in great measure in the midst of and upon the lava.

The pieces of this mineral which we picked up were
very porous and light, but extremely hard. Even the
hammer produced no impression upon them. Found
a small extent of surface where the rock in place was
limestone, with impressions of shells. This was the
last of the formation traced all along from Ooshak;
for we now were fully landed upon the mica slate,
which no longer appeared only occasionally and in a
decomposed condition, but was everywhere about us,
and under our feet, in rocky ledges of every shape. The
highest ground appeared to be covered with a layer of
lava. When we reached the greatest elevation on the
road, we had a fine view of another extinct volcano, called
in Turkish *Kara Devlit*, or the Black Inkstand, a very

Volcano of Kara Devlit.

appropriate name indeed, as can be seen from the
accompanying sketch, taken from this spot. It stands
near the edge of the plain or valley through which

flows the Hermus, not here in sight. It must bo very
high, as I judged that we could see but about one-
half of the whole, rising above the hills that hide
its base. It appears to have been thrown up entire
from the bowels of the earth, and to be wholly formed
of lava and scoriæ. The crater itself is well marked,
and many trees, apparently pines, grow upon the edge
and outer surface, whose fresh green colour makes a
strange and striking contrast with the black hill on
which they stand. Here we entered into a deep cut in
the rock, and came, at 4·45, to a guard-house, built in the
side of this cut, and thus protected from the extremely
cold blasts which must sweep over the spot, whose
elevation cannot be short of 3000 feet. We presently again descended, and travelled over level
ground, passing by many neglected orchards and fields;
there was probably some village out of sight in the
neighbourhood. The west wind now freshened, and we
reached, at 6, the isolated café situated at the head of
the well-known Cavak Dereh Pass, in a bleak spot, fully
exposed to the blast, and extremely cold and uncomfortable. But there is no other stopping place for the
traveller between Koola and the village of Salihly;
the accommodations afforded consist of two miserable
rooms and a large stable, beasts being really better
provided for than men. I did not wonder, except for
the cold, which was piercing, that a large caravan preferred to encamp in the open air. This spot is 2681
feet above the sea. It constitutes the very edge of

the plateau which occupies the most of the Peninsula
of Asia Minor. We shall now descend to the low alluvial plains which form a belt between the plateau and
the sea.

Friday, Sept. 2nd.—We started at 5·30, and plunged
at once down the rocky pass of Cavak Dereh, or Poplar
Pass, a very inappropriate name, since there is not a
single poplar in it. Our lodgings were not only very
uncomfortable, but we paid very dear for all we took,
as it had to be sent for to a village half an hour off.
The wind had fallen, but mists floated about us, and
the sky was overcast. Cavak Dereh is a steep and rocky
gorge, consisting in a great measure of the bed of a
stream; it is two hours or some eight miles in length.
We passed as many as four dried-up fountains, which had
once been erected for the comfort of the traveller, who
must greatly depend upon a refreshing draught while
going up this pass in a warm summer's day. We are
here in the midst of the mica slate formation, which
has, however, a hard texture, and contains a smaller
proportion of mica than yesterday. Emerging from
the pass, we came to hills of earth, where the road was
smooth and good. We soon caught sight of the plain
of Philadelphia on our left, watered by a tributary
of the Hormus, called the Kooza Chay, or river. It is
bounded on the south by the mountain-chain of Tmolus,
which has different names in different localities. It
commences a little south of Philadelphia, where a
chain of hills running due south joins it to the Messogis

of the ancients, the southern boundary of the plain of
the Cayster. The Tmolus runs west in a slightly curved
line, nearly as far as Voorla, the ancient Clazomene,
where two prominent conical peaks give it the name of
the Two Brothers. The group of hills attached to these
are the ancient Mount Corax. Thence, eastward, a line
of porphyritic hills runs past Smyrna on the south, and
reaches the western extremity of Tmolus himself, where
it is called Tahtaly, or the mountain of planks, from the
fact that the pines are there cut into boards and taken
to Smyrna for sale. It is now, however, mostly barren
of trees in this portion, and a line of hills running
north unites it to Sipylus. Tmolus, a little farther
east, is called Nif Dagh, from the village of Nif,
or Nymphio, at its foot; the remaining portion, the
highest of all, and still farther east, goes by the
name of Booz Dagh, the ice-mountain. Tmolus does
not, however, in these parts, come right down upon
the smooth alluvial plain, but is separated from it by
a belt of earthy hills, chiefly of a reddish hue, which
have been so worn by the rains and tumbled about by
the earthquakes of the "Katakekaumene" as to assume
all sorts of fantastic shapes. From our commanding position we could distinguish several towns in the plain;
Derasily was upon the edge of it, right before us, and
Salihly, a place of considerable size, beyond it, not far
from the opposite edge. The Binbir Tepeh, thousand
and one hills, the pyramidal tombs of ancient Sardis,
covered a vast extent of ground on the right, and behind

them rose blue old Sipylus, round and rocky. We
reached Dernsily at 9; the road constantly descending, and most of it in good condition, we had made
5 hours in 3½. Had a luncheon of fruit, grapes and
an excellent water-melon, at the miserable khan,
and were off again at 9·45. This village, like all the
rest in the region, is marked by misery, poverty,
and dilapidation. It is, however, surrounded by rich
soil, which would secure it wealth under a different
Government. We had already entered the plain,
and were soon upon the low grounds, always wet in
winter, and now grown over with a thick, rank grass.
We reached the Kooza Chay at 10·30, and found it
nearly dry; there was just water enough in it to make
the flow to the north-west perceptible. The banks are
here from six to eight feet high, and about seventy yards
apart. The stream is not fordable in winter, and has to
be crossed by a bridge, situated a little below. The
left bank is also covered with rank grass, and the soil
near the river very sandy. We, however, soon came
upon cultivated fields, whence crops of grain had been
gathered. Saw several threshing-floors; noticed several
plantations of poplars; these are sown thick, and are
thinned out as they grow; they are used for building
purposes. At 11·15 reached Salihly; it must be a
bad place for intermittent fever, for even now pools of
water are standing in the very town, swamps can be
seen all around, and the rich plantations have abundant
clusters of reeds which always indicate the presence of

stagnant moisture. There are many trees about, and extensive orchards; the land is under cultivation all around to the mountains, as far as the eye can reach, and much of it appears to produce melons and maize, which require the richest soil. The place seems prosperous; several houses were building.

We took up our quarters in the best khan in the place; it consists, as usual, of an inner square court, surrounded by buildings. In this case two sides were occupied by stables, and the two others contained rooms, the side upon the street, alone, being two stories high. The whole, like all the houses we saw in this place, is built of mud bricks supported by a wooden frame. They gave us their best room, situated on the left side of the entrance, and we had from the window a full view of a group of the *élite* of the town, who come, in the afternoon, to sit on little stools under the shade of the trees, smoke their narguiles, and sip their coffee, while some one in the company volunteers to make them stare by relating the most extravagant pieces of information, followed by a general discussion on politics, and a passing of judgment upon the doings of the great powers of Europe and the little power of Turkey. We enjoyed a doze in the midst of the hum of voices—if enjoyment it may be called, when mosquitoes and other tenants seemed to consider us as intruders. The room was ornamented with paintings *al fresco*, which are as fair specimens of the present condition of the fine arts in Turkey as can be met with. As my narrative claims to contain a true portraiture of the Turkey of the present day, I must not deny the reader the pleasure of gazing upon a specimen of the kind, the handsomest modern *tableau* I have met, which covered one side of our room. My copy is a faithful reproduction, though I confess that the beauty of the original is greatly enhanced by the gorgeous colours the Oriental artist has succeeded in applying with wonderful variety.

Specimen of Turkish Painting.

Sept. 3rd, Saturday.—An observation taken this morning at half-past four gives the position of Salihly at 417 feet above the sea, showing that we have descended 2276 feet since our last stopping place; it must be about the difference of altitude between the head of the pass at Yedi Kaleh Caïveh and Derasily at the foot, the distance between them by the road being about twenty miles. Salihly is not fifty feet higher than the Hermus. Our road took us not far from the edge of the plain, upon smooth and well-cultivated

ground. After a while, Carabed discovered he had left
his overcoat behind, and went back to fetch it; he found
the Khanji had already appropriated it and was wearing
it with great *gusto.* The road still kept in a curve near
the foot of the hills, avoiding the lower level of the
plain which is probably under water during the winter.
After a ride of an hour and a quarter we reached the
ruins of Sardis, mostly situated on the left of the road.
The citadel, rendered so famous by the history of ages
preceding the Roman conquest, was built upon a high
and steep hill; earthquakes, and the action of the
weather upon the soil, which contains no rocks, have
gradually torn it down; only a small piece of wall yet
stands erect upon the edge of the precipice to tell of
its former power, and even that may suddenly disappear. The town lay around three sides of the castle-
hill, north, west, and south. On the higher portion
are the remains which are called "the house of
Crœsus." We only saw it from the road, and it seems
more like a theatre; the lower portions appeared to be
supported by very solid arches.* There is on the east
a wall of no great solidity running up the hill. It may
have been a portion of the city wall. Lower down are
the remains of a large building, mostly of bricks, which
appears Roman; and lower still are those of another
very large edifice, consisting of four solid pilasters of

---

* A subsequent visit enabled me to ascertain that these buildings
were the theatre and stadium. The so-called "house of Crœsus"
stood much lower down the hill.

marble beneath and brick above, the marble facings
having probably fallen from the upper part. Half a
mile to the west are the remains of another, a very
massive building, partly of brick and partly of marble.
The ruins of the famous Temple of Cybele are on the
south side of the hill, as we were told, and distant from
us six or eight miles. We continued to skirt the edge
of the plain as we proceeded on our way, but now
passed over undulating and stony ground, formed by
the débris of the mountain. At 8·30 reached a café,
with a shop, well shaded by trees, which were a great
attraction to the traveller on a hot summer day.
There was here again a plantation of poplar trees,
such as we had seen about Salihly. We had also
spied two fine cypresses a little back. This tree is
not found upon the plateau, except where it occurs
wild and stunted upon some of the high mountain
ranges. We found the same to be the case with the
fig-tree, which we first saw at Salihly, covered with un-
ripe fruit; however, the ripe fruit was sold in the market.
We found the fig-tree here again, and it multiplies as
we advance toward the sea. This tree sometimes occurs
upon the lower parts of the plateau, but is stunted, and
the fruit is not good. We left the pleasant shade of
this spot at 9·15; the whole distance from Salihly
to Cassaba is eight hours, and this café, called
Ahmedly, is the half-way place. Carabed was again
oblivious, a very unusual thing for the bright fellow,
for he forgot the barometer at the café, and we waited

half an hour for him to turn back for it. As we approached Cassaba, the miserable mud houses of the town and the minarets began to peer among the foliage, while the lofty Sipylus, of a deep blue, rose apparently right behind the town, though it lies really at a distance of fifteen miles. We reached the place at 12·30. Though showing an advance in civilization to one who comes from the Interior, it has the reputation of being a dirty and unhealthy place of residence. The streets, though narrow, as in Turkey generally, have side walks on both sides of them, and between them runs a continuous dark stream of dirty water. The town is certainly highly favoured in both the quantity and the quality of its water, and artificial fountains are met with on every side. But the water runs off upon the surface, there being no sewers to convey it out of sight. Moreover the people are constantly throwing every species of offal and filth into it. They have another very dirty custom : instead of repairing the pipes which convey the water to the town and distribute it to the fountains, they frequently throw dung into them, in order to prevent their leaking. Surely a sanitary committee is loudly called for at Cassaba.

The water-supply of the town comes from a very fine and abundant spring, some two or three miles distant. It flows through an aqueduct about 40 feet below the ground, with openings for ventilation every 200 yards. It is evidently an ancient work, of remarkable solidity. Time will, however, destroy the most solid works of

men, and this aqueduct has broken down in some
places, and leaks in many more. The Turks have no
provision for repairing public works; it is one of the
beauties of the Muslem faith that such deeds are
great acts of virtue, which will meet with special
rewards in heaven. It has therefore either been taken
for granted that such things would be attended to, or
else fear has been entertained that any public provision
would take away the merit of those charitable deeds;
and it is well known that every public building or
work is going to ruin in this land. Once in a long
period a man who has amassed riches by murder and
rapine will, under the influence of some twinges of
conscience, leave a few "purses" to repair an old
bridge, or to bring water into a long dried-up fountain.
But these may truly be regarded as rare exceptions
to the general rule. And so it is that at Cassaba the
Roman aqueduct, instead of being repaired, is filled
with dung to keep it from leaking. Offers have been
made by European engineers to make the repairs, but
the Government refuse to provide the funds. The
water is remarkably fine and pure near the spring, and
many people go there to fetch their store of it; but by
the time it reaches the town through the aqueduct it
becomes a dark-coloured and filthy fluid, quite unfit to
be used as a beverage.*

* The ravages of the cholera were fearful and unprecedented at
Cassaba in 1865, a year after our visit, which is sufficiently explained
by the above description of the water supply. Who is responsible
for this dreadful mortality?

The buildings of this place, though generally of mud, show a decided advance in civilization. They are often plastered and painted, especially the side towards the street; the roofs are uniformly covered with tiles, and we meet here the Turkish *chaknisy*, a portion of the upper story projecting several feet into the street. Despite all the disfavour which this fashion meets with, especially on account of its favouring the spread of a conflagration, there is no doubt that it is a great comfort in the summer season. The end windows receive the breeze which always flows up and down the narrow streets and diffuse it through the house; not only adding much to the comfort of the inmates, but also rendering the habitation more healthy. Cassaba evidently takes its pattern from Smyrna, but it calls to mind what Smyrna was thirty years ago. The Greek language appears to be generally spoken; and as we walked about the place, we noticed that the men and women of that nation dress very much as in Smyrna. The elder women, however, very generally wear full trowsers and a jacket, while the younger and the girls use the gown; this would indicate that a few years ago the Turkish dress was still in use. Here the Rayah women drop the veil, which they are obliged strictly to adhere to through all the Interior.

We took a room in the best khan, a large structure of wood and mud bricks, consisting of an inner court with central fountain, surrounded by two stories; stables and offices below, and lodging-rooms above. We occu-

pied the corner room up-stairs, and had a good view
of two streets. Our furniture was fine in comparison
to anything the Interior had offered us—a sofa, rude
table, stool, and rickety chair. Looking about us and
taking a stroll, we noticed that fig and pomegranate-
trees were abundant, and covered with fruit. One
cannot visit Cassaba in the warmer season of the year
without being struck with the immense number of
storks. They are perched, and have their nests, upon
nearly every chimney and house-top, and are flying
about in all directions, and "tak-tak"-ing with
their bills almost incessantly. They walk about in the
streets and courts, and pick up their food among dogs
and men, with as much unconcern as would be shown
by a chicken or a turkey; we had seen the same thing
at Toorkhal and Afion Karahissar. The great marshy
plain below doubtless affords them an abundant feeding-
ground, and all the natives are compelled, by the
bigoted hospitality of the Muslem, to leave them in
undisturbed possession of the upper portions of their
premises. Such hospitality, however, is not always
well rewarded, for the stork has been known not unfrequently to introduce snakes into the house. The
same superstitious feeling has also protected the ring
or turtle-dove in Cassaba, whose cooing and fluttering
is heard on every side. This bird is only found in
towns; I have not seen any upon the plateau, nor on
the northern shores of the Peninsula, though they are
found to some extent in Constantinople; they are very

bold in the Turkish quarters of the towns, where they
are never molested. They prefer somewhat wet and
shady spots; there is one at this moment walking and
feeding right under the window where I sit, unmindful
of passers by. They are called "*dhekokhtooras*" in
Greek, which means *eighteen*, a good imitation of their
cry, for which, however, the Greeks endeavour to give
an explanation, by saying that they represent an
unfortunate daughter-in-law, whose mother quarrelled
with her about some loaves of bread from which one
was missing. The poor daughter kept asserting that
eighteen was the number, not nineteen, that had been
baked. To release her from her life of torment and
abuse she was transformed into a ring-dove, and thus is
heard ever and anon to reiterate the disputed assertion,
"It was *eighteen, eighteen!*" (δέκα ὀκτώ.) Would that the
hospitality of the Turks were confined to storks,
"eighteens," and dogs. They have their uses, and
form a part of the economy of nature in this country,
of which one broken link would doubtless cause the
whole chain to give way. But when it comes to
certain blood-suckers which patronise not the street,
and the house-top or chimney, but the interior of the
habitation itself, it becomes a question as to who shall
vacate the premises! I remember well how at Constantinople Sultan Abdool Mijid removed one day
from his winter palace of Cheragan to his summer
palace of Beilerbey, without previously asking leave
of the already-admitted tenants; and he, therefore,

the very next morning moved back again from
Beïlerbey to Cheragan. Bed-bugs were too powerful
even for his Highness the Sultan. I have been assured
that he never again stopped at Beïlerbey, at least
through the *night*, until the whole palace was *accidentally*
burned down to the ground.

Noticed a great abundance of laurel or oleander
bushes between Cassaba and the banks of the Hermus.
There are yet many crimson flowers upon them. The
first we had seen from the moment we set foot on
shore at Samsoon and throughout our land journey,
were met with between Salihly and Cassaba.

September 4th, Sunday.—The elevation of Cassaba
(434 feet) indicates a rise of ground of 27 feet above
Salihly. This town is supported by agriculture and
the raising of silk-worms. It commands a great extent
of fertile land on both banks of the Hermus; and
there, among other products, are grown the famous
Cassaba melons, which are carried in such quantities
to Smyrna, and are even offered for sale at Constantinople since the introduction of steam communication.
Cotton is also an important staple, and all the usual
grains are grown with advantage. The higher grounds
are planted with vineyards. A large surface is also
covered with gardens and mulberry plantations; but
though cocoons are raised here in abundance, there is
no local manufacture; they are all exported. The
introduction of such branches of industry by the natives
themselves is effectually prevented by the system of

robbing and extortion carried on by Government officials and Turks in authority, added to the impossibility of the Rayahs (the only class which possesses the requisite qualities for engaging in manufactures) obtaining redress in the courts—chiefly because their testimony is not received against a Muslem. The only manufactures that have succeeded in this country are carried on by foreigners, and they maintain their position only by the ever watchful protection of their respective Governments.

Monday, September 5th.—Rose at 2 A.M., and started at 4. A man led us with a lantern through the town, and it began to dawn some time after we had put our horses to their paces upon the high road. The morning was quite cool, a fresh breeze blowing from Tahtali on our left. The ground was at first sandy and pebbly, and we were told that this part is often under water during the winter, compelling the traveller to follow a more circuitous road nearer the mountain. Lines of laurel bushes closed the view of the plain on our right. At 5·15 came to a café among clusters of trees, and we soon after reached the Nif Chay, a very considerable stream, which rises in the mountain of Tahtali, and flows to the Hermus. The water is now very low; the stream meanders and turns so many times in the narrow but beautifully-shaded valley, that we had to cross it five times; the last time was by the side of a stone bridge, of which four arches alone are standing, several others having been carried away. The banks

of this river abound with the platanus or plane-trees,
of remarkable size and beauty; the oleander grows
luxuriantly in clusters, and trees of different species
form bowers and groves in every direction. Nightin-
gales must be very abundant here in the spring, for
this is just the kind of place they like best to frequent.
The mountain is so near that the river fills its bed
and becomes unfordable after a heavy rain, and travellers are compelled to follow a path upon the slope
of Sipylus on the north side of the valley, and to cross
the Nif Chay at a bridge situated lower down. This
valley is famous for highway robberies; for the thick
clusters of trees and bushes enable the bandits to hide
wherever they like, and to shoot down the traveller
as he crosses the stream. Nymphio, which gives its
name to this river, is situated on the left, at the foot
of Tahtali Mountain; and all the land between it and
the Nif Chay is green with orchards and fruit-trees,
where are gathered, among others, the celebrated
Nymphio cherries. We soon came out of this fertile
and delicious valley, and passed into another, which
shortly became as remarkable for its excessive aridity,
being stony, dry, and at last wholly destitute of verdure.
The white limestone rocks were not only hard to
travel upon, but they reflected the burning rays of
the sun with such intensity as to be even painful to
the eye. Our poor horses dragged themselves wearily
through this pass as we went along the inhospitable
slopes of Sipylus. We reached the miserable hut

dignified with the name of café, but well characterized
as Tash Café, the *rock café*, at 9·30. It lies just before
the entrance to the cut or narrow gorge that leads out
into the plain of Smyrna. We went up this pass,
and found most of it only a few feet in width, with
steep banks on both sides. It is paved throughout,
though the pavement is in a ruinous condition. As
we rode through we could not avoid reflecting upon
its eventful history. We here met some machinery,
dragged along upon wooden rollers; it was intended
for a cotton-cleaning factory, about to be set up by a
European in Cassaba. Descending from the highest
point upon the road, which was still hemmed in by
high banks, effectually closing up the prospect, we
reached Bell Café at 10·15, and suddenly emerged
upon a small platform, whence we had a complete
view of the whole plain and gulf of Smyrna, the two
lines of mountains on the right and left running
parallel to the west, while the space between them in
the foreground was occupied by a level and fertile plain
studded with villages;—the turreted hill of Pagus,
some distance off in the line of hills on the left, with
the town of Smyrna starting from its base and spreading almost across the picture, the old windmill upon
the point of land ending the line of buildings on the
north,—then the dear blue sea, the old familiar outline
of the "Two Brothers," and the sea-castle beneath
them, and far, far off in dim outline, our old friend the
weather-gauge, hoary old Carabournoo, the mountain

and cape which closes the gulf on the west. We stood
still a moment in amazement at the splendid panorama,
the sense of the beautiful and the love of "home"
conspiring to fill us with enthusiasm, and we all
spontaneously gave a shout of recognition and a hearty
cheer. I am sure the Turks and Greeks about us
must have wondered where we came from, to be so
much excited by the sight of the old place. We
could scarcely bring ourselves to rest here through
the warmest part of the day, in order to refresh both
man and beast. We waited some time, however,
before our horses came up, for we had unconsciously
pushed forward at a rapid pace. The spot was truly
beautiful. The pass behind us can be seen from quite
a distance at sea, appearing like a deep indentation in
the chain or wall of hills which rises at the end of the
valley between Tahtali and Sipylus. It is, indeed,
one of the land-marks by which vessels are steered
into the port of Smyrna. Cultivation begins at the
Bell Café, and gives freshness to the little valleys
which lead down to the plain, while the summits of
the mica and limestone hills are barren and rocky. The
café with its stable is well shaded by a clump of plane-
trees, and there are ruins of other huts. We rested
here until 2 P.M., when we started down the steep hill
over a paved road, which is sadly out of repair. The
weather would have been oppressive but for the fine
sea breeze, here called the *Imbat*, blowing right in
our faces. The wind had been from the south-east,

Distant view of Smyrna and the Gulf

and the air was charged with hot vapours; we saw
the westerly breeze coming long before we felt it,
by the sails of the boats in the gulf. Passed on
through plantations of olives and pomegranates, with
the village of Narlikeuy on the right, which derives
its name from this latter tree; and at 3 o'clock
arrived at a café which lies opposite to Boornabat, on
the south side of the plain; this is called one hour
from the city. Rode by the spring, a little sheet of
water, shaded by an ancient platanus, which is known
as "Diana's Bath," now turning a flour-mill. Here,
instead of continuing on the straight road to Smyrna,
we turned into a stony side lane, which took us to the
Booja road, on the edge of the lacustrine formation,
and thus under the walls of ancient Smyrna, through
the gap well known among the natives by the name of
Kara Kapoo, the Black Gate. We had from this spot
a fine view of the plain, which is traversed by the
Aïdin Railway, with Sedikeuy at the foot of Mount
Corax. And thus following our old beaten track over
the plain by the "white mountain," and through "the
paths among the vineyards," we were brought by God's
good providence in safety to the dear summer home
at Sedikeuy, which we had been approaching ever since
we started from Tocat on our overland journey, forty-
one days before.

CHAPTER XXVII.

IT had been our intention, before ending the long
overland journey described in the foregoing
pages, to visit two of the most interesting monuments of antiquity, and probably the very oldest to
be found on the Peninsula. But, though these lay not
far off our road, we were naturally anxious to reach
home, and, as they were near Smyrna, we easily persuaded ourselves to put off our visit to a later period.
I refer to the Bust of Niobe upon the eastern extremity
of Mount Sipylus, and to the Monument of Sesostris,
near the northern entrance of the pass through Tmolus,
from the plains of the Hermus to those of the Cayster.
The last of these is recognised and accepted by all;
but it is difficult of access, and few venture upon the

undertaking of paying it a visit, though such trouble
is rarely better rewarded. But there has been so much
misapprehension and misrepresentation respecting the
Bust of Niobe, and it is yet so remarkable a monument,
that the reader will doubtless thank me for minutely
describing it.

But first, a few introductory words respecting the
general features of this region.

The Gulf of Smyrna, which lies about the middle
of the western coast of Asia Minor, is formed by two
ranges of hills, running east and west some 3 to 5
miles apart; near their western extremity another
mountain, the ancient Mimas, running north and
south, closes up the mouth, leaving, however, a
broad entrance at the north-west corner. The two
parallel lines of hills of which we have spoken rise
higher as they tend eastward, and the southern one
becomes Mount Tmolus, while the northern is Mount
Sipylus. There is what may be called a bridge of hills
thrown across from Tmolus to Sipylus, thus completing
the enclosure wherein lies the Gulf of Smyrna. Smyrna
itself is built at the foot of a hill, called Mount Pagus,
on the south side of the enclosure, and from the city
to the eastern hills the water of the Gulf has been
displaced by low alluvial land, which is covered with
gardens, vineyards, and olive-groves, and studded with
prosperous villages. The rich valley of Nif, or Nymphio,
has already been described as of surpassing loveliness
and beauty in its central portions, though surrounded

by arid and barren cliffs. It is watered by the Nif
Chay, which flows out of the sides of Tmolus. And
the place was. doubtless, as attractive for its natural
beauties in ancient times as it now is; for the Byzantine emperors had a palace here, erected by the younger
Andronicus, whither they retired from the cares of
state.

Old Homer, in describing the Statue of Niobe on
Mount Sipylus, thus portrays the locality (we use a
literal translation, as Pope's does not faithfully render
the original). He says:—

"And now among the rocks and solitary cliffs of
Sipylus, where they say are the couches of the Divine
Nymphs, who dance upon the banks of Acheloüs, she
[Niobe] though turned to stone, still broods upon the
pains inflicted by the gods."—(' Il.,' xxiv. 614.)

There is not in all the surroundings of Mount Sipylus
any place more likely to have been the reputed resort
of the " Divine Nymphs," who retired to their couches
in the adjoining cliffs, than this valley of Nymphio. The
Nif Chay also answers to the description of the Acheloüs, rising as it does in the side of Mount Tmolus, and
flowing past Sipylus to the Hermus. And the name of
Nymphio, a corruption, no doubt, of Νυμφαίων, the abode
of the Nymphs, shortened to Nif by the barbarian Turks,
is an additional evidence that this was indeed the spot
described by Homer. It is a very ancient place, as
may be seen from the remains of a bath and a castle
on the hill, and history has never given it any other

name. All these circumstances lead us to the conclusion that we have the Acheloüs in the present Nif
Chay, and that the valley of Nymphio is the reputed
abode of the ancient Nymphs. The statue of Niobe
cannot, therefore, be far away. We now proceed with
the narrative of our first visit to the very ancient
statue, which the people of the country have always
agreed to call Niobe, but which all travellers—
Chishell, Arundel, Strickland, Hamilton, Texier, and
many more—consider to be either a statue of Cybele,
the mother of the gods, or a monument of some de-
parted hero.

There is now a railway from Smyrna to Magnesia, a
large and important town on the north side of Mount
Sipylus, occupying a recess where a prominent and
steep hill is crowned with the remains of its ancient
fortress or castle. It was an autumn day, and we had
ridden in the cars, reaching Magnesia in about two
hours after leaving Smyrna, the distance traversed by
the road being about 40 miles, winding round the head
of the gulf to Menemen, and following thence the course
of the Hermus. The road that leads from Magnesia to
Nymphio, or more directly eastward to Cassaba, Sardis,
and Philadelphia, is the ancient road of the world's conquerors from Sesostris to Timoorlenk (Tamerlane), and
skirts the plain at the foot of Mount Sipylus. As you
proceed the mountain rises more and more abruptly from
the plain, which is fertile and well cultivated ; vineyards, mulberry plantations, and fields of grain, extend

to the distant hills, and hide the course of the
Hermus, which flows from east to west about 2 miles
on our left.   I passed over this road in a rough
cart on four wheels, without springs, drawn by two
miserable horses, whose harness was made of untanned
leather and ropes, and driven by a Crimean Tartar.
Our course was between the mountain and the continuation of the railway from Magnesia eastward to
Cassaba.

After riding about three-quarters of an hour, we
crossed a mill-run by a little bridge.   This small
canal is dug out of the mountain side, and is solidly
built up with stones and cemented with lime.   It extends to a distance of 500 yards, to where it is crossed
again by another bridge, and is a far more solid structure than we generally see in the country.   A good
part of the way, a paved road for carriages, now out of
repair, lies beside it.   The water it conveys flows westward toward the plain, and is employed in working a
flour-mill.   Following this canal for about 100 yards,
after passing the last bridge, we came to a miserable
café, on the left of the road, built by the edge of a
pretty pond, which supplies the canal or mill-run.   This
sheet of water is 300 yards long, and about 50 wide,
stretching along the edge of the mountain, from which
it is separated only by the road.   It is replenished by
four springs issuing from the ground upon its brink,
and there are others, it is said, beneath the water.   This
pond is evidently artificial, being formed by an ancient

wall of solid blocks of stone, which retains the water on the side toward the plain.

We have described this spot so minutely, because some very learned men have thought it was once the site of a whole city which was swallowed up by an earthquake. Its small size is quite against this supposition.

We now go back to the narrative of our visit to this spot. When about 150 yards from the café, our driver called out, "Here is the Tash Suret!" (stone image). Looking up we saw what appeared to be a woman's rude form carved out of the rock; the arid and barren limestone, which had hitherto formed the higher portions of the mountain, here gradually descends nearer the plain, offering a ledge often quite perpendicular. Where it faces the north-east it is particularly smooth, and the figure appeared to be carved in relief upon its surface. There is an indistinctness from below especially, because the sun can light it up only early in the morning, which accounts for the fact that some people have thought it only a freak of nature, and would not take the trouble to go up and examine it. The image is colossal; from below I received the impression that it represents a woman in long robes, reaching to her feet, whose folds seemed very distinctly marked. This is the idea adopted by travellers who have written upon the subject. Had they gone up they would have seen that the statue consists simply of a *bust* set upon a pedestal, and that

what they took for folds of a robe are *Niobe's tears*,
trickling down from her face to the bottom of the
monument. Some travellers, however, have thought
the statue "represents a woman in a sitting posture,
and in *an attitude of contemplation;*" and Stewart
actually gives us a picture of the woman thus *sitting,
and with her arms folded upon her breast!*

I hastened to the café, and on inquiring about
the best path to ascend the mountain, learnt that a
Greek who stood by the roadside, and sold *yevrekia*
(cakes) to the passing camel drivers, is the *cicerone* of
the statue. I therefore set him before me, and began
a steep and fatiguing ascent, made somewhat dangerous
by the loose stones over which we had to pass.

The ascent begins at the road; I could see the
interesting object of my visit at a high angle up the
mountain, right over the pond already described. We
followed a zigzág course, first upon soil cut up by the
winter rains, and then over pieces of hard limestone
which had fallen from above. We finally reached a
small platform of earth, by the side of a large rock
standing apart from the main body, and probably fallen
from it; I had, from this point, a very good view of the
statue, in some respects the best. This spot does not lie
in front, but a little to the left and below the statue;
distance about 50 yards. I then climbed to the base
of the monument; but Pausanius had truly said of it,
"When standing close to it, the rock and precipice do
not show to the beholder the form of a woman, weeping

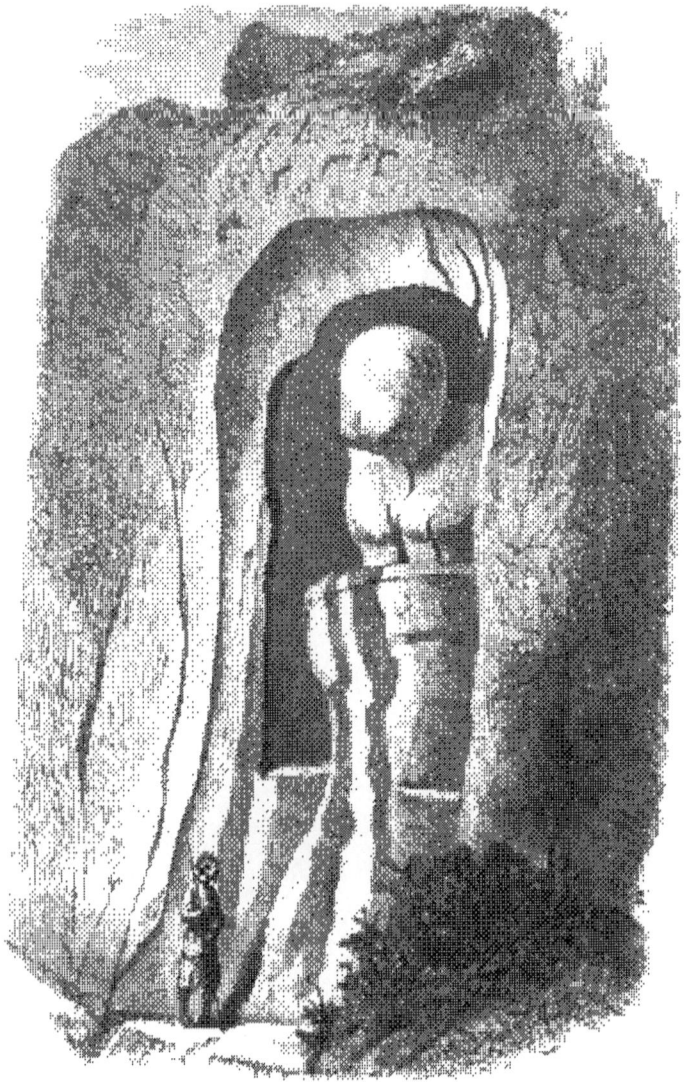

Statue of Niobe.

or otherwise; but if you stand farther, you think you
see a woman weeping and sad."—('Attica.' L. i. 21, 5.)
Viewed close by, it appears of unnatural breadth, and
such unnatural form that some have doubted whether
it was intended to represent a human being at all.
The "tears," too, streak it over with broad lines of blue
of various shades which bewilder the mind. At a
moderate distance these defects disappear, and the
design of the artist is clearly perceptible. The spot
most favourable for viewing it is on the right, its own
left or western side. The shades there bring out the
sculpture, and the desired level can be secured. The
accompanying sketch was drawn from that spot.
The description I shall now give of the statue is the
result of the examination made, not during this visit
only, but also on a subsequent occasion, when a whole
party of us came to the spot with all that was requisite
for taking precise measurements.

The soil stands some 12 feet below the base of the
monument, and a narrow platform or artificial projection is cut out of the rock. This projection, well worn
and very slippery, extends not only in front of the
work, but for a considerable distance on its eastern
side. From this projection to the top of the rock
the height is about 50 feet, over the whole of which
the surface from top to bottom has been cut smooth
with the chisel for a considerable distance on both
sides of the sculpture. An alcove, or niche, some
35 feet in height, and 16 feet 4 inches by measurement

in width, has been cut into the rock, and a smaller
alcove, of much greater depth, surrounds the bust itself.
The latter is of colossal size, representing the head,
shoulders, and breast of a female, and ending a little
above the waist. The arms are wanting. The work
stands boldly out from the rock, being in high *alto
relievo*. The features are wholly obliterated, the
marble being there completely broken off, and even
dug into at the place of the right eye and cheek.
Some traces of hair, unless it be the rough chiselings,
are visible over the left ear, which is also gone. The
bust is set upon a broad and high pedestal, upon each
side of which is a shelf, perhaps for the purpose of
receiving offerings. The whole work from the top of
the head to the base of the pedestal measures 20 feet
8 inches, the entire bust being 8 feet 3½ inches in
height, and 0 feet wide at the shoulders, while the
height of the head is 4 feet 2 inches. The two shelves
stand 7 feet 1½ inches from the bottom. But the
characteristic feature of this sculpture, that which
enables us to identify it as the bust of Niobe, consists
in the "flood of tears" which incessantly pour down
from her face to the base of the monument. The
appearance is remarkable and striking. The stone
here is of white marble, slightly tinged with red. The
general face of the rock, however, affected by the
influence of the atmosphere, is blue; the two alcoves
are white, as is the whole carved work. But from
the eyes, and especially from the right eye, a

dark blue vein descends over the lower part of the face, drops upon the breast, falls upon the pedestal, and flows thence in two broad streams down to the foot. The first time I examined this monument it seemed to me that these blue veins were portions of the rock of which the artist had availed himself in order to represent the tears of Niobe; they were hard and dry, and on being cut with an iron tool presented every appearance of a blue vein. But, upon a later visit, I found that it had just rained, and the water was yet dripping from the ledge overhead to Niobe's face, and actually flowing down the face of the sculpture, imparting to these veins a much deeper hue. They had also been softened by the moisture, and could be broken off with a sharp tool. My conclusion, therefore, was, that the water trickles down the rock so as to strike upon the face of the bust, and leaving a bluish lime deposit wherever it passes, represents a flood of tears pouring down the monument.

My cicerone informed me that, since the opening of the Smyrna, Magnesia, and Cassaba Railway, many visitors come to this spot; and, said he, the English stand at the outer rock, and fire with ball at the face of the statue! The story appeared incredible, for it seemed more likely that the Turks would commit such an act of Vandalism; but he assured me that it was so, and that he had himself repeatedly seen the English do it. The only motive I can imagine is the English

passion for a small bit of everything they see abroad
to carry home and show to their friends. I had
ocular demonstration of the number of visitors who
now come to the spot in the many initials rudely
scratched upon the accessible portions of the work.
I could perceive no trace of any buildings connected
with this sculpture; but they may have been obliterated by time. There are several tombs cut in the
rock near by.

The view from this spot is extensive and fine;
the great plain stretches to the horizon, and not far
below us meet three celebrated streams, the Gediz or
Hermus, the Nif Chay, Homer's Acheloüs, and the
Koom Chay, "the fishy Hylus" (another of Homer's
appropriate epithets). The plain is narrowest to the
N.E., the hills of Kara Dagh coming forward in this
place; but in every other direction it presents an unbroken mass of verdure which melts into the distant
mountains.

Standing at the base of this ancient monument, some
400 feet above the plain, I looked right down into the
little lake I have described. Can any one doubt, I
thought, that Homer's mind turned to this spot, and
that this was the Niobe who, weeping though turned to
stone, filled with her tears the basin beneath her feet,
of whom he sang: "Upon arid Sipylus, upon the rocks
of the desert mountain, . . . Niobe, though turned to
stone, still broods over the sorrows the gods have sent
upon her"? Such were my reflections when the

cicerone, the *yevrekji*, broke out with the following: "There is a tradition that this statue was once a woman whose children were killed, and she wept so that God changed her to stone; they say her tears made a pond down there, and still keep it full." It is indeed strange to find that all the people around here, both learned and ignorant, unite in calling this Niobe; and that all our learned European travellers, on the other hand, should agree in denying it. For my own part, I think tradition is right this time, and that the learned are wrong. I find by comparing their accounts with the statue itself, that they contain an astonishing amount of mistakes. One learned author says the statue lies 100 feet from the road, and another, equally authentic, makes it 65 feet. For my own part I am satisfied that this statue is old Niobe, one of the most ancient sculptures in existence; for it stood there in Homer's day. Others, after him, have thought the work worthy of their pen. Pausanius goes out of his way to tell us that he had seen Niobe herself when he went up the Mountain Sipylus. Strabo connects Niobe with the "Cirbesian pond," answering to the one we have described. And Ovid, speaking with still greater precision, says :—

"She weeps still, and, borne by the hurricane of a mighty wind,
She is swept to her home. There, fastened to the cliff of the Mount,
She weeps, and the marble sheds tears yet even now."

Ovid, Met. ii., 310.

An explanation, however, may be suggested which
will reconcile the two theories that this statue is Cybele,
the Mother of the Gods, and that it is Niobe. It may
be that this sculpture was executed in a very remote
antiquity to represent a female deity, Cybele, or some
form of nature worship; that the natural water-drip
from the rock above upon the marble gave it from the
first the same striking watermark which it still bears,
maintained by the same cause; and that this appearance suggested to the lively imagination of the Greeks
the whole myth of Niobe, her tears, her sorrows, her
stony transformation, her perpetual weeping. The
Greek word Niobe connects itself with "the pouring of
water" and "the falling of snow" (νίζω, and νίπτω,
and νίφω), so that "stony Niobe all tears" is probably
but a Greek impersonation of the drip-drip of the
marble rock upon the ancient rock sculpture, which
thus acquired the name of Niobe, "the weeping one."
It is also remarkable that the Greek myth calls the
oldest son of Niobe "Sipylus," the very name of the
mountain in which this statue is found. Whether this
be the true explanation or not, the great point of
interest is still the same, that the tradition which
connects this statue with Niobe is as old as Homer,
and the sculpture older still, while his mention of the
"places of the Divine Nymphs" seems to mark this
spot as the *locus* of some very ancient religious worship.
Another very curious point arises from the notice
of this sculpture by Homer. He introduces the

mention of Niobe in the speech of Achilles to Priam,
when he has consented to give up the corpse of Hector
to his father. He presses the aged king to take food
even amidst his sorrows, "for," he says, "even Niobe
was mindful of food in her deep grief, when her
twelve children were destroyed;" then, narrating the
legend, Achilles says again, "She therefore was mindful
of food when wearied with weeping." I do not know
that this pointed allusion to Niobe's unremitting care
for food has ever been explained. I venture to suggest
that the allusion may be to the offerings of food here
made to the image by her votaries, as we have already
(p. 310) noticed the shelf adapted to that purpose.
Homer seems to speak (may we suppose, with the
slightest touch of sarcasm?) as the priests of the
image were wont to speak of its votaries: "Niobe,
though ever sorrowful, is ever needing food—your
offerings," &c. Such an interpretation of the passage
brings to our minds the crafts of the priests of Bel
and the sarcasms of Daniel.

Certainly, the whole scene around us at this moment
agrees remarkably with the Grecian legend, and may
be looked upon as the very birthplace of the myth of
Niobe. She is the "daughter of Tantalus," over
whose head, remember, the rock was always hanging
ready to fall. Tantalus is nothing else than a rock
hanging poised in air (ταλαντεύω) ever threatening to
come down, an exact description of the constant dis-
integration of the face of the hills in this region.

Niobe, in her deep-cut alcove under the overhanging ledge of rock is "daughter of Tantalus." She is, as Cybele, the great mother—her very boast; and "her children, struck down to earth, slain by Phœbus and Diana," are the masses of rock, such as we have just passed over, that fall into the valley, separated from the cliffs by the action of the sun and rain. "They lie unburied on the plain," Homer tells us, "till on the tenth day the heavenly gods bury them;" the fallen rocks after a time break up under the influences of the weather. "Here, in these mountains of Sipylus are the couches of the divine Nymphs that dance, or stream, about Acheloüs," that is, in this hill now above us are the springs (which, indeed, we have just passed) from which flow down the streams that feed Acheloüs at our feet; Acheloüs, "the son of Sol," springing, that is, from the melting of the snows in summer. If we are right in thus interpreting the scene before us and the Homeric legend, then this most ancient statue is not an image sculptured to represent the story of Niobe, but it is itself the very original from which that story sprang. Carved in the most remote antiquity to represent, it may be, Cybele, the deity of a race that preceded the Greek immigration, the circumstances that gathered round it gave rise in the imaginative minds of the Greeks to the whole beautiful legend of Niobe, all stone and all tears, as we see her at this moment, and we here look upon a monument which was even to Homer an object of venerable and

unknown antiquity, a monument antecedent not only
to history, but in some sense to mythology itself.

My visit to the Monument of Sesostris was made in
the company of several very agreeable young gentlemen who desired to spend their Easter vacation in
making an excursion to some of the ancient sites of
greatest celebrity in the neighbourhood of Smyrna.
We went together not to Nymphio alone, but, passing by
Cassaba, we visited the ruins of Sardis, and the *Bin bir
Tepeh*, the numerous mounds which formed the necropolis of that capital of Lydia.

I must premise that Herodotus refers to this bas-
relief in the following terms: "There are in Ionia two
figures of Sesostris carved on the rocks, the one (by
the way) by which men come from Ephesus to Phocea,
the other (by the way) by which they come from
Sardis to Smyrna." I shall refer farther on to the
rest of his description, which is remarkably correct,
but will now observe that the other monument here
referred to has not yet been discovered. It is also
worthy of notice that there is a similar monument
of Sesostris on the remarkable rocky ledge at the
mouth of the Nahr el Kelb, the Dog River, near
Beyrout, in Syria, where his later imitators have
sought to immortalize themselves by leaving similar
marks of their passage; so that there stand side by
side the boastful inscriptions of the Egyptian, Assyrian,

and Roman conquerors, ending with Selim, Sultan of
the Osmanlics.

Monday, April 22nd.—Rode out of Smyrna going east,
and passed by "Diana's Bath," a spring which oozes
out of the ground from among the roots of a lofty
platanus, and feeds a pond which modern improvements
have successively made a paper factory and a flour
mill. A Temple of Diana and Homer's Grotto (one out
of the thousand which bear his name) are claimed to
have stood near by in ancient times. We passed below
Kookloodja, a prosperous Greek village on our right,
whose tall church steeple is a conspicuous object in all
the surrounding region. At 8 we passed an old Turkish
cemetery. The Turks have been gradually withdrawing
from the villages of the plain to the suburbs of Smyrna,
unable to resist the advance of enterprise and wealth
possessed by native Christians and Europeans. This
is always the case in Turkey wherever the too close
oversight of European eyes prevents them from robbing
people with whom they cannot enter into fair competition. Leaving the large village of Boornabat about two
miles on our left, we passed through the thick groves of
pomegranate trees which belong to and give its name
to the village of Narlikeuy, pomegranate village,
situated on the left side of the road, and beyond the
groves. The village of Hadjilar (pilgrims to Mecca)
lies further on, also upon the left. After crossing an
extensive plain, and traversing the narrow pass of Bell

Café over the mountain, we approached Nymphio, where the thick foliage of the orchards, gardens, and vineyards quite refreshed the eye. Just before going into the village, we saw a large oblong building of stone with regular layers of bricks, standing in a garden near the road. It is called the Palace of the Byzantine Emperors, and is said to have been erected by the younger Andronicus. Reached Nymphio at 11. It is a large village built at the entrance of a narrow gorge which runs up from the broad valley into Mount Tmolus. Looking down towards the north, the valley appears one broad mass of verdure extending to the foot of Mount Sipylus on the opposite side.

We sent to the Mudir, or Governor, to point us out lodgings, and were shown to the house of a respectable Greek gentleman, who offered us a pleasant and clean upper room, with adjoining piazza and terrace; and having partaken of some refreshment, we got into the saddle again at 12·40, and followed two tall and well-armed guards, dressed in the Zeïbek style, with bare legs and high caps, from which hang a profusion of little tassels of various colours. These had been furnished us as guides by the Mudir. It was evident there were expectations of making something by the job, for he refused to give us but one guide, saying it was customary to send two. We followed a path leading along the mountain side into a valley which soon becomes narrower, and observed some very peculiar hills upon its western side, which indicate great volcanic

perturbation. It was evident as we proceeded that we
were turning farther away from what must have been
"the road from Sardis to Smyrna" in Herodotus' time.
We expected, from Herodotus' statement, to find the
monument on the sides of Sipylus, and found ourselves
intently eyeing the opposite mountains to catch a
distant sight of some prominent ledge which might
contain the precious carvings. But we entered a gorge
running south-east into the very heart of the mountain.
Just before reaching this gorge, we saw a dilapidated
guard-house, whose occupants expect a bakshish from
the European visitors who come here to pay their
respects to the Egyptian monarch: we did not call
upon them now, but did so on our return. This is said
to be a bad place for robberies. It is the beginning
of a pass that leads across Mount Tmolus from the
plain of Casaba on the north to that of Eudemish
and Baïndir on the south; and on account of its
difficult and inaccessible nature, it is reported to be
the retreat of the highway robbers who ply their
trade upon both sides of the mountain. Crossed the
stream, and proceeded along its eastern bank, where
there was scarcely room enough for a path. The sides
of the gorge are rocky and steep, and the bed of the
river is filled with fallen fragments. The rock is a
red conglomerate, with hard limestone upon the top.
There are many pine trees, and the underbrush is tall
and full. At 2·10 our guides stopped under a tall
pine, and pointing up hill to the left, told us that the

object of our search lay in that direction, among the trees and shrubs. We immediately began to ascend the steep hill side, amidst an abundant vegetation. We could see around us outcropping portions of the red conglomerate. Having risen to about 100 feet from the river bank, we found ourselves suddenly ushered into the presence of the old king, panting and wet with the perspiration of our difficult ascent under a burning sun. There he was, standing as firm and unmoved as though he were still master of sea and land from the Euxine to the sources of the Nile. The carvings occur upon a hillock whose entire height above the river is about 150 feet. The lower part of it is of conglomerate, but the top is a piece of hard limestone of pretty regular shape. The face of this rock is smoothed down over a surface 45 feet high and 60 feet broad, which fronts up the stream, or south. Were all the trees and shrubs cut away, the carvings could not be seen from below by the river bank; one would have to proceed some distance up the stream; and supposing a royal road to have once existed through this pass, the image could be seen while travelling northward upon it. No better description can be given of it than that of Herodotus himself, which I began to quote above. I shall therefore content myself with a translation of his brief but apt account. Speaking of the two monuments of Sesostris existing in Western Asia Minor, he says: "Each of these figures represents a man four cubits and one spithame in

height (six feet and a half), holding a spear in his
right hand, and a bow in the left, with the rest of his
costume corresponding to these weapons, *i.e.* half
Egyptian and half Ethiopian. Across his breast and
from one shoulder to the other is carved an inscription
in Egyptian sacred characters, saying, 'I by my
shoulders gained possession of this country.'"—(Herodotus, lib. ii. 106.) There appears to be an error,
however, in this description, for an inspection of
the picture will show that Sesostris holds the spear in
his left hand, and the bow in the right. But Herodotus doubtless speaks of the beholder's right and left.
The carvings upon the breast' are gone, but there
seem to be remains of others near the corner of the
tablet, and by the side of the spear head; they, however, are too far gone to justify the exact tracings
we find in some copies made by artists whose imagina-
tions gave undue sharpness to their eyesight.

It is truly instructive to look upon a monument
which has not only stood the decaying influences of
thirty-three centuries, but more than this, has baffled
for that space of time the human passions which have
conspired to destroy it. It is an illustration of the aid
rendered by remains of this nature toward establishing
the statements of history as truths indisputable, and
never to be shaken.

We returned by the way we had come; but a second
inspection of the ground still further convinced me that
the road from Sardis to Smyrna never could have

passed within three or four miles of the monument
we had just visited. Herodotus, indeed, does not say
"*close to the road*," nor does the word "road" occur
in the original; but his expression means only that
the monument is reached by this way, or lies in the
district as men pass from Sardis to Smyrna.

When we returned to Nymphio and our quarters, our
guides began to give themselves airs of importance,
which revealed their large expectations. They came
upstairs and sat where they liked, eased themselves of
their shoes, took off their caps, and rummaged among
their folds in a way that affected the nerves of some
inexperienced ones in our company. We, for some
time, endured their freedom, in order to initiate our
young English and French companions into some of the
mysteries of Oriental life. When I, at length, handed
the high dignitaries the customary bakshish, they turned
up their noses at it, threw it down indignantly, and
went off with a great flourish of trumpets. Some of
us concluded that they must have been of the number
who had led one of the English princes to the old
Egyptian king not long ago, and took us for his
cousins. The next morning, while we were getting
ready for an early start for Cassaba, they sent a
messenger to know whether we intended to go without
giving them their bakshish. We replied that we should
give them nothing unless they came themselves for it.
One of them then appeared for both; we gave him only
his own present, which he had contemptuously thrown

away the day before, and his companion got nothing
until he, too, came for it in person. We, moreover, enjoyed teasing them by assuring them that the Zeibek
dress had been prohibited by an order from the capital
(which was a fact), and we added, with a wink of the
eye, "We know the Pasha of Smyrna well, and see
him often ; he does not know that the *zabtiehs* of Nymphio
dare to wear the costume of highway robbers!" They
must have spent a troubled day and a restless night,
poor fellows! and they probably to this hour curse the
day that brought them in contact with the "mean"
and stingy cousins of the Prince of Wales!

In a ramble about Nymphio we saw a carved slab over
a fountain, an extremely indifferent work of the later
Byzantine period. There are remains of old walls, and
of a fort or castle upon the hill overlooking the place.
We also visited the Palace of the Byzantine Emperors,
which we found to be 71 feet in length, and 24½ feet
in width within the walls, which are 6½ and 8½ feet in
thickness. The building consisted of a vaulted lower
story, with two rows of windows and two stories above.
The stones have fallen from the top in such a manner
as to present the appearance of rows of chimneys, the
tops of several of which are crowned with storks' nests,
The foundations of extensive and costly buildings
have been discovered and partly uncovered in the
gardens, indicating that the ancient town extended
some distance in that direction.

It does not enter within my plan to describe the

remainder of this journey, my object being only to draw the reader's attention to the two remarkable monuments of Niobe and Sesostris, and explain their position and some of the illustrations they afford of the venerated writers of antiquity. Sesostris is supposed to have at one time subjected the whole of Asia Minor to his arms. I have already pointed out the decidedly Egyptian features of the sculptured remains at Euyuk, whose unfinished condition seems to indicate that their authors were driven away by the irruption of a foe, so that the opportunity of accomplishing their task never recurred. The sculpture of Sesostris, near the north end of the Karabel Pass, is another and a still clearer proof of the extension of Egyptian power in the land. The first is found in Northern Phrygia, the second in Western Lydia; and as it is probable that Sesostris moved mostly upon the land, the evidence is strong that his power once stretched to the Euxine and the Hellespont.

APPENDIX.

APPENDIX A.

ON THE ORTHOGRAPHY OF ORIENTAL WORDS.

THE following system of orthography has been used in writing
Oriental words in the present work. It was prepared by a Committee of the Armenian Mission in Turkey, and adopted at its
annual meeting about twenty years ago. It will be easily remembered by persons who are in the habit of using either English or
French.

VOWELS.

a is always pronounced broad, as in *father*; in French, *bas*.

e as in *mel*; like the French *fermé*.

i   „   *sit*;   „   *ici*.

o   „   *bone*;   „   *côte*.

u like the French in *cruche*.

ŭ as in *but*; and the French mute *e*, in *besoin*.

eu like the French *eu*, *jeu*.

oo as in *room*; and the French *ou*, *croûte*.

CONSONANTS.

Generally as in English and French.

Instead of *c* the letter *k* is preferred for the hard, and *s* for the
     soft sound.

gh represents the Greek *γ*, and the Parisian *r*.

g is always hard as in *gap*, and in French *galop*.

j represents the same sound as in French, as *Jacques*.

dj is soft *g*, or the English *j*, as in *Jack*.

h is a slight aspirate, and *kh* a harsher one.

sh is sounded as in English; in French as *ch* in *cheval*.

ch as in English *cheap*; in French it is usually written *tch*.

dh is hard *th*, as in *this*.

th is always soft *th*, as in *think*.

kh represents the Greek *χ*, and is the strongest aspirate. It has
     representatives both in Turkish and Armenian, *ﻍ* and *խ*.

Although there are two r's both in Armenian and in Turkish, we have thought it unnecessary to distinguish them, on account of their comparatively rare occurrence. We have done the same with respect to the two Turkish o's and s's, and the two Armenian t's.

In order to prevent misunderstanding, we have added an *h* to a final *e*, which is to be pronounced as above indicated, and without the aspirate.

APPENDIX B.

HYPSOMETRICAL OBSERVATIONS MADE IN ASIA MINOR IN 1864.

These measurements were calculated by Professor Guyot's Tables, and were taken with an instrument made under his direction by Green of New York. Two thermometers were employed when necessary, but the one attached to the instrument was usually sufficient. The base employed was the level of the Black Sea, at Samsoon. All the observations were made between May 8th and September 5th.

LOCALITY.	ELEMENTS.		Heights in English feet.
	Barometer in English Inches.	Thermometer. Fahr.	
	°	°	
Samsoon, 40 feet above sea (mean of six observations)	30·040	59	..
Khan, 4 hrs. south of Samsoon ..	27·142	61·5	2886·57
Cavak (mean of three observations)	27·880	61	2135·60
Delinos Khan	27·000	59	3002·78
Bekjilik, above ditto..	26·426	58	3569·86
Khan, 2 hrs. west of Amasia	28·362	76	1710·86
Amasia, Krug House	28·246	74·75	1629·92
,, 12 feet above the river ..	28·498	74	1590·84
,, level of Yeshil Urmak ..		..	1578·84
Inclazar (mean of three observations)	27·311	73	2758·06
Toorkhal, 20 feet above the river ..	28·186	71	1862·04
,, level of Yeshil Urmak ..	..	..	1822·04
Torst, 150 feet above river (mean of 132 observations)	27·654	69·5	2390·16
Toxat, level of Yeshil Urmak	..	..	2240·16

HYPSOMETRICAL OBSERVATIONS—*continued.*

LOCALITY.	Elements.		Heights in English feet.
	Barometer in English inches.	Thermometer, Fahr.	
Bekjilik, 4 hrs. south of Tocat	25·201	71	5010·4
Highest point of the road between Bekjilik and Karghún	24·750	72	5512·2
Karghún	25·385	76	4830·23
Sivas (Mr. Winchester's house) (mean of six observations)	25·648	66·5	4461·76
Saru Yeri, foot of Star Mountain	25·247	71	4957·82
Top of Star Mountain	22·168	67	8556·53
Chiflik of Haji Boghos Agha	27·312	79	2850·96
Yoghin Musulman	27·280	68·5	2799·91
Kenhneh	26·400	79	3752·34
Yozghat (Mr. Farnsworth's house)	25·728	70	4418·94
Boghaz Keuy	26·635	68	3513·28
Sungurlu (mean of three observations)	27·443	71	2528·01
Aghudju Koyoonoo	27·421	78	2672·0
Izeddin	26·729	83·5	3415·85
Diskhskan	27·422	85	2707·51
1 foot above Kuzil Urmak	27·543	83	2572·28
Yozghat (village)	26·091	83	4100·93
Angora (mean of three observations), at our lodgings	26·823	71	3334·63
Halu Kooyoondjoo	26·916	63	3082·82
Chiflik	27·048	72	3020·20
Yaila of Euyuk	27·661	59	2320·35
Sakaria, at bridge, 14 feet above river	27·641	69	2387·62
Oris Keuy	27·227	80	2884·28
Hortoo	26·550	76	3265·58
Sivri Hissar	26·546	74	3778·15
Balahissar	26·908	77	3200·63
Aktash, 15 feet above Sakaria	27·160	59	2824·19
Baghludja	26·548	79	3394·37
Top of Mountain south of Beyat	25·386	70	4838·64
Seidiler	26·129	75	4018·84
Afion Karahissar (Mr. Pharson's house)	26·892	81	3886·18
Bulmainood	26·320	66·5	3878·21
Chiflik	25·807	83	4424·44
Islam Keuy	26·866	78	3250·42
Boughow	26·917	76	3185·54
Ooshak	26·915	74	3187·88
Geuneh	28·000	72	2053·13

HYPSOMETRICAL OBSERVATIONS—*continued.*

LOCALITY.	ELEMENTS.		Height in English feet.
	Barometer in English inches.	Thermometer. Fahr.	
Yenishehir	28·293°	76°	1776·88
Suriyeh	28·843	73	1710·83
Konla (12 feet above the ground) ..	27·674	79	2417·07
Yeli Kaloh Kaïveh	27·350	66	2081·64
Salihly	29·630	71	417·63
Level of the Hermus at ditto	..	..	367·63
Cassaba	29·645	82	431·73

THE END.